Education for Responsible Citizenship

Education for Responsible Citizenship

The Report of the
National Task Force
on Citizenship Education

B. Frank Brown, *Director*

Cosponsored by
The Danforth Foundation
and the Institute for
Development of Educational Activities, Inc.,
the educational affiliate
of the Charles F. Kettering Foundation

McGRAW-HILL BOOK COMPANY
New York   St. Louis   San Francisco
Düsseldorf   London   Mexico
Sydney   Toronto

Library of Congress Cataloging in Publication Data

National Task Force on Citizenship Education.
  Education for responsible citizenship.

  Includes index.
  1. Civics—Study and teaching. I. Danforth Foundation, St. Louis. II. Institute for Development of Educational Activities. III. Title.
H62.N3627 1977   320.4   77-3925
ISBN 0-07-046095-7
ISBN 0-07-046096-5 pbk.

123456789   RRDRRD   76543210987

This book was set in Century Schoolbook by University Graphics, Inc. It was printed and bound by R.R.Donnelley & Sons Company. The designer was Elaine Gongora. The editors were Thomas Quinn and Cheryl Hanks. Frank Bellantoni supervised the production.

Contents

Acknowledgments   vii

Introduction
   The Case for Citizenship Education
   B. Frank Brown   1

1 Recommendations for Strengthening Civic
   Education
   Advisory and Project Committee Members   9

2 The Total Educational Environment
   Ralph W. Tyler   15

3 Political and Social Purposes of Education
   Stephen K. Bailey   27

4 Historical Perspective on Civic Education in the
   United States
   R. Freeman Butts   47

5 The Crisis in Civic Education
   Howard D. Mehlinger   69

6 Rationale for a New Emphasis on Citizenship
   Education
   Isidore Starr   83

7 The Implications of Lawrence Kohlberg's
   Research for Civic Education
   Edwin Fenton   97

8 Citizenship Education through Participation
   Dan Conrad and Diane Hedin   133

9 Citizen Participation: Lessons for Citizenship
   Education
   Luvern L. Cunningham   157

10   The Role and Responsibility of Television in Civic
Education
Douglass Cater   165

11   Alternative Approaches to Citizenship
Education: A Search for Authenticity
Fred M. Newmann   175

12   The Crisis of Global Transformation,
Interdependence, and the Schools
*Saul H. Mendlovitz, Lawrence Metcalf, and Michael
Washburn*   189

Appendix
Citizenship Test for Secondary Schools
George Gallup   213

Index   222

Acknowledgments

The Danforth and Kettering foundations express their appreciation to the following individuals who responsibly and diligently served as members of committees giving guidance and direction to the development of this report:

Advisory Committee

Geraldine Bagby
Vice President, The Danforth
  Foundation
St. Louis, Missouri

Stephen K. Bailey
Vice President, American Council
  on Education
Washington, D.C.

George L. Brown
Lieutenant Governor, State of
  Colorado
Denver, Colorado

Chairman
R. Freeman Butts
William F. Russell Professor
  Emeritus in the Foundations of
  Education
Teachers College, Columbia
  University
New York, New York

Francis Keppel
Director, Program on Education
Aspen Institute for Humanistic
  Studies
Cambridge, Massachusetts

John C. Pittenger
Secretary, Pennsylvania
  Department of Education
Harrisburg, Pennsylvania

Samuel G. Sava
Vice President for Educational
  Activities
Charles F. Kettering Foundation
Dayton, Ohio

Gene L. Schwilck
President, The Danforth
  Foundation
St. Louis, Missouri

Roger D. Semerad
Former Staff Assistant to the
  President, Domestic Council
The White House, Washington, D.C.

Ralph W. Tyler
Vice President, Center for the Study
  of Democratic Institutions
Chicago, Illinois

Margaret Bush Wilson
Chairman, Board of Directors
National Association for the
  Advancement of Colored People
St. Louis, Missouri

Project Committee

Alla L. Bullen
Teacher, John C. Fremont High
  School
Los Angeles, California

Richard C. Clement
President, International
  Association of Chiefs of Police
Toms River, New Jersey

Jason Conviser
Student, Ithaca College
Ithaca, New York

D. Robert Graham
Senator, 33rd District, Florida
Miami Lakes, Florida

Elizabeth Rack
Vice Chairman for Voters Service,
  The League of Women Voters
Washington, D.C.

Patricia Rammer
Student, Armstrong High School
Neenah, Wisconsin

Eloise Sewell
Principal, Robert B. Green
  Elementary School
San Antonio, Texas

Robert I. Sperber
Superintendent, Brookline Public
  Schools
Brookline, Massachusetts

The project and advisory committee members are responsible for the recommendations in the report. The various chapters were written by individual members of the advisory committee and where appropriate were commissioned to an outside source.

The parts of the report which were written by individual advisory committee members and others are as follows:

Introduction
The Case for Citizenship Education
B. Frank Brown
Director, | I | D | E | A | Information
  and Services Program
Melbourne, Florida

Chapter 1
Recommendations for
  Strengthening Civic Education
Advisory and Project Committee
  Members

Chapter 2
The Total Educational Environment
Ralph W. Tyler
Vice President, Center for the Study
  of Democratic Institutions
Chicago, Illinois

Chapter 3
Political and Social Purposes of
  Education
Stephen K. Bailey
Vice President, American Council
  on Education
Washington, D.C.

Chapter 4
Historical Perspective on Civic
  Education in the United States
R. Freeman Butts
Visiting Distinguished Professor of
  Education
San Jose State University
San Jose, California

Chapter 5
The Crisis in Civic Education
Howard D. Mehlinger

Director, Social Studies
  Development Center
Indiana University
Bloomington, Indiana

Chapter 6
Rationale for a New Emphasis on
  Citizenship Education
Isidore Starr
Professor Emeritus, Queens College
Scottsdale, Arizona

Chapter 7
The Implications of Lawrence
  Kohlberg's Research for Civic
  Education
Edwin Fenton
Professor, Carnegie-Mellon
  University Education Center
Pittsburgh, Pennsylvania

Chapter 8
Citizenship Education Through
  Participation
Dan Conrad and *Diane Hedin*
Center for Youth Development and
  Research
University of Minnesota
St. Paul, Minnesota

Chapter 9
Citizen Participation: Lessons for
  Citizenship Education
Luvern L. Cunningham
Professor, Educational
  Administration
College of Education
The Ohio State University
Columbus, Ohio

Chapter 10
The Role and Responsibility of
Television in Civic Education
Douglass Cater
Director, Program on
Communications and Society
Aspen Institute
Palo Alto, California

Chapter 11
Alternative Approaches to
Citizenship Education: A Search
for Authenticity
Fred M. Newmann

Professor, Curriculum and
Instruction
School of Education
University of Wisconsin-Madison
Madison, Wisconsin

Chapter 12
The Crisis of Global
Transformation,
Interdependence, and the Schools
*Saul H. Mendlovitz, Lawrence
Metcalf,* and *Michael Washburn*
Institute for World Order, Inc.
New York, New York

Dr. George Gallup contributed significantly both in the development of the Citizenship Test for Secondary Schools and as a consultant.

In addition, we thank Dr. Peter McPhail, director of the Schools Council Moral Education Project in England, for his generous sharing of ideas and materials and for allowing us to visit schools in England experimenting with the materials.

B. Frank Brown, Director
National Task Force on Citizenship Education

Introduction: The Case for Citizenship Education

B. FRANK BROWN

In early 1975, the Danforth and Kettering foundations formed a joint initiative designed to improve the knowledge and education of children and youth in the principles of citizenship and to increase their responsibility for playing a heightened role in the affairs of government and public institutions.

This movement grew out of a number of prominent concerns: the lack of quality in conventional civic education programs, the erosion of the values and attitudes of young people, the serious and continuing pressures on family life, the rising rate of juvenile crime and the increasing violence of crimes committed by teenagers, and the general alienation of people from their institutions.

An abundance of research data indicates that the nation's young people have scant knowledge about the responsibilities of citizenship or how to become involved in government. Data also reveal an increasing disrespect among the young for the most important institutions of society. An informed disrespect would be embarrassing but encouraging. Unfortunately, every examination of young people's knowledge and opinions reveals that both the critical and the supportive attitudes of the young float atop an abyss of ignorance. The 1973 citizenship test by the National Assessment of Educational Progress indicated that seventeen-year-olds and young adults know frighteningly little about the personalities or policies of governmental leaders, and have not even begun to understand the workings of the American political process.[1]

Perhaps even more significant is the report of the Yankelovich Youth Survey, which documented sudden and startling shifts in the attitudes of American youth away from traditional values. In 1973, Yankelovich compared the values of young Americans between ages sixteen and twenty-five with those of the same group in 1967. The 1973 research found such abrupt changes in values that the researchers were forced to conclude that the six-year period marked the end of one era of values and the beginning of another. The most

1

dramatic change Yankelovich noted was a turning away from the concept of patriotism. (While 35 percent of youth thought patriotism an important value in 1969, by 1973 only 19 percent considered it significant.)[2]

The aforementioned research studies are further substantiated by the report of the National Commission on the Reform of Secondary Education which, after an analysis, reported that one of the most serious problems confronting secondary education in America is the lack of emphasis on student responsibilities and preparation for citizenship.

After an analysis of hundreds of schools' handbooks titled "Student Rights and Responsibilities," the Commission reported that over 99 percent of these publications deal with student rights and fewer than 1 percent even mention student responsibilities.[3]

The issue of student rights became well established in law in 1975 when the Supreme Court—in the case of *Goss v. Lopez*—granted students due process for violations of school rules. It is now time that attention be turned to the matter of student responsibilities to school and society.

The previously described studies of the education of youth confirm the ineffectiveness of the ways in which society and the schools are educating young people for citizenship. Citizenship preparation by the schools has long been a neglected area, but it is now in a serious state of intellectual disrepair. In the elementary schools, this subject has been allowed to disappear behind the facade of more fashionable concerns. Meeting the most vocal demands of the community one at a time, rather than attempting the hard work of building a coherent curriculum, the designers of elementary programs have been compelled to push aside civic education in favor of units on drugs, sex, and social pathology. More recently, career education (a highly complex subject requiring detailed and sequential study) has been fostered on the elementary schools in units that reach as low as the kindergarten.

At the secondary level, the major burden for teaching about citizenship lies in the narrow, lifeless civics courses which comprise the social studies curriculum in grades eight or nine. This weakness is compounded by the fact that too often the civics course is taught by the athletic coach who needs a light teaching schedule because of his after-school coaching responsibilities.

These travesties suggest that neither school nor society presently considers citizenship preparation to be an important function of the schools. This is in sharp contrast to the attitude of the founding fathers who assigned to public education a primarily political purpose—to promote the values, the ideals, the knowledge, and the obligations required of citizens in a democratic republican society.

The new goal of citizenship education is best described by the distinguished historian R. Freeman Butts, William F. Russell Professor Emeritus in the Foundations of Education at Teachers College, Columbia University, and Visiting Distinguished Professor of Education at San Jose State University. In Butts' words:

> The political goal of education is to prepare all individuals to be able to play their part in the political system by developing the values, the knowledge, and the participation required for making deliberate choices among real alternatives.[4]

The tragedy of Watergate alone is a persuasive argument that we are not achieving the political goals of education, and as a consequence, the level of morality in government and politics is dangerously low. An abundance of other evidence indicates that the majority of both college and noncollege students believe the American society is democratic in name only and that special interests run the political majority of the nation with little true participation by the mass of American citizens.

These circumstances were the topic of a lengthy discussion with Secretary of the Department of Health, Education, and Welfare David Mathews, who, during his term of office, met with members of the Task Force to explore what action could be taken to improve citizenship education.

Mathews expressed the opinion that the present state of citizenship is perhaps the most critical problem confronting the American people. He described the crisis as follows:

> Being a citizen today is essentially a spectator sport. Citizenship education is little more than learning what others do to make and execute the policies of government.
>
> Citizenship cannot be remote. The disinterested citizen becomes disengaged, the disengaged citizen becomes disillusioned, and disillusionment leads to despair.
>
> We may well be witnessing the kind of citizen dropout that Thomas Jefferson imagined when he asked, in his First Inaugural Address, if the American experiment in self-government might be withering for lack of energy to sustain it.

With reference to the cause of citizen apathy, Mathews attributed this occurrence to the disillusionment of many of the country's citizens. As he expressed it:

> We are witnessing a mass alienation of the people with their government. It is manifest in such things as sinking voter registrations and public opinion polls which reflect a failing confidence in government.

The dissonance in society which Secretary Mathews described signifies that the introduction of a new course or modest alteration in the citizenship curriculum will not materially affect student learning in civic education. What is indicated is a major reconstruction of the civic education curricula. This must begin with a new definition clearly setting forth what being a citizen means in the latter part of the twentieth century. Not until the responsibilities of citizenship are determined can new programs on how to educate for citizenship be developed.

THE CRIME PROBLEM

A relatively new phenomenon that is impelling the schools to revitalize and reconstruct citizenship education programs is the enormous and rapidly growing crime problem. The United States now has one of the worst crime records of any country in the world. This is confirmed by Gallup International, which revealed data in early 1976 relating to the quality of life of people living in different areas of the globe and embracing a large percentage of mankind. The Gallup research reported that more crimes are now committed in the United States than any place in the world except for certain disadvantaged sections of Latin America and Africa. Furthermore, recidivism in the United States is proliferating at an alarming pace.

The rate of crime in the United States doubled around 1962 and then again about 1970. If the number of crimes perpetrated continues to double every eight years, then the quality of life in America—which has already become restricted—will be seriously impaired, and the nation will have to turn to alternatives which are unacceptable in a democracy.

Crime statistics which are especially disturbing to educators deal with the acceleration in the numbers of crimes committed by adolescents. Between 1960 and 1974, juvenile arrests jumped by a whopping 138 percent. Between 1963 and 1973, the number of arrests per

100 juveniles between the ages of fifteen and eighteen increased from 7 to 13.5 percent. Arrests of persons in this age group for violent crimes have almost tripled—from about one arrest per 400 juveniles to about one arrest for every 140 juveniles.[5] Persons under eighteen now account for nearly 50 percent of all arrests for serious crimes. This juvenile crime problem alone is more than justification for including the concept of responsibility and citizenship as the fourth R in the basic competencies expected of all Americans.

THE MELTING POT REVISITED

Another characteristic of American society which bears heavily on the movement to reform civic education is pluralism. C. P. Snow defines the pluralist society as one which does not have any code of common assumptions.[6] He notes that one of its considerable disadvantages is the difficulty of achieving a common purpose.

The political implications of developing extreme pluralism are not trivial. Increasingly, sociologists are warning that society cannot forever ignore Emile Durkheim's thesis that "society can survive only if there exists among its members a sufficient degree of homogeneity."[7]

However, one of the great strengths of this country has been the various ethnic backgrounds of its people. How to retain this strength and at the same time develop the processes to achieve the "common good" is a fundamental concern for society in general and civic education in particular.

DEFINING THE TASK

With all this confusing input from society, the task is to construct a program of citizenship education for a nation where there is no longer a universally agreed-upon definition of the components of good citizenship. In an effort to make progress in this direction, the Task Force determined that the elements of late-twentieth-century citizenship contain the following components:

1. To know what the principal issues are in contemporary society

2. To know how to become better informed about the leading arguments of an issue

3. To be able to appraise the worth of the evidence on which disputes are based

4. To have a predisposition to try to do something about civic issues

5. To be respectful of the opinions and sincerity of others

Epitomized, a citizen should have the ability to analyze the political and ethical implications of any human situation.

Within this framework of citizen responsibility, a major purpose of this report is to point out that a fundamental societal dilemma exists which must be resolved if the nation is to attain its goals. There is a compelling need for high-level leadership in helping the nation's schools accept a new and greater responsibility in the important task of preparing youth for responsible citizenship.

A free political system has the obligation to give all citizens the opportunity and ability to take an active part in shaping the institutions and laws under which they are to live. If this objective is to be achieved, the nation's schools must be helped to initiate new and dynamic programs designed better to prepare young people for citizenship.

The nation has just passed its Bicentennial celebration. What better time could there possibly be to examine new concepts for citizenship education and concentrate on the idea of dynamic curricula dealing with the concepts of education for responsible citizenship? The intent is to ensure that the great principles of liberty, justice, and equality are better understood and practiced.

Both the advisory and project committees, which guided the development of this report, are acutely (even painfully) aware that the entire responsibility for civic education cannot be fostered on the schools. Other institutions—local, state, and federal governments, along with the television medium—have a major role to play in the reconceptualization of education for responsible citizenship.

NOTES

1. National Assessment of Educational Progress, *Political Knowledge and Attitudes,* 03-SS-01, Denver, Colo., December 1973.

2. Daniel Yankelovich, *Changing Youth Values in the 70's: A Study of American Youth,* report jointly sponsored by Edna McConnell Clark Foundation, Carnegie Corporation of New York, Hazen Foundation, JDR 3rd Fund, and Andrew W. Mellon Foundation, 1973. The complete narrative of the 1973 Yankelovich Youth Survey, entitled *The New Morality: A Profile of American Youth in the Seventies,* is available from McGraw-Hill Book Company.

3. National Commission on the Reform of Secondary Education, *The Reform of Secondary Education: A Report to the Public and the Profession,* McGraw-Hill Book Company, New York, 1973, p. 137.

4. "Education for Citizenship: Educational Goals and Curriculum Patterns," presentation by R. Freeman Butts to members of the Education Commission of the States, Miami, Fla., June 21, 1974.

5. "Pitfalls and Possibilities in Juvenile Justice Reform," address by John M. Greacen, acting director, National Institute for Juvenile Justice and Delinquency Prevention, at the National Conference on Juvenile Justice, Los Angeles, Calif., Nov. 21, 1975.

6. C. P. Snow, "Grounds for Hope?" *New York University Education Quarterly,* Summer 1976, p. 2.

7. Emile Durkheim, *Education and Sociology,* 1922; reprint, The Free Press of Glencoe, Ill., Chicago, 1956.

Recommendations for Strengthening Civic Education

ADVISORY AND PROJECT COMMITTEE MEMBERS

PREAMBLE

In the Constitution, certain basic principles were enunciated by "We, the people." Many citizens maintain that a central function of the schools is to assure the affirmation of these principles by each succeeding generation. The achievement of this affirmation is the task of citizenship education. With the erosion of the educational roles of home, community, religious institutions, and employment, the burden of this task falls increasingly on the schools.

RECOMMENDATION NO. 1: Citizenship education courses as they exist often are limited to the study of government and economics. The base of these courses should be broadened to include Constitutional rights and liberties, the environment, ethical values, interdependence of peoples, and human rights and responsibilities.

RECOMMENDATION NO. 2: The goals of civic education should be knowledge of the political system and how it really and ideally works, development of the skills of participation in civic life, improvement of civic competence, commitment to values compatible with the principles which underlie democratic institutions and a capacity to analyze the consequences of these values, and development of self-esteem so that all individuals feel that their participation in civic life can make a difference.

RECOMMENDATION NO. 3: In all schoolwork dealing with civic competence, and in school-directed community experiences, students should be associated heterogeneously.

RECOMMENDATION NO. 4: Programs to assist young people in becoming responsible citizens should have clearly stated objectives, be continually pursued, and be constantly reassessed. Educators must recognize that every curricular and extracurricular activity, in both the elementary and secondary schools, carries inherent components of citizenship education.

RECOMMENDATION NO. 5: Civic education in the elementary school should be considered as a multidisciplinary subject, with all teachers responsible for its practice and development. The responsibility for teaching civic education in secondary schools rests with the entire school staff. English and social studies teachers have a special opportunity to make impact in this area, because the concepts of justice, liberty, and equality are intrinsic to the subject matter.

RECOMMENDATION NO. 6: Civic education courses should lead the student to an awareness of major social and political trends; a need for balance and perspective in dealing with local, state, national, and international problems; and a recognition of the implications of the interdependencies of nations and the necessity for more compatible and compassionate relationships between developed and developing nations.

RECOMMENDATION NO. 7: The development of an effective civic education curriculum requires three elements: appropriate content for study, teachers prepared to guide student learning, and school procedures which foster the values and skills required in a democratic society. The stated purposes of citizenship education too frequently are contradicted by the "hidden curriculum"—the informal learnings which are provided through the teacher's behavior, the classroom norms, and the interactions between teacher and student and among students.

RECOMMENDATION NO. 8: Because values and ethical issues are central to civic education, schools should be encouraged to use moral-education concepts, as well as law-related materials and community-based experiences reflecting the values of the community.

RECOMMENDATION NO. 9: Among the experiences required for high school graduation should be a practicum in civic education. This requirement could be met by supervised community action-oriented volunteer service projects in hospitals, municipal departments, courts of criminal justice, or any other socially valuable area. Community service experience should be related to work in the classroom and monitored by teaching personnel.

RECOMMENDATION NO. 10: Civic education courses should involve a broad range of participants from the community in addition to school staff.

Recommendations 11 through 16 set forth responsibilities of specific groups to the total civic education program.

RECOMMENDATION NO. 11: *The Federal Effort.* A national effort in the field of civic education, with Congressional guidelines and funding, should be implemented under the supervision of the Office of Education. While the programs themselves should be designed and administered at the local level, Congress should enact civic education legislation comparable in scope and urgency to the National Defense Education Act to stimulate local efforts across the nation.

RECOMMENDATION NO. 12: *The State Effort.* Each state department of education should participate in advancing citizenship education programs based upon input from citizens and the best research in the field.

RECOMMENDATION NO. 13: *The School Board.* The school board, as the body directly responsible to the people, should form citizen advisory committees to help define the goals of the school in the area of political acculturation. Looking beyond its own community, the board should pay special attention to the instruments and conclusions of organizations such as the National Assessment of Educational Progress, which periodically conducts an evaluation of citizenship education at the national level.

RECOMMENDATION NO. 14: *The Superintendent.* The superintendent is charged with maintaining the quality of the civic education program of the schools. He must regularly evaluate progress in this area and remain alert to opportunities for expanding and improving the program.

RECOMMENDATION NO. 15: *The Principal.* The school principal is the key person in establishing a positive climate necessary for effective citizenship education in the school, and the degree of commitment by the principal usually determines the quality of the civic education program. To gain more effective leadership from its school principals, society needs to broaden the preparation and authority of those holding this position.

RECOMMENDATION NO. 16: *The Teacher.* In preparation for teaching, all teachers should receive an internship in government, municipal affairs, health service, the criminal justice system, or some other related area. Teachers should learn to deal with controversial issues on the basis of scholarship without indoctrination. They must know how to lead small groups effectively.

Authorities responsible for educating teachers should make sure that the most competent and capable people are recruited for the task of teaching civic education.

RECOMMENDATION NO. 17: Student responsibilities should be placed in the same positive context as student rights. As every right has a corresponding responsibility, the schools should place a balanced emphasis on both.

RECOMMENDATION NO. 18: School governance, separate and distinct from courses of study, should be integrated in the curriculum and in all school activities. The practices of student government should be consonant with the principles of civic education. Students should be encouraged to act on issues of concern to them—community issues as well as school issues. It is essential that the environment of the school be just and democratic.

RECOMMENDATION NO. 19: The orderly and effective transition from youth to adulthood is a prime purpose of education. The schools should encourage communication between young people and the existing adult culture. To provide for an expanding relationship between students and adults, the school should become a center for community activities.

RECOMMENDATION NO. 20: The schools should do all in their power to develop in students an analytical and inquiring mode of television viewing. Citizens should bring pressure to bear on both television networks and local channels, urging them to assume responsibility for helping the individual to deal more intelligently with public affairs, to reinforce the sense of history, and to develop a feeling of stewardship for the future.

RECOMMENDATION NO. 21: Adolescents should be taught the importance of negotiating, and the skills involved in this process, in order to guide their understanding of the meaning of compromise in the democratic resolution of problems.

The Total Educational Environment

2

RALPH W. TYLER

THE CURRENT PUBLIC MOOD

It seems a paradox that the American public focuses its anxieties about the effectiveness of education on two chief areas: the "basics" (reading and arithmetic) and citizenship, including moral education. Many educators view these as opposite poles of the educational function. They consider the acquisition of reading and computational skills to be a relatively narrow goal, while the development of constructive citizenship and character is thought to be a broad one encompassing the "whole child." If education is to contribute to the maintenance of a productive, peaceful, and just society, these goals are not in conflict.

In a modern industrial society, anyone who cannot read or compute finds few opportunities for employment, and his participation in the civic life of the nation is restricted. Much more is now required from citizens than was needed in earlier times. As always, they must develop respect and concern for others and understand how their community, state, and nation function; but they must also become aware of the problems that require attention in a rapidly changing world, and they must develop commitments to the larger society and make constructive contributions to it. The educational objectives include the development of social interests, attitudes, skills, and habits, as well as knowledge. To meet these expectations requires of each citizen a large and lifelong educational effort.

Unfortunately, complex human learning does not come easily. Learning to read and compute is not simply a matter of drill, and the learning of citizenship is not merely a matter of inculcating moral and social precepts. When simplistic views are pressed on schools, the response often takes the form of intensive drill and the reciting of platitudes, stripping the educational program of much of its meaning and attraction to students and reducing its effectiveness in stimulating and guiding significant learning.

The contemporary effort to improve education and to give more explicit attention to citizenship and character development can be a positive influence if it is based on a more realistic understanding of the total educational system. Education must not be confused with schooling, and the school cannot be the sole target of those criticizing or seeking to improve education.

THE TOTAL EDUCATIONAL SYSTEM

An educational system, of which school is only a part, furnishes the experiences through which a young person learns to participate constructively in a modern industrialized society. What he or she experiences in the home, in social activities in the community, in chores and jobs, in religious institutions, in reading, in listening to radio and viewing television, and in the school are all part of the educational system through which he or she acquires knowledge and ideas, skills and habits, attitudes and interests, and basic values. The school furnishes opportunities to learn to read, write, and compute, to discover and use facts, principles, and ideas that are more accurate, balanced, and comprehensive than what is provided in most homes, work places, or other social institutions. The school also supplements and complements learning furnished by the other institutions and is usually an environment that represents the American social ideals more closely than the larger society. In most schools, each student is respected as a human being without discrimination, the transactions in the classroom are guided by an attempt to be fair and dispense justice, and the class morale is a reflection of the fact that the members care about the welfare of others.

In the past, experiences in the home, the work situation, and the school made somewhat different contributions to the development of American youth. Most young people acquired their basic habits of orderliness, punctuality, and attention to work primarily through experiences in the home and in work settings, with helpful supplementation by the school's regimen.

People develop their values from all the experiences that have seemed significant to them, and they value what they find enjoyable: material objects, activities, perhaps even the acquisition of knowledge and understanding. As a young person develops a conception of the kind of person he or she would like to be, living up to this self-image is satisfying and valued. In brief, every human being has a very large range of potential objects, activities, relations with people, and ways of behaving that he or she may learn to value, and thus they become that person's values.

But everyone finds his or her values in conflict in particular situations, where one value can be gained only at the expense of another. For example, if a child keeps the basketball the whole play period, she gains the satisfaction of the activity, but she may lose the friendship of the boy next door who wants to share in the play. Or if a child "swipes" the pen from the teacher's desk, he gains the value of possessing an attractive object, but he loses the satisfaction of living up to his self-image. Developing a set of personal values implies a hierarchy or priority of values. This hierarchy results both from one's direct experiences and satisfactions and from observing the behavior of persons who seem attractive.

In the past, most children's social values developed initially in the home and in the experience of playing with others. Now television has a strong influence, even in the early years of life. The value children attach to unselfish sharing as against selfishness is already obvious when they enter school. But experiences in school and outside the home can have a marked influence in modifying priorities. A desirable hierarchy of values may or may not develop from exhortations or from participation in "wholesome" activities.

Attitudes are important in creating social-civic values. In the past, attitudes toward productivity and some of the basic working skills have been learned by young people through participation in family chores, and in part-time jobs where they commonly worked under close supervision with critical appraisals of their efforts— mowing lawns, shoveling snow, preparing meals, doing laundry, carrying newspapers, and working in stores and shops. Productivity in working on school assignments does not impress young people as having the same social importance as productivity in doing chores and working on other jobs. Developing the desire to be productive is important in the education of youth, but it is not chiefly acquired through school experiences.

Schools are relatively ineffective, too, in teaching children to take responsibility for a task and accept the consequences of success and failure in performing it. Responsibility for doing one's school assignments does not have the same meaning for a young person as being responsible for work directly affecting others, the consequences of which will be judged by others. Adolescents commonly vacillate between the desire to take large responsibilities and the fear of

failure. Learning to take responsibility and to bear the consequences requires considerable experience, with gradual increase in
the degree of responsibility and in the seriousness of the consequences of failure paralleling the increase in the competence and
confidence of the youth. The school alone can contribute only a
minor range of learning experiences for this purpose. Situations
which are clearly real and require adult behavior as perceived by
young people are necessary. Opportunities must be furnished in
business, industry, agriculture, health agencies, civil service, social
agencies, and the like—the institutions in the community where
adults take responsibility and where real consequences follow. The
school can help find these opportunities for youth, can help organize
them for effective and sequential learning, and can supervise them
to assure that educational values are being attained, but the school
cannot do the whole job itself.

The school can also contribute to the development of social skills
that are essential to civic life, to home living, and to effective work
in group settings. Schools are societies in microcosm where children
and youth communicate, cooperate and compete, and generally
carry on their transactions without serious conflict or the arousal of
intense antagonism. Opinion polls of youth report that they are
generally well satisfied with the social environment of their schools.
Most schools appear to contribute positively to the development of
the kind of social skills essential to many kinds of adult situations.

In educational systems of the past, the several parts had certain
interdependent features. As skills in reading, writing, and arithmetic were developed in the school, the student found opportunities for
their use in activities outside the school both in work and in recreation. Skills quickly become inoperative when their use is infrequent.
If the only reading required of youth is that assigned in school,
reading skills do not reach a mature level. If writing is limited to an
occasional note or letter, writing skills remain very primitive. If
arithmetic is not used in such home activities as consumer buying,
furniture construction, budgeting, or in outside work, arithmetic
skills and problem solving are likely to be haphazard. Hence, the
total educational system needs to be viewed as one in which practice
as well as initial learning is provided.

In the recent period of rapid social change, the educational roles of
the home, the community, the religious institutions, and employment have been greatly changed. Generally, they have been
reduced. Only the school is maintaining approximately the same

role with the same amount of time annually for its work with children and youth. The time no longer occupied by the other experiences has largely been taken up by television. Schramm and Parker report that the average American child between the ages of ten and fourteen spends about 1,500 hours per year viewing television and only about 1,100 hours per year in school. When the educational expectations of the public are not realized in the performance of youth, common opinion holds that the schools have failed, ignoring the erosion of the nonschool part of an educational system.

DIFFERENT EDUCATIONAL ENVIRONMENTS

Not only has the total educational system been seriously eroded during the recent past, but the learning experiences of children from different circumstances have become different in respects that are important for citizenship education. For example, children living in relatively affluent middle-class suburbs have generally learned to value peaceable group activities, fair treatment of peers, and unselfishness in face-to-face relations. Most of them respect constituted authority in school and community, and their adolescent rebellion does not represent a permanent separation from adult institutions, but rather a testing of their own development to adult status. The men and women in their community who are respected and are attractive for youth to emulate are those who have substantial possessions, belong to families engaged in professional or managerial occupations, and devote time to voluntary, charitable, educational, and civic activities. These children lack experiences in working constructively with people different from themselves and do not understand clearly the needs or circumstances of others. They have had few opportunities to assume responsibility and to work hard and long to achieve group goals. They conceive political activities as something going on "out there" rather than being a natural and important aspect of their own lives.

Poor children in the inner city are usually involved in learning experiences different from those in affluent suburbs. With a chronic shortage of material things in the homes and community, fighting for possession of them is common, and peaceable transactions are interspersed with quarrels and the use of force to take things. Experience with transactions guided by fair rules is usually so limited or has furnished so little satisfaction that many of the children do not value living by accepted rules or laws. Taking what one can get without serious punishment appears to many of them to be a better principle than meekly obeying laws that would deny them what they crave. The "successful" adults that attract their emulation are often the "hustlers" who drive big cars, wear flashy clothes, and live an exciting life. Parents try hard to instill a respect for law and a commitment to the Ten Commandments, but the "hustlers" seem to do better. Children in the inner city also experience only a restricted environment offering few, if any, opportunities to work constructively with persons different from their neighbors.

Working-class families emphasize the values of possessions, of "getting ahead," of holding a good-paying, steady job, of keeping clear of the law, of having and being good neighbors. These youth are likely to emulate adults who are in higher social strata, often those shown on television. Both the well-to-do and the indigent are viewed by most of this community as undesirable elements in the society, and their children are not encouraged to make friends with children from other backgrounds.

Many working-class adults are active in political clubs and in return expect special treatment by local officials. Many of the children observe firsthand the activities of the precinct captain and other local party leaders and understand some of the realities of local politics. They look favorably on the work of policemen and expect them to help protect their homes and possessions. They value "law and order."

In rural and small-town settings, the community outside the school commonly offers opportunities for children to work together in constructive activities such as 4H Club projects, Little League ball clubs, and community betterment projects sponsored by church groups. These experiences not only develop social skills, but also form attitudes favoring cooperation and beliefs that group actions can help to improve the community. Most of the adults value gaining and maintaining the respect of their community, getting ahead, education, and independence. Government is often viewed as a necessary evil to protect "good people" from the criminal element. Public schools are not perceived as government agencies but as "our institutions," while most other publicly supported activities are referred to as "the government's." Many of the youth emulate prominent community leaders or impressive high-status persons frequently appearing on television. The children lack experience with politics other than reform efforts outside the normal political institutions. They live in an environment which is much more unified with respect to economic, political, and social values than that found in urban areas.

Poor children in rural settings—those in rural Arkansas, Appalachia, or in families of migrant farm workers—have very little experience working constructively with people outside their own subgroups. Neither they nor their parents think of governments as theirs, whether local, state, or national, and they do not expect any positive benefits from government. They have learned to value material possessions, family solidarity, and independence from interference by others. They have few opportunities to develop social skills, and they view unselfishness and truthfulness as applicable within the family group but not beyond. The same is true for the injunction against stealing. The commitment to the family of origin is very highly valued. Few of these youth find adults that they seek to emulate.

RECONSTRUCTING THE TOTAL EDUCATIONAL SYSTEM

A partial reconstruction of the total educational system can be based on an initiative by the school. Particularly at the junior and senior high school level, many school systems are developing programs in which students participate responsibly in adult roles. In 1972, the National Association of Secondary School Principals sponsored a conference which led to more than 1,000 high school action-learning programs in which students worked with adults both for pay and as volunteers. The National Commission on Resources for Youth published in 1974 a book entitled *New Roles for Youth,* in which dozens of exemplary programs of youth participation are described in some detail, complete with suggestions of how to set up and conduct such programs.

The longest experience in the use of out-of-school educational activities derives from the cooperative work-study program in vocational education programs partly supported by federal funds. Typically, a student works at a job half a day and attends school half a day. A coordinator is employed by the school not only to place students in appropriate work settings, but also to help the employer develop a sequence of job assignments to give the student a chance to continue learning rather than simply to perform routine operations. The coordinator is also expected to assist the teachers in the school to relate the curriculum as far as possible to the experiences the students are having in their work. A recent evaluation of cooperative high school work-study programs was conducted by System Development Corporation. Their report furnished several kinds of evidence of the value of this program in preparing a young person for effective job performance, enabling him to obtain employment after graduation, and furnishing motivation for his schoolwork.

During the past twenty years, a wide circle of schools have sought to make real the community school idea developed by Maurice Seay, Harold Sloan, and others during the thirties. In essence, this idea conceives the school as an institution of service for the entire community, and the community as a major resource for the education of students. The embodiment of this concept in practice involves cooperation between the school and many community groups, organizations, and individuals; it also involves the utilization of out-of-school educational experiences. Major support for schools in this movement comes from the Community School Association, with headquarters in Flint, Michigan.

Important as they are, cooperative education and community school activities are not enough to furnish a comprehensive learning environment for citizenship education. A major part of this environment lies outside the school walls, where students spend most of their time. Reconstructing the total educational environment to overcome its recent erosion will require a new role for the school. In the past, the school supported and reinforced the dominant civic values of the community, without conscious recognition of its role. For his well-known readers, William H. McGuffey chose stories and essays that reflected currently accepted values, but most teachers and administrators were not aware that schoolbooks had educational objectives beyond the development of reading skills and a widening of the student's horizons as he grasped the ideas presented in the stories and essays. Now it is necessary for the school consciously to reexamine contemporary conditions, to identify the contributions it can make, and to encourage and support the efforts of other community institutions.

The school cannot easily deal with comprehensive citizenship education, because it cannot be the chief contributor to such education and cannot effectively dominate the coalition of community groups that must work out a feasible program of mutual responsibility. The school has had little practice in planning and implementing programs in which it plays a junior partner's role.

Another difficulty arises from the need to keep closely in touch with the out-of-school experiences of the students in order to focus on the real ethical situations these children confront in learning to be good citizens. Simulations cannot fully convey to students the dilemmas that tempt and torture human beings.

Nevertheless, there are contributions that the school can make, many of them in harmony with its traditional role of developing cognitive abilities and habits. The school can encourage students to reflect on the problem situations they encounter, to analyze these situations, to try to predict the consequences of several possible courses of action, to compare their thinking with what they actually did, and to note the consequences they experienced.

Furthermore, the contributions envisaged by the curriculum constructors of the last century are still possible today. Literature can illuminate social issues and help students understand and feel the significance of courage in acting in accordance with conscience. Movies, television, radio, and the press can also furnish material for this study. The school can help the student evaluate critically the offerings of these media and develop criteria for selecting what he will spend time viewing, hearing, and reading. The school, working closely with other constructive community groups, can influence the content of these media and their distribution to children.

The school can also continue its long-accepted role of providing within its environment a democratic society closer to the ideal than the adult community has yet been able to achieve. It can provide a setting in which young people can experience concretely the meaning of our democratic ideals. In the school, every student is to be respected as a person, regardless of his background. In the school, the students can experience a society where justice and fair play dominate, a society where people care about each other and where all have an opportunity to share in planning activities, executing them, and gaining the rewards of what they have accomplished. It is not always easy for teachers and administrators to provide this kind of environment, but it is crucially important for children to see firsthand a society that encourages and supports democratic values.

ADMINISTRATIVE ARRANGEMENTS FOR A COMPREHENSIVE EDUCATIONAL SYSTEM

Because a comprehensive program of citizenship education requires constructive learning activities far beyond those which can be provided within a school, some form of community council or board is necessary to assess educational needs, identify actual and potential resources, and develop an outline of educational programs. Some educational task forces or councils must be drawn from the larger metropolitan area or region for educational needs that cannot be met well by the local community.

At the state level, legislation should be enacted to authorize these community and metropolitan organizations, to express the policy of the state, to encourage and provide support for the development and maintenance of a comprehensive educational system, and to repeal any existing legislation which limits educational programs to those within the school or within certain specified time periods.

At the national level, the Congress should be asked to adopt a resolution endorsing comprehensive educational programs and stating a national policy to encourage full development of human resources through comprehensive educational experiences. The federal government should authorize support for, and appropriate funds to encourage and assist, the development of community councils and metropolitan or regional task forces to develop and maintain comprehensive educational systems.

These proposals do not envision public operation and support of all out-of-school educational experiences. The American public is not likely to vote the taxes required to furnish professionals to guide the education of children and youth in the many hours when they are not in school. Furthermore, a monolithic structure of the total educational system is inappropriate for a democratic society, particularly a multicultural one. Volunteer leaders can be secured, as has been demonstrated by out-of-school educational organizations like the 4H Clubs, the Boy Scouts and Girl Scouts, and the Junior Achievement Program.

Several surveys indicate that a large number of persons with knowledge and skills would like to teach them as a public service without remuneration. The strength and vitality of voluntary organizations in the United States have been noted frequently by foreign visitors. What is missing is the comprehensive identification of needs and authorized encouragement of those who could meet the needs.

The intent of these proposed policies is to develop a recognized and responsible educational system to replace the informal and eroding one that now exists. This nation has progressed a considerable distance in enabling a major fraction of their young people to learn the knowledge, skills, and attitudes required for a responsible and productive life in a complex society. But 20 to 25 percent of youth have not learned these competencies. They need specially designed opportunities to learn the basic skills, to develop the necessary understanding, and to take on increasing responsibility as citizens in activities that involve production and service to others. In the near future, because of the continuing erosion of learning experiences in home, in community, and in the work place, many more youth may have difficulty in making the transition to responsible adulthood. The vitality and stability of American political, economic, and social institutions are dependent upon the effectiveness of its educational system. That system must not be permitted to disintegrate.

Political and Social Purposes of Education

3

STEPHEN K. BAILEY

The American polity may be characterized as a system of state-supported capitalism, political and bureaucratic federalism, and constitutionally protected criticism.

Global and domestic economic, political, and social forces are placing unprecedented strains upon this system.

These twin propositions might simply be filed as written were it not that, currently and prospectively, they impinge massively on other existential realities.

Life begins and ends as a vital statistic of government. National security and diplomatic operations are justified as protectors of life and liberty. Publics invest in state-supported schools in the belief that schools have the capacity to contribute substantially to the cognitive and affective development of young people. Laws governing child labor affect the trauma of adolescence. Social security and medicare substantially influence the conditions of old age. All segments of the existential wheel are shaped and affected by the laws, institutions, and behaviors of the political economy: the availability and quality of jobs and the distribution of wealth outside the job market; the coping agenda, including coping with taxes and with myriad public regulations; the external supports to the free self, including the availability of educational, cultural, and recreational resources and facilities; and definitions of freedom permitting the exercise of individual options.

The American commonwealth is far too complex for rational control at the center—at least without the use of punitive government sanctions quite out of keeping with our peacetime national heritage. The result is a bizarre kaleidoscope of centers of political and economic power. Some of these centers are public, some private,

NOTE: Based on Stephen K. Bailey, *The Purposes of Education,* Bicentennial Monograph Series, Phi Delta Kappa Educational Foundation, July 1976, chap. 6.

some mixed. They exist at all levels of constitutional federalism: national, state, and local. In the eyes of devotees, the American polity provides most citizens with freedom and security and with a high standard of living. In the eyes of its critics, it promotes real freedom and exorbitant wealth for a few at the price of massive caste and class inequities, demeaning bureaucratic strictures and regulations, militarism, and a cultural crassness that dehumanizes its citizens.

The fundamental conundrum is how to overcome the evils postulated by critics without destroying the virtues claimed by devotees. For rigid ideologues of the right and the left, of course, no answer is possible. "Free enterprise" reactionaries (consciously or unconsciously using Darwinian analogues) argue that inequality is a law of nature. Social as well as individual wealth, they assert, is the product of decisions made by Prometheans motivated by the possibilities of material gain. The appropriate job of government then is minimal: to establish the framework within which a free-market economy can prosper, and to handle social and economic basket cases among the unfortunate. Critics to the left, on the other hand, believe that a free market is an illusion, that state-supported capitalism is inherently exploitative, protective of the rich, and dangerously militaristic. They believe the way to salvation is either a strong central authority organized to plan for economic justice, conservation, and peace, or a political economy atomized into pastoral communes of benign anarchy.

Most Americans appear to disavow ideological extremes. To paraphrase Justice Holmes, they have little faith in utopias and almost none in sudden ruin. They hope to find a middle way that optimizes a number of competing goods: options for the individual, a redress of the intolerable grievances of caste and class, a diplomatic and military posture consistent with a progressively ordered and equitable global network of nations and peoples, and a stable economy friendly to the ecology of the biosphere. They believe governments are needed as major instruments in a search for optimized trade-offs. They also believe, however, that governments are part of the problem as well as part of the solution. They know that statesmen can corrupt and can be corrupted. They know that, at some point, the apparatus of government monitoring and regulation becomes a cure worse than the disease being attacked. They have a vague sense that individual citizens have a responsibility to participate in the political processes. Beyond voting, letters to editors and politicians, and street protests, however, they are not clear how participation can or should be exercised.

The test of the viability of some middle way, some "vital center," has never been more severe. If the phrases in the Preamble to the Constitution are employed as bench marks for measuring the adequacy of our political economy, the shortfalls are patent.

A More Perfect Union? There are ominous signs that America is being retribalized into ethnic, religious, racial, economic, demographic, and sexual divisions. White suburbs surround black and brown inner cities. Zoning ordinances keep the riffraff out. Generations talk with each other fitfully across moats of misunderstanding. Self-interest and self-indulgence flout the very notion of community.

Establish Justice? America, in an orgy of litigiousness, has overcrowded its court dockets, pampered rich litigants, frustrated the poor and the middle class, and produced more lawyers than are compatible with a nation built on unspoken assumptions of mutual trust.

Insure Domestic Tranquility? The headlines of crime and violence and the ubiquitous ads for personal and home security devices tell the sad tale.

Provide for the Common Defense? In spite of mountains of riches spent on armaments, America is part of an international disorder that is almost bound to confront humankind with a continuation of international kidnappings, violence, and terrorism; a series of small flames of belligerency in a forest of tinder; planetary economic bargainings that America may not win; and an escalating risk of nuclear piracy and blackmail.

Promote the General Welfare? This entire chapter is directed at the disturbingly uneven state of the general welfare—psychological, economic, social, and political.

Secure the Blessings of Liberty? Here, quibbles aside, the United States on any scale of nations is still in the front rank of societies that enjoy political freedom. The question is whether the perilous state of the nation in other respects will erode and destroy this cardinal condition of its self-renewal. Fear is the most brutalizing of human emotions. If social pathologies (for example, crime, unemployment, racial conflicts, international tension) become sufficiently unsettling as to produce widespread personal fear, people will trade freedom for security by electing despots. So runs one of the oldest principles of political action. This truth is so basic that it deserves elaboration.

ANCIENT LORE ON THE CONDITIONS
OF FREEDOM

The ancient chronicles of mankind are freighted with examples of domestic turbulence. The historian Thucydides believed that domestic turbulence was inevitable. To him it was simply the overt manifestation of the cycles of history, kept revolving by what he called "excess of power." According to Thucydides,

> . . . primitive despots start the wheel rolling. The more power they get the more they want, and they go on abusing the authority until inevitably opposition is aroused and a few men, strong enough when they unite, seize the rule for themselves. These, too, can never be satisfied. They encroach upon the rights of others until they are opposed in their turn. The people are aroused against them, and democracy succeeds to oligarchy. But then again the evil in all power is no less operative. Democracy brings corruption and contempt for law until the state can no longer function and falls easily before a strong man who promises to restore order. The rule of the one, of the few, of the many, each is destroyed in turn because there is in them all an unvarying evil—the greed for power—and no moral quality is necessarily bound up with any of them.

Plato and Aristotle subscribed to elements of Thucydides' cyclical theme of history. For them the two great political evils were libertarian democracy and dictatorship, and they believed that the first led inexorably to the second. Plato, for example, devoted the entire third book of his *Laws* to an examination of the opposites, to Persian tyrant kings, and to how an unrestrained democracy in Athens ruined itself by an excess of liberty. Plato's *Laws* are far more rewarding than his *Republic*. The latter is totalitarianism idealized. The *Laws,* on the other hand, deals with real people in a real world. The good or approximately good society, to which the third book of the *Laws* is addressed, is a society which maximizes law-abiding rule—which features, in other words, domestic tranquility. For as Plato and his pupil Aristotle contended: in any good state, the law must be the ultimate sovereign and not any person whatsover. They perceived a universal moral precept: that constitutional rule is consistent with the dignity of the subject, whereas personal or despotic rule is not.

What, then, undermines the rule of law? What causes domestic strife and political decay? Was Thucydides right in stating that greed for power is the basic cause of civil unrest? Most political theory addressed to this question from ancient to modern times has identified a second causative factor: inequality.

Plato fully believed that, at least in Greek experience, excessive differences between rich and poor had been the chief cause of civic contention. Aristotle believed that revolutions are caused chiefly by inequalities in property (a theme later to be elaborated by many other political theorists, including Karl Marx).

Sir Thomas More, in his biting sixteenth-century satire *Utopia,* pointed out that crime in England was alarmingly common, but that in a grotesquely unequal society crime is the only livelihood open to a great number of persons. In as terrible a voice as his pen could conjure, More fairly shouted at the England of his day, "What other thing do you do than make thieves and then punish them?"

In the nineteenth century, in the quieter vein of a Victorian Oxford don, T. H. Green wrote, "It is idle to expect men to become responsible agents when they live in conditions that destroy the qualities of character on which responsibility depends."

When inequality and power hunger remain uncorrected by government and by private virtue, the basic corruption of the political order ensues. Machiavelli, in the sixteenth century, described political corruption as including "all sorts of license and violence, great inequalities of wealth and power, the destruction of peace and justice, the growth of disorderly ambition, disunion, lawlessness, dishonesty, and contempt for religion." And according to Machiavelli, when the necessary virtues have decayed, there is no possibility of restoring them or of carrying on orderly government without them except by despotic power. And despotic power is infinitely preferable to anarchy.

This last theme appears in stirring eloquence in the writing of Thomas Hobbes more than a century later. In his great work *The Leviathan,* Hobbes conjectured that man is basically selfish and power seeking; that the rewards of nature are in short supply; and that, in the competition for the scarce goods of life, there would be a "war of every man against every man" if it were not for a contrivance called government. Without government, life would be "solitary, poor, nasty, brutish, and short" (Hobbes' most famous phrase).

If power hunger and inequality constitute the main threats to domestic tranquility, what then are the conditions of domestic stability? Obviously the answers are (1) reduce inequality and (2) set up agreed-upon rules (including checks and balances) to ensure that power is contained and that alternations of power are peaceable rather than disruptive.

On reducing inequality, Plato wanted to limit the amount of property that anyone could hold in order to "exclude from the state those excessive differences between rich and poor which Greek experience has shown to be the chief cause of civic contention."

Aristotle believed that equality (and consequently domestic tranquility) was synonymous with a large middle class—neither very rich nor very poor. As Euripedes had said years before, the middle class is the class that "saves states." Politically, Aristotle thought that a combination of oligarchy and democracy was the most stable form of government. If not watched by the people, the oligarchs—or privileged few—would become oppressive, and this oppressiveness would breed disorder. Without the balance wheel of the privileged few, the democratic masses would be rudderless, and the ship of state would founder.

Echoes of the Greek philosophers' twin ideas of mixed and balanced government and greater equality can be heard throughout the succeeding centuries—up to and including our own. Certainly these are the golden themes of our founding fathers: the equality doctrine especially noted in our Declaration of Independence; the mixed and balanced government concept, in our Constitution.

The essential legacy of the theory of mixed and balanced government and of greater equality must constitute the bedrock of American citizenship education. The lessons are clear: there is no possibility of domestic tranquility in a free society without a progressive increase in social justice; if sufficient power is to be aggregated to make effective government possible, both institutional and political means must be found to hold such power accountable. In these terms, the realities of racial and economic castes and classes explain a sizable proportion of the lack of domestic tranquility. The trauma of Watergate is a reminder of the need to hold power accountable.

PARTICIPATION AND REPRESENTATION

Fundamental to the success of a free society is widespread citizen participation in the political process. This participation may include voting; party and interest-group activities; performing such public functions as jury duty, testifying as a witness, and serving on public boards and commissions; and carrying out honorably the mandates of obeying laws and paying taxes. Beyond this participation, citizens contribute to the polity by keeping informed about public affairs and by sharing their views with other citizens and with elected representatives. An independent press and a rich smorgasbord of information purveyed by television, radio, journals of opinion, and books, are essential to the maintenance of a politically literate society.

Much of the real power of citizens, however, is latent. It lies in the perpetual threat to politicians of retribution at the polls if citizens, otherwise passive, are outraged by the direction or corruption of public life. Former Harvard professor Carl Friedrich once called this "the law of anticipated reaction." It is a moralizing force of incalculable significance to the workings of democracy.

For reasons that are understandable in the sociology of reform, the air is filled with romantic half-truths about the possibilities and desirability of extending and increasing direct citizen participation beyond the activities and latencies just listed. Because the nation has recently been burned by abuses of power, some high-minded reformers and concerned educators have developed ("refurbished" is a better word) a democratic litany as superficially plausible as it is operationally specious and even dangerous. Two propositions seem to dominate: first, citizens should, wherever possible, participate directly in all political decision making; second, where they cannot participate directly, the decision processes of their representatives must be open to detailed and continuous public monitoring. Following in the footsteps of the reform movements at the turn of the century (especially the tarnished movements for the initiative, referendum, and recall), modern reformers seem to have little understanding of the complexity of the agenda of modern government, of the interest-group building blocks of public policy, and of the essential conditions of aggregating and exercising responsible political power. In consequence, they establish reform paradigms that are frequently irrelevant, naïve, or mischievous.

For those reformers who believe in universal, direct citizen participation in public affairs, whose model democracy is the New England town meeting (which, incidentally, usually was and is caucus rigged), technology is surely available. The government could, at modest expense, equip every television set in the nation with "yes" and "no" buttons. Every Sunday night at 8:00 P.M., three national, three state, and three local propositions could be flashed on the screen. The citizen would simply vote yes or no. On the first trial Sunday, the propositions, for example, might be as follows:

National
Proposition One: The Federal Reserve rediscount rate should be lowered by a quarter of a point.   Yes_____ No_____
Proposition Two: Five nuclear submarines should be built instead of two aircraft carriers.   Yes_____ No_____
Proposition Three: Gold should be remonetized for purposes of stabilizing international currencies.   Yes_____ No_____
State
Proposition One: State environmental protection laws shold limit sulfur emissions of factories to one particle in 10,000.   Yes_____ No_____
Proposition Two: Offender farms are 25 percent less secure than traditional prisons, but their rate of recidivism is also 25 percent less. Should the state substitute the farm system for the prison system?   Yes_____ No_____
Proposition Three: The state budget should shift from a line-item to a program-budget format.   Yes_____ No_____
Local
Proposition One: School bonds should be marketed only if the interest rate is under 10 percent.   Yes_____ No_____
Proposition Two: Most recent hirings of municipal employees have been minorities and women. Now that retrenchment is necessary, seniority should still determine who is to be laid off first.   Yes_____ No_____
Proposition Three: The local police department should be amalgamated with the new metropolitan police system.   Yes_____ No_____

Even if a packet of printed materials were delivered well in advance, or a two-page spread of editorial comment appeared in the Sunday newspaper, how reasonable is it to assume that most citizens would have the information or would take the time to master the data and to make analyses sufficient for informed judgments? Usually, propositions placed on the ballot under various referendum provisions are decided on the basis, not of study, but of simplistic reactions to public relations techniques or to calls for party or interest-group loyalty.

Because of the ultimate capacity of American citizens to make wise, fundamental value choices, attempts to induce them into making superficial technical choices are ill-advised. Representative legislators and officials are supported by an educated bureaucracy, informed by myriad interest groups and experts, checked by an independent judiciary and a free press, and held accountable to the larger public through periodic elections, intermittent correspondence, and occasional face-to-face meetings. All this constitutes not only a reasonable apparatus for conducting modern public business in an economically and technologically complex free society like the United States, but also the *only* reasonable apparatus.

But there are necessary conditions if this complex apparatus is to work effectively. One condition is that politicians and the media really work at reducing technical questions to the level of value choices that are, in fact, amenable to public discourse and to ultimate resolution at the polls through expressions of preference for persons and parties. A second condition is that opportunities be provided for interest-group inputs into the decisional processes of government, but not for interest-group vetoes of the actions of legitimate majorities and authorities. This last point needs emphasis. James Madison, in the tenth Federalist Paper, wrote of the inevitability of interests and factions in a free society. He contended that the *regulation* of these various and interfering interests forms the principal task of modern legislation (emphasis supplied). Madison's choice of *regulation* instead of *accommodation* implies authority; that is, the aggregation of responsible power capable of making decisions that are something more than a simple acquiescence to raw pressure or a primitive bartering of contending claims. At most levels of American government, the two instruments of responsible representative power for moralizing and homogenizing group pressures are: chief executives, whose legitimacy normally depends on an external party choice ratified by a plurality of electoral votes; and legislative leadership, whose legitimacy depends on the sanction of party caucuses within legislative houses. Anything that weakens the capacity of those centers of responsible power to accommodate differences, while searching for an overarching public interest testable at elections, undermines the legitimacy and effectiveness of the entire political system.

For a number of reasons (including recent abuses of executive power, administrative violations of due process, the propensity of legislators and officials to overclassify governmental information, and the unreasonable secrecy within which some public business has been conducted), various reform groups have attempted to open the entire system to immediate public scrutiny. By promoting "sunshine laws" ("sunlight purifies as well as illuminates"), reformers have succeeded in many states and at the national level in correcting some of the abuses noted above. In the process, however, the simplistic drafting of rigid sunshine laws has in many places undermined or unduly constrained essential political activity. At some point in the process of public decision making, after various groups have made their demands known, after "participatory democracy" has taken place, temporal and spatial environments must be created that permit responsible authorities to sort out claims and counterclaims, analyze trade-offs, and develop face-saving formulas that optimize a series of inevitably conflicting values. In some circumstances, this cardinal aspect of democratic politics can best take place in the open. But in many cases, enforced openness through indiscriminate sunshine laws simply drives the process underground, or provides interest groups with a monitoring opportunity that they—not the general public or even the press—will exercise, and that inhibits the free give-and-take of honest compromise. Sunshine purifies, but an excess causes cancer.

Inasmuch as the public cannot possibly know everything that is going on, even in the open, the real protection of the public interest rests in holding political authorities responsible for results—not in inhibiting the processes through which decisions are made. If the American public has become so distrustful of its public servants that it has to impose detailed surveillance techniques to monitor every moment of their public behavior, this nation will have designed a system which in truth is the "triumph of technique over purpose." As Edward Levi has put it, "A right of complete confidentiality in government could not only produce a dangerous public ignorance but also destroy the basic representative functions of government. But a duty of complete disclosure would render impossible the effective operations of government."

Similarly, government can be immobilized if demands by any group for participation in the processes of decision making become a euphemism for minority control by veto or disruption. Some weight must always be given to intensity of feeling on the part of special interests (for example, labor; business; agriculture; banking; veterans; education; and religious, racial, and ethnic groups), but democracy is meaningless if responsible majorities cannot be formed and given the power to govern. This is why the health of American political parties—the great organizers of pluralities and majorities—is so important. This is why the antiparty sentiments of the American public are so dangerous. America's general ignorance about the significance and the workings of its party system is a defect so serious as to threaten the viability of the entire democratic enterprise.

Majorities, including party majorities, must of course rule within the framework of the Constitution. Independent courts, a free press, and ultimately a committed and informed citizenry are the fundamental safeguards of this elaborate and essentially benign system.

These fundamental propositions about power and responsibility must be learned by each new generation. Schools and colleges have a particular responsibility to inform their charges of these basic necessities. But all parts of the polity (including the press, myriad interest groups, political parties, and the government itself) share the burden of instructing citizens in the conditions of preserving freedom in a big democracy. Individual courage and loyalty to high principles must be manifest in all parts of the complex system if it is to work: individual politicians; individual bureaucrats; individual judges; individual interest-group representatives; individual party workers; individual reporters, commentators, and editors; and individual citizens who are motivated only by a concern for the public weal. But these persons must learn the art of using or influencing the complex and often ponderous machinery of politics and government, if they are to make constructive changes in the substance and the procedures of the polity.

THE DEVELOPMENT OF POLITICAL SKILLS

Abstract and general knowledge about the polity is one thing; the skills and attitudes needed to make the polity work are something else. Schools and colleges do not do well at conveying the knowledge. On the matter of skill development, they are woefully deficient. How can the American society educate future generations of leaders (hundreds of thousands of them) and future generations of informed and critical followers (millions of them) to have the heart, the brains, and the guts to think and to behave responsibly as political beings? James Thurber cautioned people not to look backward in anger, not forward in fear, but around in awareness. By and large this advice has not been heeded. Schools and colleges have done little in identifying the skills, mental attitudes, moral philosophies, and social commitments needed for the survival of democratic values—perhaps even for the survival of the species.

Educational administrators and teachers do not lack the desire to be helpful in the socialization process. Considerable time and attention have been given by schools to the inculcation of attitudes of patriotism and tolerance and to the underlying political philosophies of our constitutional system. The best of America's schools, colleges, and universities have stimulated an honest social criticism that has had an important and healthy influence on both foreign affairs and recent domestic events. But when past and present educational practice is measured against present and future national and international need, an enormous educational gap becomes obvious. Educators have almost totally ignored the development of social and political skills, without which even sophisticated attitudes and compendious knowledge are inutile.

What are these social and political skills, and how can they be taught or learned? First, America needs minds that have the skills of relating one thing to another, of seeing connections. Dictionaries contain an uncommon but useful word: "syndetic," meaning "connecting" or "connective"—the capacity to encompass relationships. Syndetic skills are absolutely essential. There is a compelling need to develop syndetic courses and exercises that force students to look for connections—connections between the runoff of farm fertilizers and the death of Lake Erie; connections between the Mideast political crisis and the price of gasoline in Peoria; connections among drought in the Middle West, Soviet economic priorities, and starvation in India; connections between gadgetry and pollution; connections between corruption and inflation; connections between prejudice and domestic crime.

Only if citizens have some clear conception of the complex ingredients of social causation, and of the probabilistic rather than the certain nature of social choices, will they develop the capacity to solve the problems that beset the nation and the world, or even to live stoically with the maddening trade-offs that are not easily amenable to social manipulation. Much of America's scholastic and collegiate curriculum needs to be reexamined to see where and how syndetic exercises can be insinuated into existing materials, how new knowledge can be introduced that forces students increasingly to reckon with complex interdependencies. Educators have long sensed this need; but in view of the probable future, the responses have been insufficient in both quality and number.

Second, the educational system needs to turn out generations of negotiators. The past few centuries of Western history have seen a secular weathering down of the great peaks of despotism symbolized by terms like "divine right" or "absolute monarchy." Orders do not suffice in a world of manifold epicenters of power. In a world of 150 separate nations, myriad provincial and local authorities, tens of thousands of multinational and subnational economic entities, hundreds of professional and scientific guilds, and an immense variety of artisan trades, horizontal—not vertical—communications are the condition of cooperation. Who is willing any longer to be at the beck and call of either a domineering employer or sovereign, or even a condescending patron? J. H. Elliott reminded us that this new relationship was symbolized as far back as the early sixteenth century by the anxious attempts of that "normally headstrong Pope, Julius II, to calm down the equally irascible Michelangelo and induce him to return to Rome to paint the Sistine ceiling . . . the mere artist and the spiritual ruler of Christendom now met on equal terms."

And so it is no matter where one turns. Nobody in his right mind orders a plumber around. The United States does not order the Soviet Union around. The president of General Motors does not order the president of the United Automobile Workers around.

If common purposes are to be achieved in a world of often willful autonomies, legitimate authority must be coupled with skills of negotiation. These skills involve rhetorical abilities in the Aristotelian sense—the ability to persuade (note the comment of Aristotle's great teacher, Plato: "Persuasion, not coercion, is the divine element in the world"). Beyond rhetoric, the negotiating skill also involves both the subtleties and psychic resiliencies associated with the ability to resolve or to defuse conflicts—to talk people down from their "highs" of anger and mistrust. Negotiating also involves the most essential of all political talents: the capacity to bargain, to discover areas of agreement, and to deal (in the nonpejorative sense).

Except for limited opportunities in student government, education does little to prepare young people for the negotiating skills they will need to perform their civic obligations—let alone for the mundane realities of personal and occupational coping. American education needs to create a new facet to the curriculum—a facet that James Coleman would call "action rich"—which exercises regularly the negotiating abilities of young people. Through simulation, role playing, games, in-basket techniques, modified T-groups, and through real participation in the governance of appropriate school and college activities, young people must train their diplomatic muscles. Negotiating skills are the underlying political necessity, not just showing young people how to pull a voting lever.

This necessity for negotiating skills confronts some hardy values that are deeply implanted in the American psyche from childhood on. Americans put a high value on winning; but negotiating implies the value of settling equitably and fairly with *no* winners in the traditional, egocentric sense. Furthermore, negotiating suggests compromise, and Americans are reared to believe that one should not compromise between right and wrong. The oversimplifications of these bimodal moral perceptions tend to reject the very essence of American political process. In a universe of conflict and multiplicity of values, if two people disagree, neither need be wicked. This nation must have an enormous pool of skilled negotiators if its citizens are to have world peace and domestic tranquility. Equally important, there must exist a general population prepared to accept negotiated settlements of tough and emotion-laden issues.

THE EDUCATION OF LEADERS

Fear of the abuses of power has led many people to the insane conclusion that democracies do not need leaders equipped with the knowledge and the authority to govern. The dismal reality is that all too many parts of this nation's operating polity are in the hands of amateurs who have neither the knowledge nor the authority to govern responsibly. "Responsibly" is used here in both its moral and its political sense. Beyond educating the general citizenry to understand the constitutional and political system and to become familiar with the syndetic and negotiating skills needed to relate to the system and shape it, American education needs to place very special emphasis on the pre-service and in-service education of its political leadership.

Unfortunately, there are few useful historical or even theoretical models on education for political leadership. The cultivation of Plato's "Philosopher Kings," the education of Chinese mandarins, the training of British colonial servants—these come to mind as past attempts to articulate the special preparation needed by rulers. But each of these models was essentially undemocratic. Each had the good of the public at heart, but that good was to be determined largely by rulers, not by the ruled.

The agenda of modern public policy is almost unbelievably complex. Even a generation ago, T. Swann Harding lamented:

It is up to congressional committees and then to the Congress as a whole to grasp and decide upon the justice of appropriations for such projects as: the use of endocrines to increase egg production; the role of Johne's disease, coccidiosis, and worm parasites in cattle production; the production of riboflavin from milk by-products; spot treatment with soil fumigants for the control of root-knot nematode on melons; the use of mass releases of Macrocentus Ancylivorus to control Oriental fruit moth injury; and the conversion of lactose into methyl acrylate to be polymerized with butadiene for the production of synthetic rubber.

And those matters were cited for their complexity years before space flights, intricate issues of telecommunications, hard trade-offs between economic productivity and environmental protection, subtle links between municipal and international finance, the energy crisis, complex commodity bargains, nuclear threats, and anarchic competition in the partitioning of ocean resources. Disciplinary, multidisciplinary, and professional expertise of the highest order needs to be available to and through the elected and appointed leaders, if such issues are to be understood and intelligently resolved. The polity needs the intellectual services and, frequently, the political leadership of lawyers, doctors, biologists, engineers, chemists, foresters, economists, linguists, psychologists, social workers, military and diplomatic specialists, geologists, geographers—the list of needed specializations is as vast as the services and regulatory responsibilities of all levels and facets of government. In spite of valiant attempts of some colleges and universities to broaden their law school curricula, to create schools of public administration and public policy, and to launch in-service training courses for government personnel, most disciplinary and professional training in higher education is ill-suited to the cultivation and preparation of democratic leaders. Those who know the rigidities and the vested interests that abound in the academic world will not be surprised by this observation. Yet no issue is of greater consequence to the survival of this nation and of the world than the adequacy of the generalist political training of disciplinary and professional specialists in all fields.

Without going into specifics, it may be useful to summarize the insights that have been evolved by those who, in the past half century, have been charged with developing schools and institutes of public administration and public policy. They have been the persons most directly concerned with education for public leadership. What they have learned may serve those who feel the need to borrow.

Over the past fifty years or so, a number of major trends have been observable. Here, four curricular emphases may be noted: rational management, political process, policy analysis, and clientele service.

The management emphasis which dominated many of the early programs in public administration—at the Maxwell School at Syracuse and at many land-grant institutions—rested on the assumption that administration and policy were distinct functions of government. A fairly messy, partly ineffable, democratic political process produced goals. The function of "education for the public service" programs was to turn out tidy types who could carry out efficiently and economically the tasks set by untidy but electorally responsible political actors. The courses were labeled budgeting and accounting, personnel administration, planning, organization and methods, and the legal framework of administration. More recently, some of this emphasis has reappeared under the guise of operations research, program planning and budgeting systems, and management by objectives. The underlying philosophy has not changed: whatever the given task, it can be done more effectively with the help of sophisticated management tools wielded by public-spirited, disinterested generalists.

Of all the public figures in this century, no one did more than Paul Appleby to point out the limitations of the "impartial manager," public service ideal. In his great post-World War II books, *Policy and Administration* and *Morality and Administration*—drawn from his own rich experiences as Undersecretary of Agriculture and as Acting Director of the Bureau of the Budget—Appleby demonstrated that, in real life, policy making and public management are inextricably intertwined. Appleby's message was soft but clear: if you want to educate people for the public service, acquaint them with the realities of the political process—with congressional behavior, with human foibles and ambitions, with interest groups, with internecine power struggles, with the court life of the White House, with intergovernmental relations, and with negotiations and bargaining and compromise. Public service is not a management science at all, it is a political art—the art of utilizing complex machinery for the accomplishment of political and personal goals.

Programs and schools oriented toward public service careers do not, on the whole, do very well in educating young people in political process sophistication. Impressive books and articles (by Paul Appleby, Bertram Gross, David Truman, David Easton, Charles Lindblom, and others), and a number of biographies, novels, case studies, articles, and even plays, have provided a good and useful bibliography. But there is something almost temperamental in a generational sense that makes it difficult for many young people to view the accommodations of the political process as moral and as necessary to the survival of a democratic society. (It takes a long time to understand that the reason rain falls on the just and the unjust alike is that he is the same fellow.) It is difficult to conceive of educational programs designed to train for the public service that would not attempt in one way or another to introduce students to the fascinating and perennially unsettling realities of the political process.

The policy analysis emphasis is a fairly recent concept following, particularly, Harold Lasswell's seminal work immediately following World War II. Pioneered at the Brookings Institution in the 1920s and at Harvard's Littauer Center in the 1930s with special attention to macroeconomics, policy studies now abound in such fields as health, education, energy, environmental science, foreign affairs, and urbanism. Policy analysis activities appear more frequently in the profit and nonprofit think tanks of the nation than in universities. Policy science tends to be eclectic in methodology, although increasing emphasis is placed on sophisticated quantitative techniques and systems analysis models. Policy analysis has developed a rich and partly recondite vocabulary: inputs, outputs, feedback, evaluation, trade-offs, side effects, gaming, regressions, cost/benefit, and so on. It is laden with seductivity. It is friendly to computer play. It conveys both the hopes and the dangers of Platonic rationality in the conduct of the public's business. On occasion it edges toward demonstrable truths that are politically compelling. Most of the schools and programs of public administration and public policy in this nation spend an increasing amount of time on this only partially defined field of intellectual emphasis. The main trouble with much policy analysis work is that its products are rarely geared to a political world of unpredictables and crunch. In consequence, political process insights are especially needed by those who would pretend to predict, or to influence through highly rational policy analysis techniques, the vagrant vectors of public affairs.

All theories of public leadership in a democracy must presume to have the welfare of citizens as their ultimate goal. Reform movements, like Naderism and Common Cause, and a host of policy-oriented groups in such fields as health delivery services, compensatory education, civil rights, environmental protection, and so on, have given new life to a clientele orientation in the sense of both participation and service effectiveness. This emphasis is having a perceptible impact upon schools and programs of public affairs, law, business management, medicine, and engineering. How deep and fundamental this client orientation really is, is not known. Within limits suggested earlier in this chapter, it is found heartening, for it causes students and faculty to focus on public-interest questions too long ignored or taken for granted. It also addresses one of humankind's most difficult and seemingly eternal moral questions: how to organize a polity so that ultimate clients as well as intermediate agents benefit from public wealth—how to ensure that pupils benefit as well as teachers, patients as well as doctors, welfare clients as well as welfare workers.

These then, are four salients for education programs for public service. A judicious mixture of all of them is necessary if, in borrowed and adapted form, they are to assist disciplinary and professional specialists to prepare for the public role that will be thrust upon many of them during their careers: as congressional staff, as lobbyists, as political executives, as judges, as civil servants, as subject-matter specialists for the media. To paraphrase Don K. Price, nothing short of the total resources of the university is adequate to the task of pre-service and in-service education for the public service.

THE UNFINISHED AGENDA OF GOVERNMENTS

Effective public leadership is quite impossible without public confidence in public officials and in the political system. So often citizens view public life through clouded glasses. The public enterprise is far too important to be pulled down by the misdeeds of a few and by sensational derogations of the press. Whatever the shortcomings, the public sector has as its ultimate raison d'être:

- To continue and to hasten the process of bringing meaningful work and a fair chance to all citizens regardless of background

- To open up and recast political and economic institutions in order to free people from structural and procedural bondages that crush creativity and joy

- To revamp, in the spirit of the late Richard T. Frost, the penal system of this country in order to destroy the last vestiges of medieval torture

- To stimulate the future evolution and reworking of educational and cultural services so that they are available to all ages and types of people, and so that once again the creative work of inspired and gifted human beings will be revered

- To remind people that the squalor and famine and overcrowding of three-quarters of the world is an intolerable burden not only on the victims, but on the immediate conscience and long-range safety of the prosperous

- To work unceasingly for the eradiction of war as a means of settling international as well as domestic disputes, and to discover those mechanisms of peaceful conflict resolution that can give surcease to the nuclear anxieties of the human race

- To clean up oceans and streams and soiled winds and tawdry cities

- To discover energy sources that will enhance rather than pollute the biosphere

- To set aside and regulate areas of special beauty and felicity for the long-run enjoyment of the whole human race

Some of these desirable goals can be pursued by interested citizens within their local communities—through volunteer action; through serving on boards, commissions, and study groups; through partisan political activity; and through achieving elected office. This is the level of active citizen participation that comes closest to the ancient ideal of direct democracy. For most people, the local community or neighborhood is the first effective laboratory for political involvement, for political education by doing. Schools and colleges have a responsibility to communicate and to underscore to young and old the importance of local political involvement. It can be satisfying to the individual. It can help to solve local problems. It is the "boot camp" for larger political engagements.

Most of the great issues that affect people's lives, however, are state, national, or global in character. Here the enhanced education of political leaders and policy specialists is of the greatest moment. Here the essential functions of the larger public are to keep informed, to hold leaders accountable, to develop a capacity for steadfastness through trials, and to elevate the sense of community and civility that Walter Lippmann once called the public philosophy. The transiency of individual lives can be interpreted as nature's assurance of newness and aliveness and fleeting wonder in the world. But there is an ancient wisdom that survives all the passings of human beings, great and small. It is the wisdom that forms a sense of worth at its highest; it is the wisdom of Emerson's "incessant affirmatives"; it is the wisdom of those poets and prophets who have in fact caught the patriot dream that sees beyond the years "alabaster cities gleam undimmed by human tears"—who have always known that this is one world and that all are in truth one people, and who have always sensed that beneath the superficial skullduggery and pettiness of the human race is an unquenchable hunger for beauty and goodness and truth.

Releasing this still unrealized promise of the human race is the ultimate reason for, and condition of, a civilized polity. Ultimately, only administratively effective and politically responsible government can secure freedom, and only freedom can permit the human spirit to evolve to its next higher destiny.

> For what avail, the plow or sail,
> Or land, or life, if freedom fail?

Historical Perspective on Civic Education in the United States

4

R. FREEMAN BUTTS

The urge to promote civic education through the schools accelerates in times of crisis or rapid social change. It takes on special urgency in two quite different kinds of social situations in which the need for social cohesion and unity is seen to be particularly acute: (*a*) when liberal reformers see the need to mobilize disparate groups to achieve (in Robert Wiebe's words) "a new social integration, a higher form of social harmony," as in the Revolutionary Era, the Progressive Era, the New Deal, and the Great Society or (*b*) when conservative forces see the need for social cohesion to rally round their version of the American way of life and to stave off threats to it from alien sources, as in periods of massive immigration, militant radical movements, world war, or cold war.

THE REVOLUTIONARY IDEAL: UNUM (1776–1826)

As the founders of the Republic viewed their revolution in primarily political terms rather than economic or social terms, they viewed the kind of education needed for the new Republic largely in political terms rather than as a means to academic excellence or individual self-fulfillment. They talked about education as a bulwark for liberty, equality, popular consent, and devotion to the public good— goals which took precedence over the uses of knowledge for self-improvement or occupational preparation. Over and over again the Revolutionary generation, both liberal and conservative in outlook, asserted their faith that the welfare of the Republic rested upon an educated citizenry and that republican schools—especially free, common, public schools—would be the best means of educating the citizenry in the civic values, knowledge, and obligations required of everyone in a democratic republican society.

47

The principal ingredients of a civic education, all agreed, were literacy and inculcation of patriotic and moral virtues; others added the study of history and the principles of republican government itself. The founders, like almost all their successors, were long on exhortation as to the value of civic education; but they left it to the textbook writers to distill the essence of those values for schoolchildren. Texts in American history and government appeared as early as the 1790s. And the textbook writers turned out to be very largely of conservative persuasion, more likely Federalist in outlook than Jeffersonian, almost universally in agreement that political virtue must rest upon moral and religious precepts. Since most textbook writers were New Englanders, this meant that the texts were infused with Protestant and, above all, Puritan outlooks.

Noah Webster's spellers, readers, and grammar exemplified the combination of faith in literacy (Americanized), didactic moral instruction, patriotism, and Protestant devotion to duty. Immediately following the Revolution, the textbooks began to celebrate the values of national cohesion, love of country, and love of liberty. All things American began to be glorified. Even the staid *New England Primer,* which had brought up generations of Puritans to learn the alphabet by Biblical injunctions, changed its couplet for "W" from "Whales in the Sea, GOD's Voice Obey" to "Great Washington brave, His Country did save." Indeed, Washington became the object not only of extravagant praise but of virtually religious devotion. Ruth Elson quoted a 1797 textbook as saying of Washington: "The most unexceptionally, the most finished, the most Godlike human character that ever acted a part on the theatre of the world."[1]

In the first half-century of the Republic's life, the most influential carriers of civic education in the schools were the spellers and readers. Their paramount theme was to "attach the child's loyalty to the state and nation. The sentiment of patriotism, love of country, vies with the love of God as the cornerstone of virtue: 'Patriotism . . . must be considered as the noblest of the social virtues.'"[2]

A less flamboyant but real faith in the study of history as a preparation for citizenship was expressed by Jefferson. In reviewing the reasons for his 1779 proposal of a Virginia law to establish public schools, Jefferson stated:

> Of the views of this law none is more important, none more legitimate, than that of rendering the people the safe, as they are the ultimate, guardians of their own liberty. For this purpose the reading in the first

stage, where *they* will receive their whole education, is proposed, as has been said, to be chiefly historical. History, by apprising them of the past, will enable them to judge of the future; it will avail them of the experience of other times and other nations; it will qualify them as judges of the actions and designs of men; it will enable them to know ambition under every disguise it may assume and, knowing it, to defeat its views. In every government of earth is some trace of human weakness, some germ of corruption, and degeneracy, which cunning will discover, and wickedness insensibly open, cultivate, and improve. Every government degenerates when trusted to the rulers of the people alone. The people themselves therefore are its only safe depositories. And to render even them safe their minds must be improved to a certain degree. This indeed is not all that is necessary, though it be essentially necessary. An amendment of our constitution must here come in aid of the public education. The influence over government must be shared among all the people.[3]

Proposing a state University of Virginia, Jefferson's first two purposes were:

To form the statesmen, legislators, and judges, on whom public prosperity and individual happiness are so much to depend;
    To expound the principles and structure of government, the laws which regulate the intercourse of nations, those formed municipally for our own government, and a sound spirit of legislation, which, banishing all arbitrary and unnecessary restraint on individual action, shall leave us free to do whatever does not violate the equal rights of another. . . .[4]

Jefferson urged that two of his ten proposed schools for the new university be devoted primarily to civic education, a school of government, and a school of law. Weary but adamant over the violent drumbeat of Federalist-Republican partisanship of thirty years, Jefferson wanted his Professor of Government to expound Republican doctrines and ideals in order to counteract the Federalist biases of most of the colleges of the day. He thus raised the most perplexing questions of civic education: Should teachers indoctrinate a particular political point of view? Should teachers be selected on the basis of their political beliefs as well as their academic competence? Can political teaching be value-free or is it inevitably value-laden? In any case, Jefferson did not get his school of government, possibly because of conservative opposition in the state.

In the first half-century of the Republic, civic education emphasized the inculcation of civic values and relatively neglected political knowledge as such, with no discernible attempt to develop participatory political skills. No particular account was taken of differences in student backgrounds. Despite the call for free public schools, few were founded outside New England until the mid-nineteenth century. In fact, during the late eighteenth century, the trend was toward the voluntary approach to education through private schools for those who could afford it, separate religious schools for the respective denominations, and charity schools for the indigent poor. It was not until the Jacksonian period that the campaigns for common public schools virtually took the form of a campaign for civic education itself, harking back to the founders' affirmation of the political goal of *Unum*.

THE POST-REVOLUTIONARY REALITY: PLURIBUS (1826–1876)

In the middle half of the nineteenth century the political values inculcated by the civic education program of the schools did not change substantially from those celebrated in the Republic's first fifty years. In the textbooks of the day their rosy hues, if anything, became even more golden. To the resplendent values of liberty, equality, patriotism, and a benevolent Christian morality were now added (especially in New England) the middle-class virtues of hard work, honesty and integrity, the rewards of individual effort, and obedience to legitimate authority. Ruth Elson summed up hundreds of textbooks this way:

> Unlike many modern schoolbooks, those of the 19th century made no pretense of neutrality. While they evade issues seriously controverted in their day, they take a firm and unanimous stand on matters of basic belief. The value judgment is their stock in trade: love of country; love of God; duty to parents; the necessity to develop habits of thrift, honesty, and hard work in order to accumulate property; the certainty of progress; the perfection of the United States. These are not to be questioned. Nor in this whole century of great external change is there any deviation from these basic values. In pedagogical arrangements the schoolbook of the 1790's is vastly different from that of the 1890's, but the continuum of values is uninterrupted. Neither the Civil War nor the 1890's provide any watershed of basic values.[5]

A single long quotation from the preeminent American historian of the day epitomizes the set of values which the school texts echo and re-echo. An ardent Jacksonian Democrat, George Bancroft wrote the following introduction to his projected ten-volume *History of the United States* in 1834. He saw no reason to change it in the succeeding editions and revisions during the next forty to fifty years. This quotation is taken from the six-volume edition of 1879:

> The United States of America constitute an essential portion of a great political system, embracing all the civilized nations of the earth. At a period when the force of moral opinion is rapidly increasing, they have the precedence in the practice and the defence of the equal rights of man. The sovereignty of the people is here a conceded axiom, and the laws, established upon that basis, are cherished with faithful patriotism. While the nations of Europe aspire after change, our constitution engages the fond admiration of the people, by which it has been established. Prosperity follows the execution of even justice; invention is quickened by the freedom of competition; and labor rewarded with sure and unexampled returns. . . . Every man may enjoy the fruits of his industry; every mind is free to publish its convictions. Our government, by its organization, is necessarily identified with the interests of the people and relies exclusively on their attachment for its durability and support. Even the enemies of the state, if there are any among us, have liberty to express their opinions undisturbed and are safely tolerated, where reason is left free to combat their errors. Nor is the constitution a dead letter, unalterably fixed: it has the capacity for improvement, adopting whatever changes time and the public will may require, and safe from decay, so long as that will retains its energy. . . . Religion, neither persecuted nor paid by the state, is sustained by the regard for public morals and the convictions of an enlightened faith. Intelligence is diffused with unparalleled universality; a free press teems with the choicest productions of all nations and ages. There are more daily journals in the United States than in the world beside. A public document of general interest is, within a month, reproduced in at least a million of copies and is brought within the reach of every freeman in the country. An immense concourse of emigrants of the most various lineage is perpetually crowding to our shores; and the principles of liberty, uniting all interests by the operation of equal laws, blend the discordant elements into harmonious union. Other governments are convulsed by the innovations and reforms of neighboring states; our constitution, fixed in the affections of the people, from whose choice it has sprung, neutralized the influence of foreign principles, and fearlessly opens an asylum to the virtuous, the unfortunate, and the oppressed of every nation.
>   And yet it is but little more than two centuries since the oldest of our states received its first permanent colony. Before that time the whole territory was an unproductive waste. Throughout its wide extent the arts

had not erected a monument. Its only inhabitants were a few scattered tribes of feeble barbarians, destitute of commerce and of political connection. The axe and the ploughshare were unknown. The soil, which had been gathering fertility from the repose of centuries, was lavishing its strength in magnificent but useless vegetation. In the view of civilization the immense domain was a solitude.

It is the object of the present work to explain how the change in the condition of our land has been brought about and, as the fortunes of a nation are not under the control of blind destiny, to follow the steps by which a favoring Providence, calling our institutions into being, has conducted the country to its present happiness and glory.[6]

Of all the political values that the textbooks extolled, liberty was preeminent. Whenever they attempted to explain *why* children should love their country above all else, the idea of liberty took first place. Now this was undoubtedly of prime importance in promoting unity in an increasingly diverse and pluralistic society. Yet the loyalty to liberty was more in affective terms of feeling than in analytical terms of knowledge. Elson put it this way:

All books agree that the American nation politically expressed is the apostle of liberty, a liberty personified, apostrophized, sung to, set up in Godlike glory, but rarely defined. To discover what liberty means in these books is a murky problem. The child reader could be certain that it was glorious, it is American, it is to be revered, and it deserves his primary loyalty. But for the child to find out from these books what this liberty is would be astonishing.[7]

The predominant tone of the school textbooks of the nineteenth century was Federalist and conservative. Elson reported:

Although schoolbook authors consider themselves guardians of liberty, they can be more accurately described as guardians of tradition. On social questions the tenor of the books is consistently conservative. The United States is always identified with freedom, but this freedom is best identified as that established in 1783 after separation from Great Britain. The 19th-century child was taught to worship past achievements of America and to believe in the inevitable spread of the American system throughout the world. But contemporary problems are conspicuously absent, and reform movements which would have profound social or political effects are either ignored or derided. While Jeffersonian and Jacksonian democracy agitated the adult world, the child was taught the necessity of class distinctions. Nor are Jefferson and Jackson ever ranked as heroes; ... in the schools Hamilton and Daniel Webster governed the minds of the children.[8]

None was more eloquent than Horace Mann himself on what he candidly called "political education." In 1848, summing up his conclusions from twelve years as secretary of the State Board of Education in Massachusetts, Mann began with the assumptions of the founders that citizens of a Republic must "understand something of the true nature of the government under which they live." He spelled out the civic program in terms which will sound familiar to all teachers of civics since that time:

> The Constitution of the United States and of our own State, should be made a study in our Public Schools. The partition of the powers of government into the three co-ordinate branches—legislative, judicial, and executive—with the duties appropriately devolving upon each; the mode of electing or of appointing all officers, with the reason on which it was founded; and, especially, the duty of every citizen, in a government of laws, to appeal to the courts for redress, in all cases of alleged wrong, instead of undertaking to vindicate his own rights by his own arm, and, in a government where the people are the acknowledged sources of power, the duty of changing laws and rulers by an appeal to the ballot, and not by rebellion, should be taught to all the children until they are fully understood.[9]

But Massachusetts was already caught in a swirl of contesting forces occasioned by the immigration of Irish and Germans of Roman Catholic faith and by the changes in urban life attendant upon the industrial factory system. Mann knew all too well that "if the tempest of political strife were to be let loose upon our Common Schools, they would be overwhelmed with sudden ruin." He recognized that many would object to *any* study of political matters in the schools because the Constitution is subject to different readings. He saw the dangers of political partisanship in the appointment of teachers on the basis of their political fitness as measured by the school committee:

> Who shall moderate the fury of these conflicting elements when they rage against each other; and who shall save the dearest interests of the children from being consumed in the fierce combustion? If parents find

that their children are indoctrinated into what they call political here-
sies, will they not withdraw them from the school; and, if they withdraw
them from the school, will they not resist all appropriations to support a
school from which they derive no benefit?[10]

Mann could not admit that the public schools should avoid political education altogether, nor could he risk the destruction of the
public schools by urging them to become "theatres for party politics." His solution was similar to that which he proposed for the
religious controversies; the schools should teach the common elements that all agreed to but skip over the controversial:

> Surely, between these extremes, there must be a medium not difficult to
> be found. And is not this the middle course, which all sensible and
> judicious men, all patriots, and all genuine republicans, must approve;
> namely, that those articles in the creed of republicanism, which are
> accepted by all, believed in by all, and which form the common basis of
> our political faith, shall be taught to all? But when the teacher, in the
> course of his lessons or lectures on the fundamental law arrives at a
> controverted text, he is either to read it without comment or remark; or,
> at most, he is only to say that the passage is the subject of disputation,
> and that the schoolroom is neither the tribunal to adjudicate nor the
> forum to discuss it.[11]

`Mann was so intent upon getting common schools established for
an ever wider range of the potential school populations that he
would not risk the failure of the common school idea by bringing
political controversy into the schools. Thus, it came about that the
emerging public schools were largely content with a civic program
that initiated the poor, the foreigner, and the working-class children
into the political community by literacy in English, didactic moral
injunctions, patriotic readers and histories, and lessons that
stressed recitation of the structural forms of the constitutional
order.

As the Civil War approached, the textbooks began to speak of the
dangers of disunion, and being Northern in origin began to be more
outspoken about the evils of slavery. Still the South continued to use
Northern textbooks. During the war, Confederate books were written and published, but the political attitudes they expressed were
not much different from those in the books that continued to flow
from the North to the South—except on the subject of slavery. After
the war, a common custom was for Southern teachers to pin pages

together, expecting young readers to skip the Northern discussion of the Civil War and Reconstruction in favor of the truth delivered by the teacher. To make up for these gaps, the Southern books and teachers could easily expand on the Southern heroes in the Revolutionary War with Washington brooking no competition.

Up to the centennial celebration of 1876 the children of the underclasses were still largely blocked from the public schools and, thus, from civic education. The Reconstruction reforms had proposed extension of public school systems to the Southern states, but these hopes were largely dissipated by the 1870s. Northern states were slow to admit blacks to common schools, often preferring to establish separate schools for white and black. These evident failures of the educational system itself to put into practice the stated values of the political community helped to widen the gap between ideal and reality. Millions of immigrants were being incorporated into citizenship by civic education, despite the patronizing and often hostile ethnic images that the textbooks portrayed of Irish and immigrants from Southern Europe, but millions of racial minorities born in the United States were still beyond the pale of white citizenship education.

THE CIVICS OF PROGRESSIVE MODERNIZATION (1876–1926)

In the fifty years straddling the turn of the twentieth century, the character of civic education programs began to undergo more searching examination. The earlier stress on love of a grand, free country became a more shrill and passionate devotion to a *great* and powerful nation. The doctrines of manifest destiny, winning of the West, empire overseas, and making the world safe for democracy led to exaltation of the United States as the superior nation of the world, imbued with the mission to lead all the rest and thus deserving, nay demanding, a loyalty to "my country, right or wrong."

Not only did the Spanish-American War and World War I stimulate a nationalistic and even militaristic fervor and flavor in civic education, but the massive immigration that characterized almost the whole period added an aspect that seemed, to many conservatives and liberals alike, a basic threat to the commitments of the democratic political community, to the stability of the constitutional order, and to the functioning of governing authorities. They could point to ghettos in the cities, crime in the streets, bloody strikes in the factories, corruption in local governments, and spreading of socialist, communist, and revolutionary doctrines by radical groups.

The lurking fear of the alien and foreign that was almost ever present was exaggerated by the millions upon millions of immigrants who poured in from Southern and Eastern Europe and from Asia. While civic education programs and textbooks attributed this influx to the search for liberty and equality, they also began to turn more and more to Americanization programs that demanded outward signs of loyalty and social cohesion. Stress upon the public pledge of allegiance, salutes to the flag, loyalty oaths, patriotic songs and marching, required instruction in English, and attacks upon foreign language teaching in the schools now were added to the more traditional and prosaic instruction of the textbooks.

A third shift in emphasis was a more prominent role given to the image of the self-made men, the self-reliant individuals, who had shifted from pioneering in the West to pioneering in the development of the industrial, urban, business system that was modernizing America so rapidly and thrusting her producing and consuming capacity ahead of all the other nations of the world in such a short time. The political side of this image was, of course, that it had all happened under auspices of a free enterprise system apart from government controls

But another reaction to the social and political results of an aggressive industrial, capitalistic order led to the Progressive movements dedicated to popular political reforms in the electoral systems and civil service, social reforms in the cities, the prisons, the sweatshops, child labor, women's rights, temperance, and the rest. Underlying the Progressive reforms was a belief in the collective efforts of governments to control rampant business enterprise, protect the rights of the people, and bring about good government through honest and efficient civil service, bureaucracies, and regulatory agencies.

Meanwhile, educators had to deal with massive increases in school enrollments. Education was seen as a prime means to get ahead in American society; compulsory attendance laws were passed in hopes of abolishing the evil of child labor and achieving the good of assimilation through Americanization.

One response of the academically minded educators in the 1880s and 1890s was to stiffen up the study of history (and thus reduce the emphasis upon civil government) by introducing more rigorous scholarly attitudes into the history texts and the courses. Looking at this question in 1893, the Committee of Ten of the National Education Association (NEA), headed by President Eliot of Harvard, concluded that high school courses should provide the same strong mental discipline for the noncollege-bound majority as for the college-bound minority. The teaching of history was thus not primarily to develop good citizenship and love of country, but to teach high school students a historian's grasp of the nature of evidence.

For several decades the academic orientation of the Committee of Ten dominated curriculum thinking and curriculum making in civic education programs. In history, the emphasis was upon the use of primary sources to develop in pupils a historic sense and to train them in the search for historical materials, the weighing of evidence, and the drawing of conclusions. In the effort to get children to think like historians, the flamboyant nationalistic and patriotic history of the previous century was to be counteracted. In 1899 a Committee of Seven of the American Historical Association urged the use of primary sources as supplementary to the textbook. *The History Teachers Magazine* (founded in 1909) and the work of Henry Johnson at Teachers College, Columbia University, both contributed to the new movement to stress historical problem solving and reasoned judgment in a laboratory or workshop setting.

Meanwhile, the study of civil government had an upsurge in the early 1900s as new ideas about civic education began to appear among political scientists, economists, and sociologists. In 1916 a committee of the American Political Science Association, reflecting the Progressive reform movements, argued that the standard courses in civil government should be shaken up. Existing courses started with the study of the United States Constitution and the formal organization of national government, and then proceeded to a similar study of state constitutions and governments. The new courses should reverse the order. The committee endorsed the study of "community civics," assuming that political affairs nearest to home are the most important and should be considered first. The Progressive-inspired Municipal League promoted this idea.

In the long run, however, the "social studies" movement was more influential. Its sponsor was the NEA's Commission on the Reorganization of Secondary Education, whose final report, *Cardinal Principles of Secondary Education,* was published in 1918. Its civic education sections had been developed from 1913 to 1916 by the Committee on Social Studies. Again reflecting Progressive views of reform, the committee explicitly brought citizenship to the forefront of the social responsibility of the secondary school. In a preliminary statement in 1913 the chairman of the committee, a sociologist, revealed the social reform intent to make civics much more than a study of government:

> Good citizenship should be the aim of social studies in the high school. While the administration and instruction throughout the school should contribute to the social welfare of the community, it is maintained that social studies have direct responsibility in this field. Facts, conditions, theories, and activities that do not contribute rather directly to the appreciation of methods of human betterment have no claim. Under this test the old civics, almost exclusively a study of Government machinery, must give way to the new civics, a study of all manner of social efforts to improve mankind. It is not so important that the pupil know how the President is elected as that he shall understand the duties of the health officer in his community. The time formerly spent in the effort to understand the process of passing a law over the President's veto is now to be more profitably used in the observation of the vocational resources of the community. In line with this emphasis, the committee recommends that social studies in the high school shall include such topics as the following: community health, housing and homes, public recreation, good roads, community education, poverty and the care of the poor, crime and reform, family income, savings banks and life insurance, human rights versus property rights, impulsive action of mobs, the selfish conservatism of tradition, and public utilities.[12]

In the final report of the committee, the term "social studies" was used to include not only history, civics, and government but also concepts from sociology and economics. History still held a major place in the course proposals for grades 7 through 12, but a problems approach was to infuse the whole program. Civics was proposed for junior high school years as well as a new course in "problems of democracy" for the twelfth grade.

Hazel Hertzberg summarized the influence of the committee's report this way:

> Instruction in the social studies should be organized around concrete problems of vital importance to society and of immediate interest to the pupil, rather than on the basis of the formal social sciences. . . . the social studies should contribute directly to the "social efficiency" of the student, helping him "to participate effectively in the promotion of social well-being" in the groups of which he is a member, from his own community to the "world community". . . . The skills to be learned by pupils were those

of good citizens participating in the building of an invigorated society, not those of historians carefully interpreting evidence, developing criticism, and arriving at synthesis. . . .

The Report of the Committee on Social Studies had a significant impact on the direction of educational reform. It represented many of the deepest, most pervasive, and most characteristic viewpoints of the Progressive period. No doubt it would have been exceedingly influential in any case, but the circumstances—that it was issued just before American entry into World War I—created a climate favorable to its concern with personal and social immediacy and utility and what is today referred to as "relevance."[13]

While the general impact of the final, overall commission report in the *Cardinal Principles* of 1918 was great indeed in making citizenship one of the cardinal goals, the report tended to reduce the *political* concerns of civic education in favor of social and economic and practical personal problems:

Civics should concern itself less with constitutional questions and remote governmental functions and should direct attention to social agencies close at hand and to the informal activities of daily life that regard and seek the common good. Such agencies as child welfare organizations and consumers' leagues afford specific opportunities for the expression of civic qualities by the older pupils.[14]

At last, however, the skills of civic participation became part of the objectives of education. The *Cardinal Principles* found valuable

. . . the assignment of projects and problems to groups of pupils for cooperative solution and the socialized recitation whereby the class as a whole develops a sense of collective responsibility. Both of these devices give training in collective thinking. Moreover, the democratic organization and administration of the school itself, as well as the cooperative relations of pupil and teacher, pupil and pupil, and teacher and teacher, are indispensable.[15]

While this approval of the study of problems and "socialized recitation" in classrooms may seem to be a modest proposal to modern teachers, it by no means swept the profession off its feet. Teaching by the book, lecturing, note taking, question and answer, recitation, memorizing, essay writing, and examination passing continued to be the prime methods of history and civics classrooms.

And venturing out into the community was still more radical, especially if a zealous civics teacher actually ran up against the local politicians. Schools found that the study of "remote governmental functions" could be conducted more freely than projects treading on local political toes.

But at least the *idea* of participation could now take its place alongside the inculcation of values and political knowledge as the main ingredients of a civic program in the schools. And the way was being prepared for distinguishing and comparing the stated values of the political community with the actual operation of the governmental authorities, at least at the municipal level of community civics.

Above all, *Cardinal Principles* recognized that the high schools had to deal with a population very different from that of the secondary schools of the first 100 years of the Republic, that is, the non-college-oriented students. Assimiliation of vast numbers of foreign immigrants, both youthful and adult, nearly engulfed the schools and exhausted their energies. Teaching English and the rudimentary structure of government were the easiest ways. For all the protestations of the progressives and the national committees and the teachers of teachers, the courses in American history, civics, and civil government (which were engrossing to countless thousands of adult immigrants) were boring to millions of high school students pushed through ritualized cycles of social studies: "communities" in the third and fourth grades, civics in the ninth and twelfth grades, American history in the fifth, eighth, and eleventh grades, with geography, state history, and European or world history sandwiched in, probably in the seventh and tenth grades.

The following fifty-year period was given over to all kinds of attempts to reform and break out of the social studies cycles on behalf of a better civic education, and, even more belatedly, to incorporate at last minority and disadvantaged groups that had long been "outsiders" to the mainstream of American political and educational life.

RECURRING CALLS FOR REFORM OF CIVIC EDUCATION (1926-1976)

The outpouring of proposals and projects to create more effective civic education programs during the past half-century would take volumes to relate. The variations of details are infinite, yet there is a sameness to the lists of goals and objectives set forth by one commission after another. After the brutal realities and disillusionments of Vietnam and Watergate, some of the earlier statements seem blatantly and grimly superpatriotic (others exude the bland optimism of Pollyanna herself). All that can be done here is to suggest the range of political outlooks that seemed to motivate some of the major approaches to civic education.

In the wake of World War I, citizenship education programs were subjected to almost constant attack by conservative civic and patriotic organizations whose views were antiforeign, antipacifist, anti-immigration, and antiradical. In the 1920s the American Legion led the campaigns to get Congress and the state legislature to require civic instruction, flag salutes, military training, and loyalty oaths. The dominant mood of civic education in the 1920s was to "rally round the flag," extoll the merits and successes and say nothing derogatory about the greatest country on earth.

In contrast, the 1930s witnessed a social reformist outlook sparked by the economic depression, the New Deal, and the onset of totalitarianism in the world. One of the most impressive examples of educational response was the Commission on the Social Studies of the American Historical Association, which was funded by the Carnegie Foundation for five years from January 1929 to December 1933, and which issued seventeen volumes between 1932 and 1937. The dominant tone of the most widely read volumes (those by Charles A. Beard, George S. Counts, Bessie L. Pierce, Jesse H. Newlon, and Merle Conti) was set by the *Conclusions and Recommendations of the Commission* (1934): the age of individualism and laissez-faire in economics and government was closing and a new collectivism requiring social planning and governmental regulation was emerging. The marshalled arguments struck now familiar notes: deprivation in the midst of plenty, inequality in income, spreading unemployment, wasted natural resources, rising crime and violence, subordination of public welfare to private interest, and international struggle for raw materials. No particular curriculum was promulgated; but it was clear that this view of life and this political/economic frame of reference were to guide specific curriculum making for civic education programs. The clear implication was that youth should be inculcated with the values of economic collectivity and interdependence in place of economic individualism, while promoting personal and cultural individualism and freedom.

Like-minded proposals were stemming from George S. Counts,

John Dewey, Harold Rugg, William H. Kilpatrick, John L. Childs, and other social reconstructionists. Counts' *Dare the School Build a New Social Order* came out in 1932; *The Educational Frontier* edited by Kilpatrick, in 1933; and the magazine *The Social Frontier* in 1934, the latter specifically endorsing the *Conclusions and Recommendations*.

Naturally, the social frontiersmen set the profession by its ears and elicited vigorous and shrill counterattacks. But the major professional organizations responded on the whole positively in giving renewed attention to civic education. The National Education Association and the American Association of School Administrators jointly sponsored the Educational Policies Commission in 1935, enlisting Counts to membership along with several more conservative administrators. The pronouncements of the Educational Policies Commission softened the social reconstructionist economic views, but they did emphasize, over and over again, education for democracy. Charles Beard wrote the first draft of the Commission's historical volume entitled *The Unique Functions of Education in American Democracy* in 1937.

When *The Purposes of Education in American Democracy* was produced in 1938 (written by William H. Carr, executive secretary), the seven cardinal principles had been reduced to four objectives, but "civic responsibility" was retained as the fourth (in addition to self-realization, human relationship, and economic efficiency). The stated objectives of civic responsibility do not sound particularly daring today—there was little emphasis upon liberty or equality or due process—but for all the bland language there was scope for realistic civic studies (if teachers or communities had the stomach for them):

Social Justice. The educated citizen is sensitive to the disparities of human circumstance.

Social Activity. The educated citizen acts to correct unsatisfactory conditions.

Social Understanding. The educated citizen seeks to understand social structures and social processes.

Critical Judgment. The educated citizen has defenses against propaganda.

Tolerance. The educated citizen respects honest differences of opinion.

Conservation. The educated citizen has a regard for the nation's resources.

Social Applications of Science. The educated citizen measures scientific advance by its contribution to the general welfare.

World Citizenship. The educated citizen is a cooperating member of the world community.

Law Observance. The educated citizen respects the law.

Economic Literacy. The educated citizen is economically literate.

Political Citizenship. The educated citizen accepts his civic duties.

Devotion to Democracy. The educated citizen acts upon an unswerving loyalty to democratic ideals.[16]

World War II broke into this movement, mobilizing the schools for the war effort. After the war, education for good citizenship became a rage in school systems in response to the cold war crusade against communism in the world and as a kind of defense against the onslaughts of McCarthyism at home. The hope was obviously that children could be taught the values of consensus on the principles of political democracy and the values of a free enterprise economy, reflecting the spirit of accommodation and good will of the Eisenhower years.

One volume admirably reveals these twin drives—a fierce opposition to communism in the world, and a hope that good will, cooperative actions, and positive democratic attitudes would strengthen democracy at home. Sprinkled with pictures of smiling, clean, well-dressed groups of white pupils and teachers, the 32nd Yearbook of the American Association of School Administrators, produced by its Commission on Educating for Citizenship, had this to say in 1954:

> At his best, the American citizen has always sought to realize the nation's historic ideals. Now, when communist imperialism threatens all security, he feels a new appreciation for the old ideals as a stable element in a shaky world. The public schools are the means on which the American leans most heavily to make sure that all children carry forward the American heritage. So now, even more urgently than in the past, the citizen demands that the schools educate for citizenship.[17]

Echoing the *Cardinal Principles* of forty years earlier, the Commission opted for a broad concept of citizenship education that would include "all the mutually helpful social relationships with others which democracy assumes should be characteristic of human life and living." By opening the door of citizenship education to all kinds of social and personal relationships, the Commission forecast what often did happen in social studies programs. Whether adopting some version of the popular core curriculum that mushroomed in the 1950s or sticking to specific courses in civics and problems of democracy, these programs often drifted off to "problems of democratic living" involving the behavior and psychology of adolescents; their personal, marriage, and family problems; vocational interests; and personal values. The broad social conception of citizenship often became so broad and so social that it watered down or neglected the basic *political* questions of power, influence, and decision making.

This, of course, was not true of all proposals or projects having to do with citizenship education in the 1950s. The 22nd Yearbook of the National Council for the Social Studies in 1951 listed twenty-four characteristics of the good citizen, reflecting the composite thinking of 300 public figures as well as educators. The first thirteen stressed the values of equality, liberty, basic human rights, the law, and other political competencies; the other eleven had to do with economic, family, community, and international matters. One project in the 1950s focused upon the concept of liberty. The Citizenship Education Project (CEP) at Teachers College stressed the values and knowledge appropriate to the free individual, the free government, the free economy, and the free world. It documented from Constitution and law in great detail the premises of liberty under each of these headings.

What was most interesting to professional educators in the Teachers College project was the stress on participation skills, identified by the neutral term "laboratory practices." Hundreds of laboratory practices detailed how teachers and students could engage together in action-oriented problem solving in the schools and in the community. Workshops and training programs were conducted across the country for hundreds of schools and thousands of teachers during the decade of the 1950s. Taken seriously, the suggestions could have led to much more than bland good will: that is, studying the local congressional district to see if it provides fair representation of minority groups, making a tax map of the community to see if tax assessments are equitable, getting young people to join political clubs, helping to get voters to register and to cast ballots, providing citizens with nonpartisan political information, informing the community where candidates stood on issues, actually campaigning for candidates, drafting a real and not a sham school constitution, and the like. Unfortunately, the CEP had to combat a political neutralism and caution among educators during the McCarthy 1950s, its funds ran out just before the rise of political activism of the 1960s, and it never was incorporated well into the mainstream of teaching and research at Teachers College.

A curious coincidence of forces saw a general relaxing of explicit calls for more and better civic education in the 1960s. The "new social studies movement" and the rise of student unrest and activism undercut patriotism as an argument for civic education. Responding to the successes of the new math and the new science stimulated by Sputnik and funded so generously by the National Defense Education Act, the National Science Foundation, and the foundations, the new social studies took on the patterns of the social science disciplines: cognitive analysis, systematic acquisition of sequential and organized knowledge, conceptual analysis, "inquiry learning," "discovery method," and in general a stress upon thinking like a social scientist (reminiscent, as Hazel Hertzberg pointed out, of the primary sources movement in history teaching of the 1880s to 1900).

It is too early to make judgments about the relative value of various projects that could come under the heading of the "new social studies." But it is clear that the revived disciplinary approach to knowledge tended not only to belittle "soft," diffuse, and superficial programs of social studies in the schools, but also to downgrade citizenship education as a proper goal of the school curriculum. One of the most forthright and explicit statements of this view was made by the executive director of the American Political Science Association and his wife in 1962:

> There is a long-standing tradition according to which secondary school instruction in political science, or instruction based upon the knowledge political science provides, has as its main objective the making of good citizens. This tradition appears to be based on the belief that instruction in government, politics, the political process, and the important issues of public policy will produce citizens who will discuss, act, and vote rationally and intelligently and that we may thereby achieve a sane and effective democratic society. Without asserting that education in the field of government, politics, and public policy has no role to play in helping to form better citizens, we feel required to state at the outset, in the interests of clarity, that we regard this tradition and the beliefs upon which it is based as mistaken and misleading: first, because it is based on a distorted conception of how citizens are made; second, because it is based on a distorted conception of democracy; and, third, because it is based on a misconception of political science.[18]

In other words, citizens are made by the total process of political socialization outside the schools; democracy like all big governments must rest upon the expert knowledge of specialists which cannot be encompassed by the average citizen; and political science is a very complicated intellectual discipline about political behavior, not a set of maxims about good citizenship. Caught between this view from the academic departments and the raucous nonnegotiable demands for relevance now from militant student activists, the traditional programs of civic education seemed pale, irresolute, and outmoded. Whether the new social studies could provide the answer was in doubt.

It is surely true that much of the work of the many curriculum development projects was more realistic than the civic education of the 1950s—more sophisticated, more analytical and skeptical, and more attuned to minority claims for equality and the struggles for civil rights. Whether they will emphasize sufficiently political values, political knowledge, and political behavior remains to be seen. Of twenty-six major curriculum centers and projects reported on and analyzed in *Social Education* in 1972, seven or eight seemed to put special stress upon citizenship objectives.[19] Some had headquarters at colleges and universities (Amherst, University of Southern California at Los Angeles, Carnegie-Mellon, Harvard, Indiana, and Tufts); others were independent projects of the Educational Development Center in Cambridge, Massachusetts, and the Law in American Society Foundation in Chicago.

In the 1970s, law-related approaches to citizenship education have been dominant. In 1975, Norman Gross and Charles White summarized recent developments as follows:

In 1971, statewide programs were being organized or were under headway in only six states. Now (1975) 26 states have at least incipient statewide projects. In 1971, no more than 150 law-related education projects were active in the schools. Today there are almost 400. In 1971, only seven summer teacher-training institutes were held. Last year, 26 such institutes were offered. . . .

Curriculum materials have multiplied dramatically in the past decade. . . . 500 books and pamphlets suitable for classroom use. . . . 400 films, filmstrips and tapes. . . .

However, these developments do not necessarily mean that law-related education will ultimately become a part of the schools' permanent course of study . . . most of the task remains to be accomplished.

Probably no more than five percent of American students have had the opportunity to take meaningful law-related courses, and most teachers have not yet received training enabling them to instruct effectively in this area. . . .

Most projects are not yet a part of the regular program and budget of school systems. . . . It is important to train large numbers of future teachers while they are still in college. . . . projects now in existence must become institutionalized. . . .

It has been estimated that any major educational reform cannot be accomplished without at least one generation of effort.[20]

What will the historian of year 2000 be saying about efforts in the generation following 1976?

NOTES

1. Ruth Miller Elson, *Guardians of Tradition: American Schoolbooks of the Nineteenth Century,* University of Nebraska Press, Lincoln, 1964, p. 195.

2. Ibid., p. 282.

3. Thomas Jefferson, *Notes on the State of Virginia,* 2d American ed., Philadelphia, 1794, pp. 215–216.

4. Saul K. Padover, *The Complete Jefferson,* Duell, Sloan & Pierce, Inc., New York, 1943, p. 1098.

5. Elson, op. cit., p. 338.

6. George Bancroft, *History of the United States of America* from the *Discovery of the Continent,* 6 vols., Little, Brown and Company, Boston, 1879, vol. 1, pp. 1–3.

7. Elson, op. cit., p. 285.

8. Ibid., p. 340.

9. Lawrence A. Cremin, *The Republic and the School: Horace Mann on the Education of Free Men,* Bureau of Publications, Teachers College, Columbia University, New York, 1957, p. 93.

10. Ibid., p. 95.

11. Ibid., p. 97.

12. From Daniel Calhoun (ed.), *The Educating of Americans: A Documentary History,* Houghton Mifflin Company, Boston, 1969, p. 495.

13. Hazel W. Hertzberg, *Historic Parallels for the Sixties and Seventies: Primary Sources and Core Curriculum Revisited,* Social Science Education Consortium Publication 135, Boulder, Colo., 1971, pp. 11–12.

14. National Education Association, Commission on the Reorganization of Secondary Education, *Cardinal Principles of Secondary Education,* U.S. Bureau of Education Bulletin 35, 1918, p. 14.

15. Ibid., p. 14.

16. Educational Policies Commission, *The Purposes of Education in American Democracy,* National Education Association and American Association of School Administrators, Washington, D.C., 1938, p. 108.

17. *Educating for American Citizenship,* American Association of School Administrators, Washington, D.C., 1954, p. 5.

18. Erling M. Hunt et al., *High School Social Studies: Perspectives,* Houghton Mifflin Company, Boston, 1962, pp. 99–100.

19. *Social Education,* vol. 36, no. 7, November 1972.

20. Law, Education and Participation, *Education for Law and Justice: Whose Responsibility? A Call for National Action,* Constitutional Rights Foundation, Los Angeles, Calif., 1975, pp. 46–48.

The Crisis in Civic Education

5

HOWARD D. MEHLINGER

The overarching purpose of civic education* is to provide youth with the knowledge, values, and skills they require in order to function effectively as responsible adult citizens. A successful civic education program must be linked to the kinds of experiences students are likely to encounter upon leaving school. To the extent that civic education prepares students for conditions that no longer prevail or avoids informing students of the true state of affairs, it fails in its mission.

The crisis in civic education results from the apparent discrepancy between changing social and political conditions and the preparation American youth receive to help them function in the adult world. Resolution of the crisis involves bringing civic education more in line with objective social conditions. This chapter points out a few of the conditions that seem unaccounted for by current civic education programs and suggests some actions that might be taken to remedy the current crisis.

*It is important to indicate how the term civic education will be used in this chapter. Civic education is a process shared by many social institutions. It begins with the family. The media, churches, youth groups, service clubs, and others contribute. Nevertheless, this chapter is limited to the role that schools play in civic education. More than other institutions, schools have civic education as a major responsibility, because schools reach all of the children, and because civic education will not improve until schools behave differently.

Within schools civic education is interpreted variously. Some fail to distinguish civic education from social studies courses, but civic education is both more and less than social studies. To the extent that courses in history, geography, and economics contribute to students' political knowledge, values, and skills, they are a part of civic education. To the degree that they further goals unique to the separate disciplines, they are not. Instruction in courses outside the social studies department may also contribute to civic education. Nor is civic education bounded by the formal curriculum. Civic education is a process permeating the entire school. It exists in many planned and unplanned ways through extracurricular activities, the pattern of school governance, and the informal school culture.

Civic education has sometimes been used to stand for moral education or character education. Being a "good citizen" sometimes has meant being polite, obeying school rules, submitting homework on time, and not cheating on exams. Clearly, values and ethical issues are at the heart of civic education, but the narrow interpretation of "good citizen" suggested above is not the focus of this chapter.

Civic education is concerned with the knowledge, skills, and values citizens need to

IMPACT OF NEW CONDITIONS ON CIVIC EDUCATION

Civic education programs vary from place to place and from time to time. Nations with different political and social experience, different ideologies, different political structures, and different needs understandably vary in their approach to civic education. Programs suitable to China, Great Britain, India, Tanzania, Switzerland, or Mexico would be inappropriate to the United States. Within a particular nation altered circumstances can prompt reforms in civic education programs. The type of civic education programs practiced by Germany and Japan prior to 1945 seemed wholly inappropriate to the goals of the American occupation authorities, and they soon established programs more consistent with their values and conceptions of democratic government.

While drastic shifts of the type that occurred in Germany and Japan are not typical of the United States, such experiences as the Civil War, the industrialization and urbanization of America, the mass movement of immigrants to the United States, the enfranchisement of women, and participation in two world wars prompted changes in conceptions of society, in personal and social values, and in social processes. Ultimately, civic education programs had to change in order to reflect these altered conditions.

It is common for discrepancies to appear between what a society is experiencing and what people believe or are taught to believe about their society. Sometimes beliefs precede practice, drawing practice in new directions. For example, the "new culture movement" in China was aimed at changing Chinese attitudes in order that the public might participate in creating a society that did not exist, except in the minds of its architects. Changing people's values and conceptions was seen as a necessary condition toward the establishment of a new society. More typically, people's perceptions lag behind new conditions. The industrial revolution was long underway before people had adequate means to describe it, understand it,

---

function effectively as political participants in various social settings. It involves respect for law as well as an understanding of how to affect legislation, support for public officials as well as a capacity to help select the best available, and loyalty to institutions and institutionalized procedures as well as a commitment to make them work more justly in line with the principles that legitimate them. Civic education is also directed toward helping students acquire the capacity to take effective action on behalf of personal and group interests in various social settings, while considering the implications of their actions on others.

and cope with its consequences. Louis XVI went to the guillotine holding fast to a belief in "divine right."

Today, traditional civic education programs are under siege. While they continue to survive in a great many schools, they are gradually being eroded as the assumptions on which they are based are overwhelmed. Yet the need for strong civic education programs has never been greater. The survival of civic education in schools depends in large measure upon finding intellectual foundations more in keeping with current and future conditions.

SOME EXAMPLES OF HOW TRADITIONAL CIVIC EDUCATION BELIEFS HAVE BEEN UNDERMINED BY ALTERED SOCIAL CONDITIONS

In the previous chapter, Dr. Butts provided a detailed description of traditional civic education programs and of how such programs have been affected by rapidly changing social conditions. In this chapter, three examples may be useful to support this main point: As conditions change, programs aimed at preparing students for adult life in the society must also change.

One characteristic of traditional civic education has been the promotion of mainline political values and beliefs and the projection of a single set of traits that characterize Americans, distinguishing them from citizens of other nations. Fostering a view of the "American" as a product of the "melting pot" was a conscious effort to hasten the assimilation of immigrants from diverse cultures and social backgrounds. The civil rights movement of the 1960s challenged the "melting pot" concept. Because black people had not been fully assimilated and treated as other Americans, they began to stress black pride and the uniqueness of the black experience. Black leaders demanded that special courses about black people be introduced into schools; soon other groups demanded separate and equal treatment in the curriculum. As a consequence "ethnic studies," based on assumptions quite inconsistent with the notion of a "melting pot," became an important part of the civic education experience of many American youth.

Traditionally, civics courses have focused primarily upon governmental institutions and the formal rules that direct their operations. "Government" rather than politics has held the spotlight. The typical voter has been cast as a rational person, independent of mind, attentive to public issues, and capable of influencing policy outcomes through the election process and direct communication with public officials. These conceptions are inconsistent with the findings of behavioral research on political life in the United States. Understanding the "twelve steps" by which bills become laws is less important than understanding the political processes that surround legislation. The constitutional requirements for becoming President are less significant than other factors in determining presidential "availability." Studies of the American voter make it difficult to identify the rational voter popularized by civics books.

In the last decade new instructional programs based upon recent social science findings and embracing newer conceptions of American political life have entered the schools. To the extent that they are understood and accepted by school officials, they undercut more traditional beliefs about the conduct of American government and about citizens' relationships to government.

A third example: Many adolescents have experienced the police in ways quite different from the friendly, courteous policeman they learned about in elementary schools—the person who gives directions when people are lost, who helps children across busy intersections, and who protects children in their homes at night. The arrest experience of some adolescents because of antiwar demonstrations or drug raids, for example, made "Officer Friendly" a "pig." In response to these conditions, new materials and courses have appeared that focus on the rights of the accused, on what to do when one is arrested, and so on. In a similar vein, courses in practical law suggest ways that students can protect themselves against unscrupulous merchants, cold-hearted landlords, and devious moneylenders. Certainly the attitudes about law promoted by such instruction are at variance from those featured in traditional civics courses.

SOME PROBLEMS THAT HAVE NOT RECEIVED ADEQUATE ATTENTION

These illustrations indicate that some of the assumptions supporting civic education in the schools have been challenged. Thus far, civic educators have responded by isolating discrete problems of greatest concern to themselves, and by developing instructional materials and approaches aimed at bringing instruction more in line with current attitudes and conceptions about society. But they have failed to create overarching theories of civic education based upon careful social analyses and accommodating all the forces that influence the civic education of youth. Some key elements of the present situation have been neglected. Two of these omissions—there are others—are discussed in this section.

1. *Changing public attitudes about government and the political process.* In February 1976, *The Wall Street Journal* published an article summarizing recent public opinion poll data regarding the mood of the public toward the concurrent presidential campaign, in particular, and toward government and politicians in general. Among the findings reprinted in that article:

- By a margin of two to one, Americans believe that "most politicians don't really care about me." (Cambridge Survey Research)

- 58 percent believe that "people with power are out to take advantage of me." (Louis Harris Survey)

- 49 percent believe that "quite a few of the people running the government are a little crooked." (Market Opinion Research, Inc.)

- 68 percent feel that "over the last ten years, this country's leaders have consistently lied to the American people." (Cambridge Survey Research)

These findings reveal a shocking degree of cynicism by Americans toward public officials. According to the same article,

Increasingly . . . voters see the election as merely an exercise to resolve the ambitions of politicians . . . a power struggle essentially irrelevant to the problems of inflation and unemployment that intensely concern the people themselves.

While a great many Americans despair about the increase in crime, most Americans do not believe politicians' promises that they will strengthen law enforcement. Indeed, according to Louis Harris, "A majority now believes that such a candidate won't make the streets safe from crime, and chances are that he will end up being proved a crook himself." So much for "law and order" candidates!

The decline in effect toward public officials is matched by a decline in political party identification. According to Gallup polls, since 1937 there has been a more or less steady growth in the percentage of voters who identify themselves as "independent," from a low of 16 percent in 1937 to a high of 35 percent in June to August 1975. In the latter period, 21 percent of the people interviewed classified themselves as Republicans; 44 percent, as Democrats. The "independents" were more than half again larger than those affiliating with the Republican party and were approaching the size of the Democratic bloc.

These data, taken together, have led some to conclude that there is a growth in political alienation and a decline in political interest and political activity on the part of Americans. But other data confound this conclusion.

Although reliable indicators for the following phenomenon remain elusive, there is mounting evidence of a proliferation of nonpartisan, public interest organizations at local, state, and national levels, focused on single or multiple public issues of concern to their members. While Common Cause is a well-known example of a public interest group at the national level, it is matched by a great variety of other organizations—many very loosely organized—at all three levels of government. Of course, labor unions, trade associations, and professional organizations have long used the power of their collective membership to bring pressure to bear for the favorable resolution of issues of greatest importance to them. What seems to be especially striking, today, is a growing interest on the part of many Americans to organize around issues and to work for appropriate solutions. Skepticism about politicians' claims and awareness that political parties frequently blur issues in order to hold together a diverse membership have led an increasing number of Americans to invest their political energies in organizations that seem committed to solutions they favor. Also, unlike political parties or professional associations, for instance, many of these organizations do not require long apprenticeship before people can exert leadership.

Take the campaign for and against the Equal Rights Amendment (ERA) as an example. While individual politicians are on record with regard to this issue, the positions of the two parties are vague. The campaign is being carried on locally, in the state legislatures, and nationally, by concerned men and women who have mobilized because of their dedication to the issue. Many people have been drawn into political combat over ERA who would not otherwise have been active in politics.

If the trends continue in the manner outlined above, what are the implications for civic education? Clearly, civics instruction that emphasizes governmental institutions to the exclusion of other political processes lacks contact with reality. It seems shortsighted to emphasize traditional forms of political participation—voting in elections and writing letters to members of congress—while avoiding other kinds of participation. The kinds of knowledge, skills, and attitudes citizens require to be active participants in small or large political groups are probably quite different from those needed to play the role of passive observer of governmental activities. Only recently have efforts been launched to identify what such knowledge, skills, and attitudes are and to devise programs that would foster their development. Much more work remains to be done.

2. *Civic education, nationalism, and an interdependent world.* A main goal of civic education has been to promote national identity, loyalty, and commitment to national goals and policies. Traditionally, civic educators have stressed the uniqueness of the American experience, the superiority of American institutions and social processes, and the obligation of citizens to protect the United States from encroachment by other nations. The primary focus of allegiance has been the United States as represented by the federal government.

After World War II, American nationalism changed somewhat to accommodate the new international role required of the United States. Americans accepted the necessity to extend "freedom" wherever possible. Military alliances to restrict the spread of communist control seemed to be a reasonable part of a modern American defense. Helping Europe rebuild its economic structure and subsequently assisting former European colonies to become economically viable seemed sensible, not only as part of the cold war defense strategy, but also with relation to long-range American business interests.

For much of the postwar period, the United States was unmatched in physical resources and political power. In the beginning it also enjoyed nuclear monopoly, and its citizens counted on steady, continuous economic prosperity. It appeared to be the golden age for the United States, if not for the planet as a whole.

Today, to the surprise and dismay of a great many Americans, the future no longer seems so rosy. The appetite for raw materials to feed the American industrial machine has outrun American resources. While the United States remains an undeniably strong political power on the world scene, it no longer always has its way. The Eisenhower-Dulles doctrine of strategic nuclear deterrence seems inadequate and dangerous in the face of the Soviet nuclear arsenal and the growing proliferation of nuclear weapons in other nations. Problems of high inflation, severe recession, and high rates of unemployment have gripped developed and developing nations alike. For the first time, Americans are beginning to realize that saving may be more virtuous than consuming, and that their overall standard of living may not reach a level much greater in the future than it is presently.

The world is different from what it was fifteen or twenty years ago. Global interdependence is a fact of life. The United States has become the major supplier of food in international markets, with between a quarter and a third of land planted by American farmers being used for grain exports. The United States counts for more than one-half of a total estimated stock of foreign investments of about $165 billion. One-quarter of the gross national product of the noncommunist world is earned by multinational corporations out-side their home countries, and eight of the ten largest multinational corporations are based in the United States. Of the seventy-four nonenergy commodities essential to modern industry, the United States is now highly dependent upon foreign sources for twenty-two.

To quote from a Department of State publication:

> The world is extraordinarily different and more complex than the world we knew in 1950, and so are the problems confronting it. However, one striking parallel remains: Once again, as after World War II, we are at a watershed in history. We are living in a period which, in retrospect, is going to be seen either as a period of extraordinary creativity or a period when the international order began to come apart—politically, economically, morally. We are at one of those rare moments when, through a combination of circumstances and design, man is in a position to shape his future.[1]

What does this have to do with civic education? Civic education has traditionally been concerned with promoting nationalism. While nation-states will not suddenly disappear or lose their influence, nevertheless students must increasingly find *identification* with the species as a whole and not with American citizens only, be *loyal* to the planet as well as to the fifty states, and be *committed* to policies and goals intended to ensure the survival of the species rather than merely increasing American power and prestige at the expense of others. What is required is a civic education that would lead students to be as enthusiastic for the principles underlying a "Declaration of INTERdependence"[2] as they have been for those embodied in the "Declaration of Independence."

SOME THOUGHTS ON HOW TO MEET
THE CRISIS IN CIVIC EDUCATION

Civic education has no powerful, vocal constituency demanding improvement. Colleges complain when high schools fail to prepare students adequately with the skills needed for college success. Employers support vocational and career education programs because they expect to gain by improved results. But who cares whether students have a better understanding of current social conditions and are more capable of acting in their social world? Surely, everyone cares a little; but no one has cared enough to move civic education to a high priority in American education.

At least three national professional organizations labor on behalf of civic education. The American Bar Association's Special Committee on Youth Education for Citizenship has succeeded in mobilizing lawyers and educators across the nation behind the need for law-related education materials in schools. The American Political Science Association (APSA) Committee on Pre-Collegiate Education has launched a variety of activities to direct attention to the need for reform in citizenship education. And the National Council for the Social Studies, holding citizenship education as a main concern throughout most of its history, has sponsored conferences and published books and articles on the needs of citizenship education. But despite the worthwhile efforts of these groups, their outreach is too limited. All have been successful in working within their own client members; none can make civic education a national priority without assistance from others. Moreover, there is always the risk that a professional organization will define the problem too narrowly, in response to the special interests and concerns of its members.

To launch a reform in civic education adequate to the challenge will require the visibility and effort that has been given to "Career Education" and "Right-to-Read." Anything less will lack sufficient power, because the reform of civic education requires more than altering the content of the twelfth grade American government course, of inserting moral reasoning exercises into the curriculum, or of establishing new courses in law-related education (as meritorious and helpful as each of these efforts might be). The reform of civic education requires that schools confront the entire schooling process from K through 12—its formal and informal activities, its curricular and extracurricular programs—and assess the contributions they are making to the preparation of competent citizens.

Moreover, schooling must be linked to other socializing agencies in the community to judge the cumulative impact of their efforts.

High visibility is required not only because the task is complex, requiring the support and contributions of many actors, but also because the ground is slippery. Civic education is somewhat like sex education. As soon as a teacher moves from statements of lofty ideals to explicit instruction about how the society actually works, instruction becomes controversial. Sex and politics appear to be two subjects that many parents are willing to have students learn by experience; the less said in class, the better. While civic education programs will doubtless vary from community to community in response to local needs, there are a number of national issues (such as the fact of global interdependence) that will be controversial. The same degree of national public support will be needed on behalf of civic education that was employed following the launching of Sputnik in 1957 to effect wide-scale reforms in science, mathematics, and foreign language instruction.

Support is often a euphemism for cash. Clearly, financial investment will be needed as people are hired to plan and conduct new programs. But many of the financial resources already exist. Once civic education becomes a national priority, it should be relatively easy to nudge financial resources into needed activities. The first priority is to elevate the reform of civic education to a major concern in education and to build the political support necessary to sustain it during its early development.

New conceptualizations. In September 1975, the Conference on Political Education in the Federal Republic of Germany and the United States was held in Bloomington, Indiana. The conference participants included leading civic educators from the two nations. The main conference purpose was to compare work underway within the two nations in order that each could learn from the other.

The Americans overwhelmed the Germans with their curriculum projects. During the last decade or so, curriculum centers and textbook publishers have combined to produce an impressive array of instructional materials on a great variety of topics. The materials are attractive and interesting to use; they employ nearly every imaginable pedagogical device. The Germans had nothing to match the richness of the American materials.

On the other hand, the Germans had much to teach the American participants. The German approach to civic education reform seems more intellectually rigorous. They insist that reform proposals should be based upon careful analyses of society and its needs, and be rooted in philosophical inquiries into human nature. To the degree that American civic educators engage in such reasoning, the results tend to be more narrowly circumscribed, limited primarily to explanations and justifications for particular project activities. The American participants in the conference agreed that this was a peculiar American deficiency. The Germans are long on theory and short on interesting products representative of their theories. Americans have attractive products directed at discrete problems, but lack compelling statements indicating how their products contribute to long-range educational purposes.

There has been little incentive for American educators to try to grasp a total picture. For the past decade and a half, projects and project mentality have been dominant. On the assumption that education will be enhanced by increasing the range of tested alternatives available to schools, project directors have sought to isolate discrete instructional problems and to devise tested solutions to these problems. They accepted no responsibility for how their programs fit with others under development. The responsibility to fit various elements together to make an integrated program rested with teachers and school officials. Project directors did not see their role as one of planning the banquet; their task was to put tested products into the supermarket from which teacher-cooks planned a feast appropriate to their students.

In the future, funds must be found to support those willing and able to assume the task of creating alternative conceptions of civic education, grounded in philosophical views about human beings and realistically linked to careful analyses of society. The gap between civic education and social reality will not be closed if the field is restricted to outmoded ways of conceptualizing society and civic education.

Any effort to reconceptualize civic education in the schools must include the *process* of civic education as well as its content. Formal classroom instruction accounts for only part of what students think and believe about politics and society. Agencies outside of school influence students' knowledge, values, and skills, and the school itself functions as "civics teacher" in quite unanticipated ways. Considerable thought needs to be given to ways that the schools can be linked to those other agencies. Schools must also consider how the school itself can be used as a simulator of society to help students practice skills that will be relevant and useful in the political world they will face as adults.

Some groups are experimenting with aspects of the civic education process.[3] The APSA Committee on Pre-Collegiate Education has been searching for ways to link classroom instruction to what the committee terms the "natural political world of children." The High School Political Science Curriculum Project, sponsored by APSA, is attempting to use school, work, and community settings as sites for students to observe political activities and practice political skills. In Boston and Pittsburgh, Lawrence Kohlberg and Edwin Fenton are attempting to tap the informal organization of schools as well as the formal curriculum to enhance students' skills in moral reasoning (see Chapter 7). At Hanover, New Hampshire, Principal Robert McCarthy administers his school as if it were an operating political system.

Despite these interesting efforts, too little is known and too little is being attempted. A reconceptualization of civic education will depend not only upon fresh ideas for the content of civic education, but on new ways of linking the various civic education "instructors" within and outside of school.

New approaches to reform. During the 1960s, American education drew heavily on an engineering model for the promotion of innovation. This model has been described in various ways, but four stages are commonly noted: research, development, diffusion, and adoption. Each of these stages is seen as having discrete functions. Those responsible for research typically leave development, diffusion, and adoption duties to others. While the model is not necessarily linear, it is often perceived that way—with ideas originating in universities, special institutes, and laboratories, and gradually seeping down into the schools.

The engineering model was widely accepted by curriculum developers. They used knowledge acquired through the research of others; they created attractive instructional packages, tested them in the schools, and ultimately disseminated them to schools through conferences, in-service workshops, and demonstrations. The schools were left with the responsibility to adopt the programs they deemed desirable.

Some authorities have questioned whether the engineering model has worked effectively as a device for curriculum reform. Clearly, the development projects have often produced high-quality materials; but their adoption rate in schools frequently is less than expected. Moreover, the developers are often aghast at the ways schools use their materials once they have been adopted.

In the 1960s, a massive effort was launched to improve instruction via in-service institutes for teachers. The notion was that teachers would be introduced to new ideas in their in-service courses and would transfer their new knowledge to their own courses upon returning to their schools. Certainly some examples of significant change can be found. However, the overall results of the institute program were disappointing. Indeed, a study of U.S. Office of Education (USOE) civics institutes found that teachers knew *less* after attending the institutes than they had before.[4]

What seems to be overlooked in all of these efforts at massive change on a national basis is that each school interacting with its community is a culture of its own. Developers can produce improved materials that will float in pilot school settings, but they may founder on unfamiliar reefs and sandbars in other schools. Teacher trainers can provide the best instruction possible, but various pressures that operate on teachers following a return to their classrooms will affect how their new knowledge will be employed.

It seems unlikely that a reform of civic education (requiring a commitment by an entire school or school system with the support of its community) can be achieved by the development of new curriculum materials or by in-service teacher education alone. New patterns for working with schools as total social systems must be invented and tested. Ways must be found to enable civic education reformers to work with a limited number of school systems on a more direct and intimate basis, hopefully leading to strategies and techniques that can be employed successfully by others.

The kind of civic education program that any school accepts will probably combine elements borrowed from others and components unique to that school. Each school will have to shape its civic education program, in some degree, to fit the interests and needs of its community and the abilities of its staff. In short, there can be no single, unitary civic education program in a nation as diverse as the United States. The reform's success will depend in large measure on the capacity of civic educators to help schools shape their programs to goals they have identified and to which they are committed. Curriculum development and teacher in-service education will also be required. But the truly effective civic educator will need to combine the skills of a technical consultant and political adviser, for the school and community must feel they are in control if the programs are to be successful.

It will be necessary to identify individuals who can play such roles and create institutional settings from which they can operate. These settings must sustain the reformers' professional needs, make available technical and intellectual resources appropriate to the task, and command the trust of the schools and the community. Existing procedures, by themselves, will not be adequate.

NOTES

1. *United States Foreign Policy: An Overview,* U.S. Department of State, January 1976.

2. Henry Steele Commager, *A Declaration of INTERdependence* (draft), World Affairs Council, Philadelphia, 1975.

3. See Chapter 11, note 9, for information on youth participation and community involvement.

4. As far as is known, the study was never published or distributed. One explanation of the negative result is that teachers, confident of their knowledge before attending the institutes, were unsettled by the new information they encountered. They returned to their classrooms at the end of the summer dissatisfied with what they had taught before, but unable to apply their new knowledge in situations requiring that they continue to use outmoded textbooks.

Rationale for a New Emphasis on Citizenship Education

6

ISIDORE STARR

During the past two decades, the American people have experienced a series of crises which has seared the conscience, troubled the mind, and shocked the emotions. The Vietnam conflict posed the issue of just and unjust wars, while at the same time casting doubt on the legitimacy of executive and legislative conduct under the Constitution. Charges and countercharges clouded the traditional concept of loyalty to country. Watergate exposed lawlessness on the highest levels of government, while little Watergates marred the landscape of local and state politics. At times, it seemed that the law enforcers had forgotten that they are not above the law. *Brown v. Board of Education* wrested the idea of equality out of the books and thrust the American Dilemma on to the local, state, and national scenes. The persistence of poverty, which has spread from people to governmental units, has divided the nation on the policy of public assistance, while posing the Biblical cry: "Am I my brother's keeper?" Violence and crime have led to fears that the social contract, which has cemented America into a constitutional democracy, may now be transforming it into a police state or armed camp. There has developed, understandably, a crisis of confidence in American institutions.

The problems confronting American society seem like tidal waves about to engulf the nation. Present discontents, however, are not unique. They have ancient roots; the issues of the past mesh with the issues of the present. To focus on one to the exclusion of the other is either to drown in the murky waters of antiquarianism or to wallow in the shallow streams of presentism.

To avoid this predicament and, at the same time, to restore confidence in American institutions, five major ideas in the constellation of democratic thought could be selected for inquiry. Liberty, justice, equality, and property are, to use Paul Freund's phrase, "moral standards wrapped in legal commands." Each of these four ideas operates within the context of the idea of power. Responsible citizenship entails, in large part, grappling with these ideas, publicly and privately, in the search for answers to persistent dilemmas: liberty versus license, justice versus injustice, equality versus inequality, property rights versus human rights, and the uses of power versus the abuses of power.

THE IDEA OF LIBERTY

The idea of liberty wends its way through American history and literature. It is proclaimed on the Liberty Bell, it is designated an inalienable right in the Declaration of Independence, it is pronounced a blessing in the Preamble, it is protected in the Fifth and Fourteenth Amendments against arbitrary acts by government, and it is recited daily as part of the Pledge of Allegiance. But nowhere is it defined in the traditional sense.

Why is the First Amendment first? Was it intent or style? Perhaps it heads the constellation known as the Bill of Rights because it is basic to all the other rights. Those who drafted the first ten amendments knew firsthand the importance of freedom of thought, belief, inquiry, expression, petition, and assembly as a means of guaranteeing the other rights against the capricious or malicious whims of rulers. The First Amendment remains the best operating definition of liberty, and, as such, it contributes to the delineation of the dignity and integrity of the individual. It is understandably the first of what Madison referred to as the "Great Rights."

Why do the first ten words of the First Amendment prohibit an establishment of religion? Why did the drafters begin with this commandment rather than with one relating to speech or press?

Separation of church and state has been sought in America by both religious and political leaders. Roger Williams advocated "the wall of separation between the garden of the church and the wilderness of the world," and Thomas Jefferson supported "a wall of separation between church and state." One sought the wall to protect the church, the other the state. The result was the construction of a constitutional barrier to an establishment of religion and the beginning of a series of controversies which would carry over into the future. The use of public funds for busing parochial school students, released time, required sectarian prayers and Bible reading, religious practices in public schools, various forms of parochial aid, tax exemptions for church properties, and the teaching of the theory of evolution continue to find their way into the public forum and judicial tribunals.

In wrestling with these issues, the Supreme Court has formulated a number of principles: child benefit, neutrality, complete separation, and nonpreference. The Court's rulings have been attacked as atheistic, communistic, and secularistic. In a disturbing number of instances, school authorities have deliberately disobeyed the Bible and prayer decisions. One can only speculate on the relationship between the educator as a lawbreaker and the educator as a model of responsible citizenship.

On the other side, the religious freedom clause has been invoked to ensure parochial school education, to safeguard the educational objectives of selected religious sects, to permit schoolchildren to refuse to engage in patriotic ceremonies contrary to their religious beliefs, and to excuse conscientious objectors from military service where strongly held beliefs were comparable to traditional religious faith.

These are questions which responsible citizens will have to face for years to come. A pluralistic society with its contemporary condemnation of the melting pot is dedicated especially to respecting differences in customs, beliefs, and traditions. To what extent can education remove or moderate the prejudices and biases, which often emerge as barriers to the fulfillment of the ideal and practice of respect for the beliefs of others?

Freedom of speech and of the press, like the religion clauses, are basic liberties that help to define the dignity and integrity of the individual. The citizen who fears to express his views on public issues, whether within the school or in the public forum, is a diminished man or woman. Living in fear of governmental officials—national, state, or local—or apprehensive of what the community will think, means that quiet desperation or silent surrender becomes a way of life. There may be many who have little or nothing to say; but that may be due, in part, to an education which discouraged public discourse of moral-ethical questions and encouraged self-censorship and self-preservation. When this happens, the freedom of expression clauses become mere "parchment barriers."

The *Tinker* case, popularly known as the Black Armband case, brought a freedom of speech issue from school surroundings into the Supreme Court. Widely criticized and just as widely unread, the decision held that freedom of speech is a preferred right in school as elsewhere; and that the imposition of restraints will be justified only upon reasonable prediction by school officials that the expression will substantially interfere with or materially disrupt discipline in the school. The schoolhouse gate does not bar the Bill of Rights from the school, declared the Court, but students do not have a blank check to interfere with the conduct of an educational system.

Students have gone to court to seek legal clarification of such freedom of expression issues as dress, hairstyle, "underground" newspapers, and "provocative" language. Resort to the courts rather than to the streets indicates a commendable trend toward responsible citizenship. On the other hand, it can be argued that school issues should be settled within the confines of the school. If that is to be done with any degree of success, both students and educators must have some understanding of the historic, philosophical, and constitutional dimensions of freedom of expression in the world at large.

An unpopular speaker is confronted by a hostile audience, or by a generally friendly audience with a few vociferous hecklers. Policemen are present; what action should they take, if any? Is there a constitutional right to listen without interruption to what a speaker is saying on a street corner, in a hired hall, in a school classroom, or in a school auditorium? Does a student body, invited to hear a speaker, have the right to interrupt if they find the views expressed an appeal to intolerance and hate? Does a speaker have any obligation to the audience in particular and to the community in general? Does freedom of speech protect the right to say anything, anywhere, and at any time? Is there a constitutional mandate to grant tolerance to those who preach intolerance? What are the ethical and moral issues involved in these tormenting queries?

Freedom of the press is freedom of speech written large both on newspaper stands and on the television screen. The power of the press has been used, however, to whip up public opinion against an accused and to cater to the prejudices of the community in the interest of circulation. The right to a fair trial and the right to a free press are in collision; which has priority?

How far should the press be able to proceed in criticizing public or prominent officials? Does the press have the right to disclose policy decisions which may embarrass the government? Should the press have the right, daily and nightly, to invade the privacy of homes, as well as people's thoughts and feelings? What is the relationship between the press, public morality, the law, and the issue of obscenity?

Issues concerning freedom of the press have become a part of the life of the school. School newspapers have commented on school policy and administrative rulings in rhetoric which is, to say the least, unflattering to the educators. In turn, school officials have censored the newspapers. In their turn students have produced so-called underground papers, and the response has been more restraints. In extremis, the courts have been asked to rule on whether school officials have the legal authority to censor student newspapers. If they do, is prior or post restraint the best way to conduct education for responsible citizenship?

THE IDEA OF JUSTICE: DUE PROCESS OF LAW

Like liberty, justice is mentioned in these great documents. The Declaration of Independence speaks of justice and injustice; the Preamble aims to promote justice; and the Pledge of Allegiance promises justice for all. Finally, like liberty, the operative definition of justice must be sought in the Bill of Rights. The Fourth, Fifth, Sixth, and Eighth amendments speak directly to the idea of criminal justice by reference to the principles of due process of law.

The due process model, laboriously constructed through the ages, poses dilemmas for the citizenry. Does it require an adversary system—complicated, deliberate, expensive, and frequently marked by overacting? If law is the best hope, how can society respond to the charge that in this country there is a law for the rich, a law for the poor, and a law for the middle class? Has the jury system outlived its usefulness? When does a criminal proceeding become a political trial? Is a magisterial system of justice preferable to ours?

While the debate goes on, the due process model is being gradually supplanted in criminal justice by plea bargaining, which in some cities disposes of 80 to 90 percent of the cases brought to court. The gap between the professed principles of due process and the actual practices of criminal justice raises questions concerning the integrity of a political system which sanctions bypaths to justice. Once again, decision making will have to weigh the merits of the controversy. To be ignorant of the issues or to abdicate the responsibility of choice is to approve the transformation that is taking place.

While plea bargaining is displacing trial for adults, in juvenile justice the trend is in the other direction. The juvenile courts came into existence when reformers argued, for a variety of reasons, that youthful accused should be tried and treated differently. (The good intentions went astray, as the *Gault* case so vividly demonstrated.) To protect the juvenile, the Supreme Court mandated substantial due process principles in juvenile court hearings with the proviso that each state had the option to offer the accused the right to a jury trial. The informal proceedings of the recent past are now subject to formal hearings measured by traditional due process.

Two recent five-to-four rulings by the Supreme Court have carried the due process mandate into school buildings and school systems. In dealing with controversies involving ten-day suspensions and three-month expulsions, a majority of five of the justices imposed on school authorities minimal due process: notice of charges and a hearing in which each side has a right to present evidence before the imposition of punishment. The expulsion decision warned school board members and officials that they will be held personally liable if they violate the constitutional rights of students. A subsequent lower-court opinion affirmed by the Supreme Court upheld paddling, provided minimal due process preceded it.

At the very moment when the judiciary is extending due process procedures to juveniles, acts of violence by the young, especially in the ten- to sixteen-year-old group, have become increasingly common. At present there is probably no topic of greater personal significance to students in the schools. To disregard these developments in the courses of study is to leave untouched matters of vital concern to students and their parents. To treat the subject superficially and gingerly is to contribute to the growing disrespect for education.

THE IDEA OF EQUALITY

The Constitution, in its unamended state, made no reference to equality. Using the euphemism "people" for slaves, the Founding Fathers sought to circumvent the uncomfortable implications of "the peculiar institution." If slaves were referred to indirectly, women were not mentioned at all.

With the Fourteenth Amendment and the guarantee of equal protection of the laws, the issue of equality took on a constitutional dimension, but it was not until 1954 that the Supreme Court declared de jure segregation unconstitutional. Congress followed with civil rights laws and the issues were joined in education, employment, housing, and public accommodations.

The playing fields of the schools, as well as the streets of communities, became the battle grounds of the desegregation-integration rulings of the courts (which continue to assume the leadership in the quest for equal educational opportunity). When the orders of a court run headlong into the cherished mores of a community, "the sparks fly upward." To counter the idea of equality, an appeal was made to another basic principle. The confrontation has taken the form of liberty versus equality: the right to choose the neighborhood school as the institution for learning against the right to an equal education through the use of buses, if necessary.

Explosive issues are involved in the equality controversy. Can the citizens of a community engage in selective law obedience with immunity? Can educators do so? If educators can do so, can students follow their example? If a state closes some of its public schools to avoid compliance with a court ruling on desegregation, is it in violation of the Equal Protection Clause? Can parochial or private schools be used to circumvent judicial rulings on racial balance?

A recent study indicates that socioeconomic status is a far more important factor than schooling in personal success and that the idea of equality can become a reality only through reorganization of the economic system. This discomforting conclusion, referring to the schools as "marginal institutions," cannot be swept away.

What Gunnar Myrdal called the American Dilemma has spilled over into business, labor organizations, and the schools and colleges—with charges of discrimination against women, blacks, and other minorities in appointments, assignments, and promotions. The recent *DeFunis* case, dealing with so-called reverse discrimination in admission to a professional school, found the Supreme Court indecisive in resolving the dilemma of adjusting the inequities of the past with the demand for equal treatment for all today. While educators are dealing with the practical consequences of affirmative action, they must design units or courses which confront students with these dimensions of civic responsibility.

THE IDEA OF PROPERTY

The Founding Fathers showed a healthy respect for property by prohibiting the impairment of contracts. The idea of property was subsequently sanctified by the Fifth and Fourteenth amendments, which prohibited deprivation without due process of law and just compensation.

Property relationships dominate American society in a variety of ways and are of great concern to students in the schools, who must differentiate public from private property. If students were asked, for example, to sign formal contracts relating to the use of school textbooks or lockers, the rights-responsibilities equation might be clarified and transferable to other transactions.

Consumer law, landlord-tenant disputes, and welfare problems are especially close to students in the inner cities; for them, ignorance of the law can mean disaster. Consumers, confronted by false advertising, shady business practices, complicated installment buying contracts, exorbitant prices, and shoddy merchandise, have a range of available remedies. In landlord-tenant cases, a knowledge of the nature of a lease and the mutual obligations involved can contribute to a reasonable resolution or to legal recourse, instead of to violence and destruction of property. The welfare debate, punctuated by charges of laziness and cheating, takes on meaning only when the nature of poverty in the midst of plenty is studied seriously. In this sense government assistance to big business, which has been labeled welfare for the rich, calls for comparative analysis.

Some states mandate a course of study on the essentials and benefits of the free enterprise system. Based on the accomplishments of American capitalism, such a course would probably cover such topics as private property, individual initiative, competition, the profit motive, and the policy of laissez-faire. The intent seems to be to develop an understanding of the system with special emphasis on its superiority to other economic systems.

Education for responsible citizenship, of necessity, does have to raise questions about the content of such courses. Scholars, businessmen, workers, and farmers have found the free enterprise system far from perfect. The antitrust philosophy, buttressed by major legislation, was designed to preserve the substance of competition within the economy. Despite efforts of many administrations, industries have fallen under the domination of monopolies or oligopolies and, finally, multinational corporations whose property base makes them richer than many of the states and nations in which they have branches. The small private entrepreneur is overshadowed by economic giants.

The same development from the small to the big has marked labor and agriculture. The small-craft union has been merged into the powerful industrywide labor organization, and the small farmer has been swallowed by agribusinesses.

To confront what was once called "the curse of bigness" and to uphold the tenets of the free enterprise system, policy decisions have to be made. Is the antitrust philosophy obsolete? Should giant corporate units be dismantled into moderate and manageable enterprises? Should the activities of labor organizations be restricted? Have technology and automation transformed the nature of property and property ownership so that new forms have to be created?

In recent years, propertied interests have found themselves involved in legislative and judicial jousts with environmental interests. This confrontation between the sanctity of property and the quality of life is complicated by such issues as jobs, costs, prices, and progress. Among the factors to be considered in resolving this major issue of today and of the future is Justice Douglas's proposal that the forests and mountains ought to have their legal representation when confronted by counsel for corporations.

Friction between the idea of property and the ideas of liberty and equality will continue to trouble thinking citizens so long as they are free to inquire into controversies, to evaluate the solutions on a hierarchy of values, and to influence decision makers. The schools are the training grounds for these activities, and they must open their doors to the currents of controversy.

THE IDEA OF POWER

In discussing the Greek myths relating to the birth of power, Adolf Berle intimated that there is a love-hate relationship between power on the one hand, and liberty, justice, equality, and property on the other. At times, power nurtures and sustains them; at others, it opposes and restricts them. The idea of power takes its most conspicuous forms in the police power of the state and in the power of the people. The former is utilized by government to protect the lives, health, morals, welfare, and safety of the people; the latter evidences itself in elections, protests, passive resistance, and revolution.

The Founding Fathers were keenly aware of the nature and scope of power. In drafting the Constitution, they were determined to separate power among the three branches of government and to divide power between the states and the newly created national government. By creating a system of checks and balances, they hoped to limit the power of each branch of government without immobilizing the system. By dividing power, they planned to keep the national government within its place. Today the states have become petitioners and supplicants, while government by executive hegemony has weakened the separation of power.

The power issues confronting the American citizenry demand decisions relating to the form and substance of government. Shall the American people drop the pretense of a federal republic and recognize that they have taken, wittingly or not, the road to a unitary government? Is the road back to the federal system still viable and relevant for the solution of problems which transcend state lines? Since poverty and welfare, energy, ecology, employment, and education now have nationwide dimensions, would it be desirable to experiment with a regional rearrangement of states as an alternative to the federal system?

The crisis resulting from the Great Depression of the 1930s elevated the presidency to a position of awesome power. Leadership in war and in domestic emergencies strengthened the hand of the Chief Executive and diminished the power base of the Congress. Recent revelations relating to Watergate, the CIA, and the FBI bring to mind Justice Brandeis' memorable warning:

> In a government of laws, existence of the government will be imperiled if it fails to observe the law scrupulously. Our government is the potent, the omnipresent teacher. For good or for ill, it teaches the whole people by its example. Crime is contagious. If the government becomes a lawbreaker, it breeds contempt for law; it invites every man to become a law unto himself; it invites anarchy.

Government abuse of power can be overlooked no longer in the history books and in the social studies classrooms. To face this issue fairly is to encourage confidence in a system which is periodically self-correcting.

The power of judicial review tends to be troublesome periodically. More than a century ago, de Tocqueville declared, "Scarcely any political question arises in the United States that is not resolved, sooner or later, into a judicial question." This acute observation has been reflected in the unique role of the Supreme Court in American history. Its landmark rulings are, more often than not, moral-ethical pronouncements on value conflicts, rather than traditional legal decisions. As such, it is inevitable that its critics condemn judicial review as government by judiciary, while its defenders proclaim it as the conscience of the nation. The fate of the Court as an institution of closure will be dependent, in part, on the quality of the debate with reference to its role as clarifier of the ideas of liberty, justice, equality, property, and power.

Ultimate power rests in the hands of the people. That the presidential elections of 1800, 1828, and 1932 have been referred to as revolutions attests to the power of the ballot. Voting, however, is more than marching hypnotically to the polls to the tune of an ideological drummer. It involves the ability to distinguish demagogue from democrat, capricious promises from realistic platforms, and short-run perspectives from long-term ones. Responsible decision making in the leader-follower relationship is obviously a major mission of education for responsible citizenship.

The most ominous form of people power is the resort to the streets. The American Revolution and the Civil Rights Revolution of the 1950s and 1960s represent case studies of refusal to obey the law with intent to change the law. The refusal of many communities to obey the Supreme Court prayer ruling can also be seen in this light. It is preferable to examine such events fully and frankly to discover causes and consequences rather than to hide behind the bland treatments of textbooks.

CONCLUSION

Probing the nature and scope of liberty, justice, equality, property, and power will not preclude inquiry in depth into the myriad of ideas which gives meaning to our lives: self-preservation, peace, democracy, right, good, and beauty, among others. The five ideas were selected for special attention because they are of special relevance in the days ahead. In the next fourteen years the American people will be celebrating two more Bicentennials: in 1987, the drafting of the Constitution, and in 1991, the ratification of the Bill of Rights. Each document is a historic landmark, a constitutional classic, and a philosophical response to a great challenge. The Declaration explains the breaking of a social contract, the Constitution represents the making of a social contract, and the Bill of Rights sets forth moral-ethical principles protecting the secular natural rights of individuals against oppressive government. It is simply not possible to understand and appreciate these events without analyzing the ideas imbedded in the texts.

The global scene today reflects crises rooted in the clash of ideas. The democratic ethos is being confronted daily by the threat of authoritarian and totalitarian models. The capitalist system is on the defensive in a world turning toward socialist and communist economies. The quest for world peace involves issues of liberty, justice, equality, property, and power.

Each of the five ideas can be studied in a variety of contexts, ranging from the simple to the complex. Liberty can be seen as simple restraints of physical movement or complex distinctions between "liberty to" and "liberty from." Justice can be viewed as a simple law and order and "hang-em" solution or as a network of due process rights. Equality can start with the sharing of a pie and lead eventually to the problem of equitable distribution of wealth. Property can be studied as "mine and thine" and proceed to an analysis of competing economic systems. Power can be seen as a policeman's club or as the role of law. The possibilities are endless.

BIBLIOGRAPHY

Liberty

Chafee, Zacharias, Jr.: *Free Speech in the United States,* Harvard University Press, Cambridge, Mass., 1954.

Handlin, Oscar, and Mary Handlin: *The Dimensions of Liberty,* Harvard University Press, Cambridge, Mass., 1961.

Howe, Mark DeWolfe: *The Garden and the Wilderness,* The University of Chicago Press, Chicago, 1965.

Pfeffer, Leo: *Church, State and Freedom,* rev. ed., Beacon Press, Boston, 1967.

Justice

Hunt, Morton: *The Mugging,* New American Library, Inc., New York, 1972.

Packer, Herbert: *The Limits of the Criminal Sanction,* Stanford University Press, Stanford, Calif., 1968.

Equality

Jencks, Christopher, et al.: *Inequality,* Basic Books, Inc., Publishers, New York, 1972.

Konvitz, Milton R., and Theodore Leskes: *A Century of Civil Rights,* Columbia University Press, New York, 1961.

Property

Berle, Adolf: *Power without Property,* Harcourt, Brace & World, Inc., New York, 1959.

Power

Berle, Adolf: *Power,* Harcourt, Brace & World, Inc., New York, 1969.

Moral Education

Beck, C. M., et al. (eds.): *Moral Education,* University of Toronto Press, Toronto, 1971.

Childs, John: *Education and Morals,* John Wiley & Sons, Inc., New York, 1967.

Kay, A. William: *Moral Development,* Schocken Books Inc., New York, 1969.

Political Philosophy

Rawls, John: *A Theory of Justice,* Harvard University Press, Cambridge, Mass., 1971.

The Implications of Lawrence Kohlberg's Research for Civic Education

7

EDWIN FENTON

During the past twenty years, Lawrence Kohlberg, his colleagues, and their graduate students have been carving out new fields of psychological and educational research. They have also made substantial contributions to moral philosophy and to the philosophy of education.[1] Three words—cognitive moral development—capture the essence of their work. "Cognitive" stresses organized thought processes. "Moral" involves decision making in situations where universal values, such as the sanctity of life and the need for authority, come into conflict. "Development" suggests that patterns of thinking about moral issues improve qualitatively over time.

Within the past few years, Kohlberg and his colleagues have begun to investigate the educational implications of their research. They have intervened in correctional institutions to determine whether or not deliberate programs of cognitive moral development would improve the lives of inmates. They have also intervened in educational institutions, particularly in public schools, in order to facilitate cognitive moral development. These efforts, still in their beginning phases, have attracted widespread attention.

Kohlberg's research has significant implications for civic education.[2] For example, his findings suggest that most high school students do not understand the principles underlying the American Constitution. Many of them do not even understand the Constitution as a societal maintenance or "law and order" document. Moreover, the two intervention techniques which Kohlberg and his colleagues have developed—discussions of moral dilemmas to change the formal curriculum in social studies and English, and the establishment of schools-within-schools organized as participatory democracies in order to change the hidden curriculum—hold great promise for civic education in the nation's secondary schools. This

97

chapter summarizes Kohlberg's research, examines its educational implications, and describes two programs of civic education based on cognitive moral development principles.

PART I: THE RESEARCH FINDINGS

People think about moral issues in six qualitatively different stages arranged in three levels of two stages each.[3] Table 1 delineates these levels and stages.

Table 1. Levels and Stages of Moral Development

THE PRECONVENTIONAL LEVEL (Stages One and Two)
At this level, people consider the power of authority figures or the physical or hedonistic consequences of actions, such as punishment, reward, or exchange of favors. This level has the following two stages:

Stage One: The Punishment and Obedience Orientation
At this stage, the physical consequences of doing something determine whether it is good or bad without regard for its human meaning or value. People at Stage One think about avoiding punishment or earning rewards, and they defer to authority figures with power over them.

Stage Two: The Instrumental Relativist Orientation
At Stage Two, right reasoning leads to action which satisfies one's own needs and sometimes meets the needs of others. Stage Two thought often involves elements of fairness, but always for pragmatic reasons rather than from a sense of justice or loyalty. Reciprocity, a key element in Stage Two thought, is a matter of "you scratch my back and I'll scratch yours."

THE CONVENTIONAL LEVEL (Stages Three and Four)
At this level, people value maintaining the expectations of their family, group, or nation for their own sake and regardless of immediate consequences. People at the conventional level show loyalty to the social order and actively maintain, support, and justify it. This level has the following two stages:

Stage Three: The Interpersonal Sharing Orientation
At this stage, people equate good behavior with whatever pleases or helps others and with what others approve of. Stage Three people often conform to stereotypical ideas of how the majority of people in their group behave. They often judge behavior by intentions, and they earn approval by being "nice."

Stage Four: The Societal Maintenance Orientation
Stage Four thought orients toward authority, fixed rules, and the maintenance of the social order. Right behavior consists of doing one's duty, showing respect for authority, or maintaining the given social order for its own sake.

THE PRINCIPLED LEVEL (Stages Five and Six)
At this level, people reason according to moral principles which have validity apart from the authority of groups to which the individuals belong. This level has the following two stages:

Stage Five: The Social Contract, Human Rights, and Welfare Orientation
People at Stage Five tend to define right action in terms of general individual rights and standards which have been examined critically and agreed upon by the society in a document such as the Declaration of Independence. Stage Five people stress the legal point of view, but they emphasize the possibility of changing laws after rational consideration of the welfare of the society. Free agreement and contract bind people together where no laws apply.

Stage Six: The Universal Ethical Principle Orientation
At Stage Six, people define the right by the decision of their conscience guided by ethical principles such as respect for human personality, liberty compatible with the equal liberty of all others, justice, and equality. These principles appeal to logical comprehensiveness, universality, and consistency. Instead of being concrete rules, they are abstract ethical principles.

The most reliable way to determine a stage of moral thought is through a moral interview.[4] A trained interviewer presents a subject with three dilemmas, each of which sets forth a situation for which the culture lends some conventional support for a number of actions which the protagonists could take. Here is one such dilemma from one of the interview forms.[5]

Joe is a 14-year-old boy who wanted to go to camp very much. His father promised him he could go if he saved up the money for it himself. So Joe worked hard at his paper route and saved up the $40 it cost to go to camp, and a little more besides. But just before camp was going to start, his father changed his mind. Some of his friends decided to go on a special fishing trip, and Joe's father was short of the money it would cost. So he told Joe to give him the money he had saved from the paper route. Joe didn't want to give up going to camp, so he thought of refusing to give his father the money.

After presenting the dilemma, the interviewer asks the following questions:

1. Should Joe refuse to give his father the money? Why?

2. Is there any way in which the father has a right to tell his son to give him the money? Why?

3. What is the most important thing a good father should recognize in his relation to his son? Why that?

4. What is the most important thing a good son should recognize in relation to his father? Why that?

5. Why should a promise be kept?

6. What makes a person feel bad if a promise is broken?

7. Why is it important to keep a promise to someone you don't know well or are not close to?

Over a period of twenty years, Kohlberg and his colleagues have identified typical responses to the questions of the moral interview at each of the first five stages of moral thought. Scorers compare the responses given by the subject to these typical responses in order to determine moral stage. Trained scorers show 90 percent agreement in identifying stage despite the difficult and sophisticated scoring techniques involved in scoring qualitative, open-ended data.

A stage is an organized system of thought.[6] Presented with several moral dilemmas, a person who reasons predominantly at Stage Three will consistently give Stage Three answers, although the content of the dilemmas may vary widely. For example, Stage Three thinkers will argue that they should do what pleases or helps others, whether the issue involves obeying the law, affection between friends, or reasons to punish people.

Three responses at one stage to a single moral problem may illuminate the nature of a psychological stage. Suppose that Jill steals a sweater from a store. The store's security officer accosts her companion, Sharon (who is Jill's best friend). He tells Sharon that she will get in trouble unless she reveals her friend's name. Here are three responses to this dilemma, all at Stage Two:

Sharon ought to tell. After all, Jill walked out and left Sharon to take the rap. Sharon should give as good as she got. That's fair. Why should she get in trouble for Jill when Jill walked out on her?

Sharon shouldn't tell. The store probably charges enough to cover a few rip-offs. All the stores do that. It's just for Jill to get back something that she and all the rest of us have paid for anyway.

Sharon shouldn't tell. Neither the store owner nor the security guard ever did anything for her. So it wouldn't be right for her to help them out by giving Jill's name.

These three responses differ in the act they recommend (which Kohlberg calls the content of thought), since two say that Sharon should not give Jill's name and the third says that she should. They also define what is fair or just or right in different terms. But the underlying structure of thought is the same. Each response invokes an element of fairness based on reciprocity, on mutual back scratching. This common element in the thought is its structure, its underlying organizational pattern.

An individual reasons predominately at one stage of thought and uses contiguous stages as a secondary thinking pattern.[7] For example, a young teenager might respond to moral dilemmas in Stage Three terms 70 percent of the time and employ Stage Two thought the remaining 30 percent. This person is finishing the transition from Stage Two thought to Stage Three thought. Another person who responds at Stage Three 70 percent of the time and at Stage Four 30 percent probably stands at the beginning of the transition to Stage Four thought. (One stage of thought does not merely replace another. Instead, a new stage transforms the old one and incorporates its main elements into the new thought pattern. This phenomenon helps to explain why contiguous stages of thought often emerge in an interview.)

These stages are natural steps in ethical development, not something artificial or invented. To find them, Kohlberg gave moral interviews to people of different ages and then classified responses on the basis of the similarity of the reasoning process that was used.[8] Subsequently he conducted a longitudinal study, interviewing the same fifty subjects every three years. The longitudinal data helped him to revise and clarify his statements of the stages.

Kohlberg's research was conducted originally in the United States. Parallel cross-sectional research, however, has been conducted in a number of additional countries including Turkey, Mexico, Taiwan, Israel, Canada, and India.[9] In each of these countries, researchers have found the same stages of moral thought that Kohlberg discovered in the United States. However, the principled stages (Stages Five and Six) do not appear among respondents interviewed in traditional societies.

People can understand moral arguments at their own stage, at all stages beneath their own, and sometimes at one (and occasionally two) stages above their own. They generally prefer the highest stage of thought that they can comprehend. James Rest interviewed forty-seven high school seniors using the standard Kohlberg moral interview. He was able to determine the stage of moral thought that they could generate spontaneously in this way. Then he gave them a set of prepared statements giving responses to a moral dilemma at all six stages of the Kohlberg scale. He asked them to recapitulate the statements in their own words and to rank the statements in the order of how convincing they were.

Rest drew four conclusions about the comprehension of moral stages from this experiment. First, subjects tended to get nearly all the statements at a stage right, or to get nearly all of them wrong. Second, subjects who got nearly all statements at a given stage right also successfully recapitulated the statements at all stages lower than their own. Third, comprehension scores declined rapidly for stages higher than the subject's own. Most Stage Three subjects comprehended Stage Four thought, but not Stage Five; only 40 percent of Stage Four thinkers comprehended Stage Five arguments. Fourth, the highest stage used on the responses to the moral interview was a better predictor of comprehension than the predominant stage which a subject used.

There were two major findings about preference. First, 80 percent of the subjects preferred the highest stage of thought which they comprehended. Second, subjects tended to prefer the higher stage statements in their developmental order—that is, they preferred a Stage Five argument to a Stage Four argument.

Think of the implications of this research for civic education. The Constitution is based on a Stage Five morality. It assumes the existence of basic rights—life, liberty, equality—which antedate the formation of the government. The government comes into existence to guarantee these rights to citizens. The Declaration of Independence, another Stage Five document, puts the case in this way:

We hold these truths to be self-evident, that all men are created equal, that they are endowed by their Creator with certain unalienable rights, that among these are life, liberty, and the pursuit of happiness. That to secure these rights, governments are instituted among men, deriving their just powers from the consent of the governed. That whenever any form of government becomes destructive of these ends, it is the right of the people to alter or to abolish it, and to institute new government, laying its foundation on such principles and organizing its powers in such form, as to them shall seem most likely to effect their safety and happiness.

As a minimal goal of civic education, educators should aim to raise the level of moral thinking to the level at which students can understand the principles behind the Constitution and the Declaration of Independence. For many people that will be Stage Five; for others it will be Stage Four. Getting most high school seniors to use Stage Four thought predominantly will be no easy task.

People move through these stages in invariant sequence, although any individual may cease developing at any stage.[10] Everyone reasons as a young child at Stage One. Most people then move to Stage Two. As early as age nine, but usually later, most Americans enter Stage Three; some of them then pass into Stage Four in middle or late adolescence. The transition to Stage Five takes place, if at all, when people are in their late teens or early twenties, or even later in life. Very few people attain Stage Six, and those who do are usually older than thirty. As far as is known, no one ever skips a stage, and once someone has attained a particular stage, he never retrogresses to earlier ones. (No person in Kohlberg's longitudinal sample of fifty has regressed during the twenty years of that study.) However, people can have their development arrested at any stage. Most adult Americans think at the Conventional Level, Stages Four or Three, and only a small minority—perhaps 5 or 10 percent—attain full Stage Five thought. Few, if any, high school students reason mainly at Stage Five.

Two major factors limit the development of higher stages of moral thought. The first is limited cognitive capacity, a limited ability to use formal, abstract thought.[11] Beginning formal operational thought on the Piagetian scale is a necessary but not sufficient condition for Stage Three moral thought, and more complete formal operational thought is a similar prerequisite for Stage Four and

Stage Five thought on the Kohlberg scale. The second factor is a limited social perspective or role-taking ability.[12] Kohlberg's colleague Robert Selman defined role taking in two ways: by the way in which an individual differentiates his or her perspective from that of other individuals, and by the way in which an individual relates these perspectives to others. The first four stages of perspective taking may be described in the following terms (Table 2). They parallel levels and stages on the moral scale.

Table 2. Levels and Stages of Perspective Taking

THE PRECONVENTIONAL LEVEL (Stages One and Two)
At this level, a person has the perspective of an isolated individual rather than of a person who belongs to a group or social system. This level has the following two stages:

Stage One
At this stage, the person focuses only on his own interests and does not think of himself as a person with responsibilities to others or as a person who belongs to a group.

Stage Two
At this stage, the person still wants to serve his own interests, but is able to anticipate another person's reactions. Here there is willingness to make a deal to get what one wants.

THE CONVENTIONAL LEVEL (Stages Three and Four)
At this level, a person assumes the perspective of a member of a group or a society. This level has the following two stages:

Stage Three
At Stage Three, people can see things from the point of view of shared relationships, such as caring, trust, and respect, between two or more individuals who know each other.

Stage Four
Here a person can take the point of view of a member of a social system or a society as a whole. The person is able to see a situation through the eyes of many actors, including people in the society whom he does not know.

Higher stages are better than lower stages.[13] Psychological evidence supports this claim. As has been seen, people develop through the stages in invariant sequence. If lower stages were better cognitively than higher ones, one would be forced to argue that the quality of thought deteriorates as a person matures (a proposition difficult to maintain). But the psychological argument of higher stages being cognitively better than lower ones rests on a firmer basis than this argument provides. Problems can be solved better at higher stages than at lower ones. Higher stages of thought are cognitively more differentiated, more integrated, and more universal than lower stages. More differentiated means that, at higher stages, people draw distinction between such different things as the value of life and the value of property. At Stage One people do not make this distinction. More integrated means that, at higher stages, people place such values as life, law, and property in a hierarchy. Life logically ranks higher than property because property sustains life, not the reverse. More universal means that higher stages appeal to more universal principles, such as the social contract, equality, or justice. Lower stages stress less encompassing principles, such as avoiding punishment for oneself or gaining a personal reward. Hence, higher stage thought is cognitively better because it is more consistent than thought at lower stages.

Stage transition takes place primarily because real life or hypothetical moral dilemmas set up cognitive conflict in a person's mind and make the person uncomfortable.[14] Let's take Mary who customarily reasons at Stage Two. Mary thinks in terms of reciprocity—"I'll help her because I want her to help me next time." Then she hears another argument—"People will like you more if you help them. They will approve of you because good people help each other, and that's a good thing to do for its own sake." This higher level reasoning makes Mary uncomfortable because it challenges her customary belief, and it appeals to her because people prefer the highest stage of moral thought that they can comprehend. She sees the difference in the two arguments and prefers the one at a higher stage.

Stage change takes place slowly. Typical elementary school students stay in Stage Two for several years, but most of them encounter Stage Three arguments constantly. Their lives in the community revolve increasingly around their peer groups, whose members expect them to be faithful to friends, to behave in ways of which other children and teenagers will approve, and to help others whenever they can. Their parents often raise similar arguments. And so, over a period of several years and on one moral issue after another, Mary is won over to a new organized system of thought, a new stage.

Deliberate attempts to facilitate stage change in schools through educational programs have been successful.[15] Within the last decade, more than a score of investigators have attempted to facilitate stage change by leading moral discussions. They have worked in elementary schools, in junior and senior high schools, and on the college level. Although results vary in detail, one generalization about this research stands out: compared to the students in control groups, students in experimental groups—who participate in moral discussions—show significant increases in the stage of moral thought they commonly use.

In these programs Kohlberg and his colleagues use hypothetical moral dilemmas to trigger moral discussions, particularly in social studies and English classes.[16] The dilemmas present situations for which the culture lends some conventional support for a number of actions which the protagonists could take. Teachers present dilemmas in a variety of forms: orally; in writing; by recordings, sound tapes, film, or video tape; or as skits or role-playing exercises. The discussion leader then attempts to get students to confront arguments one stage above their own. This confrontation takes place either when students who think at contiguous moral stages discuss reasoning or when the teacher poses a higher level argument through a probe question or a comment.

Beginning in 1971, the Kohlberg group began to intervene in a new way by setting up a unit which was run as a participatory democracy within a women's prison at Niantic, Connecticut.[17] The inmates and staff members of the prison developed their own governmental structure and carried out the rules they evolved through community meetings in which each person—staff members and inmates alike—had one vote. Discussion of hypothetical moral dilemmas combined with discussion of real-life dilemmas became the heart of the community meetings, since the community handled such issues as stealing, the use of drugs or alcohol, and personal relationships among inmates.

In 1974, the Kohlberg group opened a participatory democratic unit in a public school.[18] About seventy students and their teachers compose this school-within-a-school, which is located in Cambridge High and Latin School, a few blocks from Harvard. Staff and students together drew up a constitution. They govern themselves through community meetings in which each person has one vote. Most of the issues which come up in the community meetings involve problems related to stealing, absence from school, the use of drugs, or disruptive behavior. Each of these problems has a moral dimension. Hence, students constantly process real-life moral dilemmas in their community meetings. They also learn to take other people's perspectives, as they think about what to do when an individual has broken a rule and they imagine themselves in that person's place.

The students take their social studies and English courses within their community school. They take the remainder of their courses with other students from Cambridge High and Latin School. Both the social studies and the English courses include a moral development program based on the discussion of moral dilemmas.

Moral judgment is a necessary but not sufficient condition for moral action.[19] On the surface, this statement seems simple enough. It implies that one must understand and believe in moral principles before one can follow them; it also implies that a person can reason in terms of moral principles and not act upon them. Beneath the surface, however, the relationship of moral thought to action is not as simple as it appears for four major reasons.

First, at preconventional and conventional moral levels, it is possible to recommend either of two possible courses of action in a moral dilemma and to support these recommendations by reasoning at a single stage. Here, for example, are two Stage Four responses to the shoplifting dilemma involving Sharon and Jill, described earlier in this chapter:

> Sharon ought to tell for everyone's sake. She ought to help enforce the laws against stealing and help Jill to learn what her responsibilities to a society as a citizen are. How could society hold together if everyone went around ignoring laws when it pleased them?
>
> Sharon shouldn't tell. Society is built upon the principle of trust. If you couldn't rely on people, then no business, school, or family would be able to work.

As these responses imply, merely knowing a person's stage of moral thought, or raising thought from one stage to the next one, usually will not enable anyone to predict what action a person will take in response to a particular dilemma.

At the principled level (Stages Five and Six), however, it becomes very difficult to construct equally forceful yes and no responses to a dilemma. One of Kohlberg's classic dilemmas raises the issue of whether a man is justified in stealing a drug to save his dying wife. A local druggist has developed the drug and charges ten times what it costs to produce. He refuses to reduce the price, grant credit, or make any concessions, and the man has exhausted every means to raise the money. The overwhelming majority of Stage Five thinkers argue that he should steal the drug, and they find a Stage Five argument that he should not steal it, unpersuasive. Here is such an argument:

> It would be wrong for the man to steal the drug. Although the druggist's position seems unreasonable, he is entitled to the drug since he did not violate anyone's rights when he discovered and produced it. It is agreed that no one has the right to take or seriously interfere with another person's life. But this is different from saying that anyone who gets sick has a right to force others to help them if the others are unwilling to do so freely, or that it is all right to steal.

The argument that he should steal the drug strikes most Stage Five thinkers as far more reasonable since it is more firmly grounded in basic, presocietal rights:

> Yes, he should steal it. A human life is infinitely valuable, while any material object—in this case the drug—is not. The woman's right to live exceeds the druggist's right to make a profit.

Stage Six thinkers, given agreement on the facts and circumstances of the dilemma, will arrive at the same decision about action—that the man should steal the drug.[20] At Stages Five and Six, then, the structure of thought will be likely to recommend a single action in a dilemma, a statement which is not true of thought at either the preconventional or the conventional levels.

Second, and despite the above statements, at least two experimenters have found a high correlation between moral thought and action in experimental situations. In one of them, the experimenter asked subjects to fill out and return a questionnaire. She provided a stamped, addressed envelope, paid the subjects in advance, and told them that failure to send the questionnaires back on time would cause her to fail her research course. There were no Stage One or Stage Six subjects. Of Stage Two and Stage Three subjects, only about 30 percent did the moral thing—that is, mailed the questionnaire on time. But more than 70 percent of the Stage Four subjects did so, and 100 percent of the Stage Five thinkers faithfully filled out and mailed the questionnaire. The second experiment determined whether students would cheat when they were relatively sure they would not be caught. About 70 percent of the preconventional students cheated; about 55 percent of conventional subjects also cheated; but only about 15 percent of subjects showing some principled thinking on a moral interview cheated. Note three aspects of these experiments: neither placed the subjects in situations involving much emotional or situational stress; in each case people acted as individual moral agents without being able to diffuse responsibility for moral decisions and without observing the examples of others; and the situations were simple ones so that the moral issue was clear and the facts of the case unambiguous.

Third, at least three factors in addition to moral thought influence moral action: situational stress, diffused responsibility, and the complexity of the moral issues involved. My Lai offers an example of all these factors. Soldiers there faced severe emotional and situational stress since many of their buddies had been killed, and they believed that any Vietnamese person from the village might well be an armed enemy. Rather than being solely responsible for making a moral decision, the soldiers could diffuse responsibility to all the officers and men at My Lai; one man's shot could act as a releaser to others. The moral issue was extremely complicated and unclear: officers' orders, every person a potential guerilla, loyalty to buddies who had died, the sanctity of life, and the very nature of war itself. Would the men who shot under these circumstances fire at American civilians in peacetime, no matter what their moral stage? Or do particular circumstances help to explain their actions?

Fourth, the development of Just Community Schools has brought a new perspective to the matter of moral action. Observers report that these schools influence the behavior patterns of many of their students. They attend class more regularly. They take greater responsibility for their own behavior and for the behavior of others. They show greater respect for students in the school who come from different racial, religious, ethnic, or social backgrounds. These changed behaviors are probably the result not only of changes in the moral stages of the students involved. Some of them are probably the indirect result of a better moral atmosphere developed in a school based firmly on the findings of research in cognitive moral development. In the long run, these changes in action may hold great significance for civic education in American schools.

PART II: THE IMPLICATIONS

A comprehensive program of civic education should have five sets of goals.[21] They are knowledge about the political system and the way it works, the development of intellectual skills essential for solving civic problems, the development of other skills required for full participation in a democratic society, the development of a value system compatible with the principles which underlie democratic institutions, and the development of self-esteem so that an individual will feel worthy and able to participate in civic life.

The psychological, philosophical, and educational findings of the Kohlberg group speak to all five of these sets of goals. They do not, however, provide a complete rationale for civic education. For example, they do not tell what specific political knowledge a student should acquire or what works of literature students should read. Nor do they suggest effective ways to teach reading or speaking, two vital participatory skills. Although they provide educational situations (the community meeting and moral discussions) in which self-esteem can be enhanced, they do not specify what techniques teachers should use in these settings to improve students' images of themselves.

Part II of this chapter examines the constructive implications of Kohlberg's research for each of the five sets of goals which have been identified. Part III also indicates the ways in which Lawrence Kohlberg and his colleagues in the Boston area, and Edwin Fenton and his colleagues in and near Pittsburgh, are attempting to organize programs of civic education based on the ideas discussed here.

Knowledge Goals

The research of the Kohlberg group makes three vital contributions to the teaching of political information. This research specifies the level of cognitive development required to understand the Constitution as either a societal maintenance document (Stage Four) or a social contract document (Stage Five). It also indicates the levels of social perspective (Stage Four) required before a person can understand how a single political system can embrace fifty states and more than 215 million people. Finally, it demonstrates how stage development will lead to a more sophisticated understanding of basic concepts, such as justice or authority, involved in civic education.

Part I contained the argument that the principles behind the

Constitution were Stage Five principles. The Constitution can be viewed as a social contract designed to guarantee the rights of citizens. These rights, Kohlberg argues, are not merely the ones on which Americans agree; they are universal rights—justice, liberty, equality, and the greatest good for the greatest number—which should be valued in all complex societies.[22] One glory of the Constitution is that a small band of gentlemen farmers and business people recognized the universality of these principles. They wove them into a document which set up a government designed to protect basic rights. The founders must have known that people who did not understand or agree with the principles they espoused would sometimes hold the reins of government. They built into the Constitution a variety of devices to protect fundamental rights when they were threatened. The most recent dramatic demonstration of these constitutional provisions—the resignation of President Nixon under pressure from the Congress and the Courts—vividly illustrates the wisdom of the members of the Constitutional Convention.[23]

Most students who graduate from American high schools do not understand the Constitution as a Stage Five document. Although there is no national sample, experience with a large number of high school juniors and seniors suggests that most of them have not attained full Stage Four moral thought, and that almost none of them think predominantly at Stage Five.[24] Many people can comprehend one stage of moral thought above their own, and they prefer the highest stage of moral thought they comprehend. As a major goal of civic education, every student should develop the ability to understand the Constitution and to be able to subscribe to it with informed consent. In order to achieve informed consent, students must attain at least Stage Four thought on the Kohlberg scale. They will not do so without a comprehensive program of civic education extending throughout their school experience and designed specifically to raise the stage of moral thought they customarily employ.[25] These experiences should start during the elementary school years.

The Constitution also can be viewed as a Stage Four societal maintenance document. The government it sets up and the laws passed by that government attempt to prevent the outbreak of domestic discord, protect the nation from its enemies, and promote the general welfare. In order for this government to succeed, citizens must be willing to take part in governmental activities and to obey the laws the legislators have passed. The research by Rest indicates that many but not all Stage Three thinkers can understand this position.[26] As an irreducible, minimal goal of civic education, educators should strive to bring this understanding within the grasp of high school graduates.

Many programs in civic education teach the Constitution over and over again—in the fifth grade, eighth grade, ninth grade, eleventh grade, and twelfth grade. The Constitution bores many students. Who would not be bored by reading a document whose true meaning he or she cannot understand? Rather than "teach" the Constitution repeatedly to younger children, civic educators should help them develop the formal operational thought, full societal perspective, and higher stages of moral thought they will require to grasp the meaning of our basic governmental documents. They then can study these documents meaningfully in senior high school.

Now to the matter of understanding how the political system works. Many teachers assume that students have a sophisticated understanding of such terms as "the society" or "the nation." Most students do not. They have limited social perspectives and limited role-taking abilities. They think of themselves as isolated individuals or as members of small groups of people with whom they are personally acquainted. One is struck over and over again with the limited social perspective of typical high school students engaged in moral discussions.[27] Students argue that a person should lie to protect a friend who has been shoplifting, because one owes something to a friend but not to a shopkeeper, who is a stranger. They find themselves unable to take the storekeeper's place in this situation or to empathize with his problems. They also are unable to recognize what sort of society they would live in if everyone condoned stealing and no one helped to enforce laws. What does the term "society" mean to such students?

A person cannot understand how the political system works if he or she lacks full societal perspective. At its best, the American political system tries to promote the welfare of all citizens—of farmers, laborers, storekeepers, students, and older Americans. These people's lives and their well-being are inextricably interrelated. But students without societal perspective lack the cognitive capacity to understand this interrelatedness. Many of the generalizations in the civics and history texts are beyond their comprehension. A societal perspective is a necessary but not sufficient condition for understanding how the political system works.

Most programs in civic education assume that this understanding exists, or that it will develop without special learning experiences during a year-long course in government or civics. Any proposal for a new senior high school course in the political process implicitly assumes that students will reach the eleventh or twelfth grade with the capacities to understand the materials they will use.[28] Most of them will not. A fully effective civic education program must cultivate students' cognitive abilities, perspective taking, and moral development through a number of years. In this way most students may reach the twelfth grade with the societal perspective they need in order to understand how the political system works.

Kohlberg's research also bears on the ability of students to deal with concepts fundamental to the political system. People define concepts in stage-related terms. An example may make the point clear. Here are five definitions of the word "fair" at five stages of the Kohlberg scale:

1. "Fair" means that you were rewarded by an important person for doing something good.

2. "Fair" means that if you helped me out, I should help you out.

3. Something is "fair" when all of us in the group agree that it was the right thing to do.

4. "Fair" means that something was done according to the rules, even if the rules may have seemed wrong.

5. "Fair" means that people have the rights that they were guaranteed in the Constitution.

When a teacher uses the word "fair" in class, students may take the word to mean any of the five definitions given here. Large numbers of the vital civic education terms—"law," "authority," "justice," "rights," and "equal treatment," for example—will be defined by students in stage-related terms. One must ask if it is possible to study civic affairs intelligently with any definition of these terms under a Stage Four (societal maintenance) level. If the answer is no, then students must begin to facilitate stage development at an early age and press the matter with every resource at their command.

Intellectual Skills

Intellectual skills mean primarily problem-solving abilities (often called analytical inquiry skills by the New Social Studies projects of the 1960s). Here are two statements of inquiry processes taken from the rationale for a four-year curriculum developed under the direction of Edwin Fenton (before he studied Kohlberg) at Carnegie-Mellon University:[29]

A Mode of Inquiry for History

1. Recognizing a problem from data
2. Formulating hypotheses
   a. Asking analytical questions
   b. Stating hypotheses
   c. Remaining aware of the tentative nature of hypotheses
3. Recognizing the logical implications of hypotheses
4. Gathering data
   a. Deciding what data will be needed
   b. Selecting or rejecting sources on the basis of their relevance to hypotheses
5. Analyzing, evaluating, and interpreting data
   a. Selecting relevant data from the sources
   b. Evaluating the sources
      (1) Determining the frame of reference of the author of a source
      (2) Determining the accuracy of statements of fact
   c. Interpreting the data
6. Evaluating the hypothesis in the light of the data
   a. Modifying the hypothesis, if necessary
      (1) Rejecting a logical implication unsupported by data
      (2) Restating the hypothesis
   b. Stating a generalization

A Mode of Inquiry for Public Policy Problems

1. Define the problem to be solved. This process includes understanding the problem thoroughly, deciding what goals should be reached, and recognizing the values implied in the decision.

2. State all possible ways to reach the goals.

3. Evaluate carefully the probable effects that each possible solution might have, discarding those that seem impractical or harmful in the process.

4. Choose the policy that appears likely to achieve most of the goals aimed for, remembering that no policy is perfect.

5. Review the choice to see whether the setting of the problem has changed and whether the goals and values of the decision makers have remained the same.

These inquiry processes failed in the classroom with less able students for three major reasons.[30] First, they require full formal operational thought—the ability to hypothesize, to see all possibilities in a situation, to relate evidence to inference, and so forth. (Only about half of American adults reason at full formal operational levels, according to a study by the Kohlberg group.[31]) Second, they require a full societal perspective when they are applied to most civic problems: Should we have forced busing? Should we close factories which do not abide by pollution regulations? Third, they require a sophisticated understanding of social science concepts which, as has been seen, many students lack.

Although the New Social Studies represent a significant advance in civic education, the curriculum projects have not provided a satisfactory solution to its problems. Traditional civic education taught students facts and generalizations about American society and its history and attempted to instill in them a love of country and its institutions. The social studies projects shifted the focus of civic education toward the intellectual processes required to solve civic problems. But the projects failed to provide the antecedent conditions which would enable students to use these sophisticated intellectual processes. Civic educators must now find ways to facilitate the development of formal operational thought, societal perspective, and higher stage moral thought if they expect to educate students who can use the inquiry processes stressed during the 1960s. The work of Kohlberg and his colleagues provides guidelines for this difficult, demanding, and important task.

Participatory Skills

Good citizens require participatory skills which can be classified into two levels. The first level consists of data-gathering and communication skills essential for playing an active part in any civic organization. The second level uses these basic skills for negotiation, working out compromises, or influencing political decision makers.[32] Both of these levels of skills must be taught carefully.

The community meetings, which are the heart of the civic education schools being organized by the Kohlberg group in Cambridge and Pittsburgh, provide a setting in which these skills can be learned and practiced. To participate effectively in a community meeting, students must have the following skills: reading, listening, speaking, reporting, chairing a meeting, doing committee work, working constructively in small groups, and controlling disruptive persons. Taking part in community meetings demonstrates the need for all of these skills and provides instructors with an opportunity to teach them. Students learn skills far more rapidly and thoroughly when they learn them for a purpose than they do when these skills are taught divorced from an immediate need to use them. Most students, however, require carefully planned educational experiences before they can master basic communication skills.

Community meetings also provide a forum in which students can practice higher level participatory skills. In community meetings, staff and students together develop rules to govern themselves; they also carry out the rules they have made. In both of these processes, they must develop the ability to compromise when differences of opinion arise. They must develop negotiation skills if they wish to persuade others to support their point of view. And they must learn how to influence key people in the decision-making process. These second-level skills should transfer to the wider political system outside the school.[33] To assure transfer, they should be buttressed with formal study of such issues as how to influence decision makers in the city council or a labor union.

Developing Self-Esteem

Preliminary anecdotal evidence indicates that participation in community meetings in the unit in Cambridge has fostered self-esteem.[34] Many students there reported on interviews that they believed other students in the school respected their opinions. The chance to participate in community decision making, where academic excellence is not an indispensable requirement for success, evidently increased self-esteem particularly among students who had limited academic potential. Being able to join teachers in decision making also had an impact. In community meetings it is clear that each vote counts for something, since all decisions are made by majority rule and since the size of the electorate (about seventy students in Cambridge) is small. Everyone may contribute something to such a group, and everyone can recognize the contribution that he can make. The fact that students knew they had a considerable degree of control over their environment seems to have contributed positively to their self-esteem.

Properly led, moral discussions can also enhance self-esteem.[35] In a moral discussion, the students and the teacher should sit in a circle in order to encourage the exchange of opinions and to facilitate sensitive attendance. The teacher should consistently acknowledge the contributions of students by attempting to clarify what they say and by making a student's comment the focus of discussion. Everyone, even students who cannot read or those who never do homework, can contribute constructively to a moral discussion. The stimulus material, a dilemma in written or audiovisual form, can be introduced in class. Everyone has an opinion about a dilemma because everyone has an opinion at some moral stage about every moral problem. A skillful teacher can encourage nonvolunteers to take part, for example, by telling them before class that they will be called on from time to time to paraphrase a comment by another student or to identify a point of difference between two students who disagree with each other. Many students testify that they took a more active role in a moral discussion than in any other classroom activity, and that they enjoyed it.

Like community meetings, moral discussions can be used to work toward several sets of objectives simultaneously. All these objectives will contribute to a well-rounded program of civic education in American schools.

Many of the exercises developed by the proponents of values clarification can contribute positively to the development of self-esteem. An example may make the point clear:[36]

Another strategy that helps teachers show young people what unique and precious human beings they are is called the coat of arms. They divide a diagram of a coat of arms into six large spaces and ask each person to make drawings as follows in all but the last space:

First space—something you are very, very good at and something you are struggling to get better at

Second space—a value about which you would never budge

Third space—your most significant material possession

Fourth space—your greatest achievement of the last year and your greatest setback or failure

Fifth space—what you would do if you were guaranteed success for a year in any undertaking

Sixth space—three words you'd like people to say about you if your life ended today

Young people often gather in small groups to share their coat of arms with each other, thoughtfully and respectfully, or they enjoy taping them to the wall and taking each other on gallery walks. It can also be played with a number of variations.

Through such exercises, students become aware of some of their good qualities. A small body of research indicates that values clarification exercises help students to feel more positive about themselves.[37] Civic educators should adapt the intriguing catalog of values clarification techniques to their own purposes. They should eliminate moral problems from these exercises and make sure the issues which remain focus pointedly on personal growth and self-understanding.

Kohlberg's research suggests that comprehensive civic education programs must have six interrelated elements. First, they must extend over many years of schooling. Stage change develops slowly. No one single course, no matter how carefully constructed or taught, will do the job.

Second, a comprehensive program of civic education must extend well beyond the social studies. Every discipline in the school can facilitate the development of formal operational thought which is a prerequisite to Stage Four (social maintenance) moral thought. Every teacher, as many athletic coaches well know, can help to improve the self-esteem of students. The entire instructional staff can make lower-level participatory skills an explicit curriculum goal. In addition to social studies teachers, English instructors can give moral development and the development of social perspective a central place in their course goals.

Third, a comprehensive program of civic education must change the hidden curriculum as well as the overt curriculum. The hidden curriculum involves all the institutional arrangements from which students learn in school.[38] These arrangements include the ways in which school rules are made and enforced, the ways in which teachers and administrators use their power and their ability to praise or sanction, and the ways in which the sheer size of large, impersonal schools affects students' learning. In many schools the hidden curriculum denies what formal courses in civic education affirm. Student governments lack the power that elected bodies possess in a democracy according to civics textbooks. School rules are made autocratically instead of through the democratic process studied in government class. Schools fail to provide the checks and balances and the mechanisms of appeal from the decisions of authorities, which students read about in the Constitution. These conditions emphasize the importance of the fundamental changes in school governance which have taken place in the democratic unit at Cambridge High and Latin School.

Fourth, a comprehensive program of civic education must include an intensive, long-run teacher preparation program.[39] Traditional teachers will have much to learn—and much more to unlearn. They must learn to think in terms of new sets of educational objectives. They must learn how to facilitate the development of social perspective and moral stage by leading moral discussions and participating in community meetings. They must learn to relinquish some of their power to a community in which each person, faculty member and student alike, has one vote. And they must learn to use and to develop new curricular materials. These instructional, administrative, and curricular skills grow slowly, and they must be learned through experience. Educators cannot prepare teachers for their new roles in Civic Education Schools by giving them a book to read and organizing workshops on occasional in-service days.

Fifth, a comprehensive program of civic education requires new curricular materials organized for developmental goals in both social studies and English. These new materials should provide sequential and cumulative learning experiences throughout the student's high school career. They do not exist, even in prototype form, at the present moment.[40] But a psychological, philosophical, and educational rationale for the materials does exist. In addition, a large number of individual curriculum artifacts have been developed by the curriculum projects of the 1960s, and they can be adapted to developmental goals.

Finally, a comprehensive program of civic education must be evaluated carefully. This evaluation should assess progress toward all five sets of goals discussed previously—political knowledge, intellectual skills, participatory skills, values, and self-esteem. Evaluators already have the tools for this task. They have developed test instruments and techniques of participant observation which can be turned to this purpose. A truly comprehensive evaluation should follow at least one sample of students far beyond the end of their high school careers. A civic education program can be proclaimed successful only if the students who participate in it become more effective citizens than those who do not. Perhaps the time has come for another Eight-Year Study, this one directed to one of the primary goals of education in a modern democracy—the preparation of young people to contribute constructively to the democratic processes, which have sheltered and weaned them and given them opportunity to grow as free and responsible human beings.

PART III: TWO CIVIC EDUCATION PROGRAMS

Two closely related programs, one at Harvard University and the other at Carnegie-Mellon University (CMU), are now attempting to implement Kohlberg's research findings in the schools.[41] Both these projects are supported by the Danforth Foundation. The Harvard project involves two high schools: Cambridge High and Latin School and Brookline High School. The CMU project has four associated school systems: Keystone Oaks School District, Chartiers Valley School District, the Pittsburgh Public Schools, and South Side Catholic High School. These two efforts to develop new civic education programs should provide guidelines for future activities.

The program in Brookline began in the fall of 1974 as an attempt to introduce moral discussions into the curriculum.[42] Brookline is an unusually good school system with an exceptional faculty and administration. Most of the guidance counselors, many of whom teach psychology, and most of the social studies teachers knew about Kohlberg's research even before the project began. Yet only two guidance counselors had actually incorporated moral education into their work, and no one in social studies had done so.

The Harvard project staff (Lawrence Kohlberg, Ralph Mosher of Boston University, and Edwin Fenton, on leave for a year from CMU) decided to begin work with the members of the social studies and guidance staffs from Brookline High School who volunteered to attend after-school workshops during the 1974 fall semester. This group included ten social studies teachers, ten counselors, the school principal, a key English teacher, and the directors of guidance, independent studies, and social studies for the Brookline system. The workshop met twice monthly from October 1974 through January 1975. It had three objectives: to help teachers learn the major research findings of Kohlberg and his colleagues, to examine curriculum materials for moral education in social studies and psychology, and to begin to create new moral education curriculum materials.

The participants did some reading in preparation for each workshop session. Kohlberg himself presented his theory and answered questions about it. Demonstration video tapes introduced the teaching process and gave teachers an introduction to the skills they and their students would need to conduct moral discussions. Teachers examined existing materials carefully and spent a session or two critiquing moral dilemmas which they had developed for their own classes. In January, about two-thirds of the participants committed themselves to continue work during the spring.

During the spring semester, the director of the Brookline project, Ralph Mosher, continued the bimonthly workshops for social studies and guidance teachers, assisted from time to time by Kohlberg and by a graduate student. Through this process, moral education materials were incorporated into ten social studies and psychology courses in all four high school grades. The consultants critiqued dilemmas written by the staff, taught demonstration classes, observed teachers conducting moral discussions, and analyzed teaching recorded on video tape. The demands for consultants' time increased steadily throughout the spring as teachers tried their wings with new pedagogical techniques. The project continued during the summer of 1975, when sixteen teachers worked from a week to a month each to develop courses of study. The materials on which they worked were used in about ten social studies, psychology, and English courses during the fall. The staff is now helping an already existing school-within-a-school to set up a participatory governmental structure modeled after the one called the Cluster School in Cambridge. Staff members have also been holding workshop sessions for middle school teachers.

While this work progressed in Brookline, another educational intervention began in a far different setting in Cambridge High and Latin School.[43] Cambridge High and Latin School is located in an old building which houses a thoroughly heterogeneous student population. A group of parents whose children had not been able to obtain entrance to an already existing school-within-a-school there asked school officials to open another alternative school unit. The officials turned to Lawrence Kohlberg in the summer of 1974, and he agreed to become a consultant. He had the full support of the superintendent and the high school principal. But he did not have the active support of department heads, nor could he find faculty members who knew about his work. In Cambridge, Kohlberg started from scratch on an exceedingly difficult task, setting up a self-governing unit within a traditional urban high school with relatively untrained people.

About seventy students were recruited for this school-within-a-school which became known as the Cluster School. They were drawn from all four high school classes and from the varied social, economic, and racial groups of the wider school population. Among them were eighteen black students and about an equal number of working-class whites, many of whom were not doing well in school. Eight faculty members volunteered and were accepted without screening. They had a variety of academic backgrounds—science, physical education, social studies, counseling, and so forth. Within the Cluster School they conducted the community meetings and taught the social studies, English, and physical education courses. On the whole they were unprepared for these tasks. None of them had ever led a community meeting or conducted a moral discussion, none of them was familiar with Kohlberg's research, and most of them were not trained in either English or social studies.

Early in the school year, the staff and the student body began to draw up a constitution by making a set of rules and developing a method to enforce them. Each person in the community, staff and student alike, has one vote on the adoption of the rules and each gets one vote in the community meetings. Long discussions in which everyone participates precede any action by the community. During these discussions, students and staff alike constantly encounter real-life moral dilemmas: How should you punish a student who has broken the rule against stealing when you know that other students have also stolen and not been caught? Should you suspend a member of the community who constantly disrupts classes but who has found for the first time a real home in the community?

Students take only their social studies, English, and physical education courses within the Cluster School. They take the remainder of their academic work within the wider Cambridge High and Latin School. But the staff of the Cluster School had had no time to prepare a new curriculum in social studies and English. Hence, like the faculties of so many alternative schools, they decided to teach minicourses, partly in response to what students requested. These courses enroll students from all four high school classes who are enrolled in the Cluster School. Because of this heterogeneity in ages, as well as in social and ethnic backgrounds, a typical class includes students at several stages of the Kohlberg scale. The same generalization, of course, applies to the community meetings.

Kohlberg attended the weekly community meetings throughout the fall. The student body was divided into small advisory groups which met to discuss issues scheduled to come before the community meetings. After these sessions, the entire community met in a single room under the leadership of either a staff member or a student. Much of the in-service training took place in these community meetings as staff members learned by doing. In addition, Kohlberg conducted weekly staff meetings in the evening to discuss what was happening in the school and to help to build skills. He used recordings and transcripts of community meetings as the basis of many discussions in staff meetings. After a hectic beginning, the community meetings slowly took form, and by the end of the year, ran very well.

Procedures for conducting the community meetings evolved slowly. Some of them were developed in a short course on democracy taught by one of the staff members. In this class, students learned how to chair community meetings fairly and to control disruptive students. The democracy class perfected the institution of the straw vote, which the community uses on major substantive issues to determine whether the members have arrived at consensus or need additional time for discussion before calling for a binding vote. The community also learned how to use advisory groups well. These groups consist of about ten students and a staff member. They meet to discuss the issues which will come before the community meeting later and to make recommendations for action.

The other major governmental institution is the discipline committee composed of one staff member and one member, chosen on a rotating basis, of each of the eight advisory groups. This committee holds hearings and assesses punishments when students break the rules which the community has established. The major issues which bring students before the discipline committee have been stealing, disturbing classes or community meetings, unexcused absences, the use of drugs, and cutting classes. Appeals to the community meetings of decisions by the discipline committee have touched off some of the most heated and constructive sessions of the year.

The formal curriculum in social studies and English, however, has not fared well. Teachers had no time to prepare interesting minicourses, because each of them taught a full load and had the new responsibilities of community meetings to worry about. Nor did they have time to learn how to lead moral discussions in their classes. Hence, the formal curriculum of the courses and the informal or hidden curriculum of the governance structure never merged to become a single educational experience.

Elsa Wasserman, a member of the Cluster School staff and a

doctoral candidate at Boston University, has undertaken a participant evaluation of the development of the Cluster School. She has
recorded meetings of the advisory group, the discipline committee,
and the community meetings and has gathered data through interviews with staff and students. Recently, a grant from the Ford
Foundation has provided funds for a full-scale evaluation of the
effects of the Cluster School on its students. That full-scale evaluation is sorely needed.

Two additional parts of a comprehensive civic education program
are located at Harvard. First, Kohlberg and four of his colleagues,
working with support from a grant from the National Institute of
Child Health and Development, are developing a definitive version
of the scoring manual for the Kohlberg scale. This manual will
speed and standardize research efforts in the field. Second, Kohlberg
himself is preparing several publications to disseminate the
research findings in the field. These publications, long awaited by
the profession, can become a key part of a wider dissemination effort
once the intervention experiments at Harvard and CMU have borne
fruit.

The projects in Brookline and Cambridge have each developed one
major aspect of a comprehensive civic education program. Brookline
tested a format for a teacher preparation and curriculum development program in moral discussions; Cambridge established a program to prepare teachers for new roles in civic education schools
organized as participatory democracies. A third project, in the Pittsburgh area, is now trying to incorporate these two elements with
others, in an attempt to see whether comprehensive civic education
programs can be organized and disseminated successfully without
prohibitive financial costs.[44]

The Pittsburgh area program has five of the six interrelated
elements of a comprehensive civic education program discussed in
Part II of this chapter. It envisions a three-year experience for
students. It includes both the social studies and the English curriculum. It changes the organization and administration of the school in
order to alter the hidden curriculum and to bring the hidden and
formal curricula into congruence. It includes an intensive, long-run
teacher preparation program. And it posits the development of an
entirely new three-year curriculum in social studies and English.

The core staff of the project includes Edwin Fenton as director
(half-time), a full-time social studies curriculum consultant (Dr.
Georgia Schneider), a full-time English consultant (Dr. Josephine
Harris), a half-time historian who is also an expert in moral discus-

sions (Dr. Linda Rosenzweig), four graduate students, and one teacher from each of the four schools involved. Each of these teachers joined the staff on a full-time basis during the spring 1976 semester. A staff of this size need never be duplicated in future projects if the curricular materials developed and the staff development plans underway prove successful.

Each high school sends between ten and twelve volunteer teachers, administrators, counselors, and community members to a twenty-week Staff Development Seminar. This seminar meets weekly after school. Participants are not paid, but they receive three hours of graduate extension credit from CMU at no expense to themselves.

The seminar has several goals. First, the teachers should learn enough about the research findings of Kohlberg and his associates to be able to develop a rationale for a developmental civic education program. Second, each of the social studies and English teachers in the seminar should be able, at its conclusion, to conduct a moral discussion to the satisfaction of the core staff. Third, the members of the seminar will adapt the curriculum work of the core staff to the particular needs of each of the four schools. (These schools differ widely in the nature of their student population and faculty.) Finally, the participants from each school will work out guidelines for recruiting students, interpreting the new civic education programs to the community, and organizing programs.

The core staff members have carefully planned the educational experiences for the seminar.[45] They have written or adapted much of the material which the participants will read, keeping in mind the limited amount of time available to devote to reading during the school year. They have planned each two-hour seminar so that several activities, which involve teachers in a variety of groupings employing diverse hands-on materials, will take place weekly. (Teachers need this variety when they attend classes at the end of a busy day.) Each member of the CMU core staff (Fenton, Schneider, Harris, and Rosenzweig) spends one full day each week in the schools, in order to work closely as colleagues with the teachers in the seminar and to get to know the student audience for whom they are designing materials.

Two graduate students act as participant observers during this seminar. They interview participants and make evaluations, and they will later convey their findings to the core staff, who can then make plans for future seminars more intelligently. The seminar was repeated for a different group of participants during the second semester of the 1976–77 school year, giving the staff an opportunity to test a revised seminar format.

The core staff assisted by two graduate students has begun to develop new social studies and English courses for the first year of these civic education programs. Planning for the first social studies course is farthest along.[46] This course will help students to gain the information and skills they require to understand principles which underlie social contracts and to establish and run a participatory democracy. The weekly community meeting will become the heart of the social studies course and will meet during the social studies period; hence, formal social studies classes will meet only four days weekly.

The students in these programs will take the regular academic offerings of their school programs in the ongoing classes of their schools with the exception of social studies and English. This arrangement will make it possible for students to take the wide range of courses in fields such as math, the sciences, foreign languages, home economics, or shop which many alternative schools fail to provide because the size of their student body is so small. Students in the civic education program will also be able to participate in schoolwide extracurricular activities such as varsity sports or the glee club.

The content of the course will vary from one school to another, but each course will focus on the ways in which a number of groups, past and present, have organized and governed themselves. For example, students will study patterns of leadership, decision making, and sanctioning, both in historical situations and in local organizations which students can study firsthand. The answers that other groups have developed to problems of governance can then be considered as possible solutions to the problems of governing a civic education school. A special unit will explain the rationale for civic education on which this program is based.

Major attention will be devoted to the development of participatory and intellectual skills. Students will be taught to gather data through interviews, questionnaires, and observation, as well as through reading. Special exercises will help to develop skills such as listening, reporting clearly in written and oral form, working cooperatively in small groups, and using discussion techniques effectively. These exercises will also stress how to chair meetings, take minutes, and keep records—three requirements for leadership in civic organizations.

All these skills will be called into play in a major investigation of educational institutions as an example of the political process. Working in small committees, students will examine such problems as how vocational education began in their school district, the origin of the local community college, or some similar innovation. This project will begin the process of transferring higher-level participatory skills to the wider community outside the civic education school.

The writing which students do in this course will probably become part of a core curriculum with English. The literature section of the English offering will be built mainly around literary works placed in settings similar to those studied in the social studies courses. The CMU core staff is selecting a wide range of literary works at various levels of difficulty. They are choosing them partly with an eye to the moral issues they raise, and are making a special effort to find literature which raises moral dilemmas at Stages Two, Three, and Four of the Kohlberg scale. Moral discussions can then become a natural part of the English as well as the social studies curriculum. If the courses succeed, the distinction between the formal curriculum and the hidden curriculum should disappear completely.

The CMU core staff has tentative plans to develop second-year courses in American history and American literature. For the third year, they plan a one-semester course in ethics as the culminating experience in moral development and a one-semester government course with a special emphasis upon political knowledge and intellectual skills. As a literature component, they tentatively plan to develop units around nine of the universal moral issues which Kohlberg has identified: punishment, property, affection, authority, law, life, liberty, distributive justice, and truth.

The CMU project conducted a formative evaluation during the 1976–77 school year. The staff utilized data from a series of tests designed by the Commonwealth of Pennsylvania to assess citizenship, self-esteem, and basic skills. Moral interviews were used to assess moral stage change. The staff will also plan a full summative evaluation to begin in September 1977 in an attempt to measure all five curricular goals.

NOTES

1. Lawrence Kohlberg, *Collected Papers on Moral Development and Moral Education,* 2 vols., Moral Education Research Foundation, Cambridge,

Mass., 1975; *Social Education,* vol. 40, p. 4, April 1976; *Phi Delta Kappan,* vol. 56, p. 10, June 1975; Thomas Lickona (ed.), *Moral Development and Behavior: Theory, Research and Social Issues,* Holt, Rinehart and Winston, Inc., New York, 1976.

2. Fred M. Newmann, *Proposal for Development of Citizen Participation Curriculum,* University of Wisconsin, Madison, Wis., October 1975, p. 21 (mimeographed); Rodney F. Allen, *But the Earth Abideth Forever: Values in Environmental Education,* Florida State University, Tallahassee, 1975, pp. 3–10 (mimeographed); Judith Gillespie and Stuart Lazarus, *Controversial Political Issues: Providing the Participant's Eye-View,* Indiana University, 1975, p. 10 (mimeographed); *Comparing Political Experiences,* Social Studies Curriculum Center, Bloomington, Ind., n.d., p. 6 (mimeographed); Lee F. Anderson et al., *Improving Political Education in Elementary Schools: Challenges and Opportunities,* Ohio State University, Columbus, n.d., p. 6 (mimeographed); Jama Laurent and Bennett Ross, *A Literature Review of Major Theoretical and Practical Approaches to Moral Development and Political Socialization,* Constitutional Rights Foundation, Los Angeles, 1975 (mimeographed).

3. L. Kohlberg, "Stage and Sequence: The Cognitive-Developmental Approach to Socialization," David Goslin (ed.), in *Handbook of Socialization Theory and Research,* Rand McNally & Company, Chicago, 1969, pp. 347–480; Kohlberg, "Moral Stages and Moralization: The Cognitive-Developmental Approach," in T. Lickona (ed.), op. cit., pp. 31–53; Elliot Turiel, "Stage Transition in Moral Development," in Robert W. Travers (ed.), *Second Handbook of Research in Teaching,* Rand McNally & Company, Chicago, 1973, pp. 732–758.

4. The techniques for conducting and scoring a moral interview have been described in a Scoring Manual available in a preliminary edition from the Moral Education Research Foundation, 3rd floor, Larsen Hall, Appian Way, Harvard University, Cambridge, Mass. 02138. The staff of the Harvard center is preparing a definitive version of the manual for publication. Another method of determining moral stage, developed by a former student of Kohlberg's, James Rest of the University of Minnesota, is described in James Rest et al., "Judging the Important Issues in Moral Dilemmas—An Objective Measure of Development," *Developmental Psychology,* vol. 10, no. 4, pp. 491–501, 1974. Copies of his instrument, the *Defining Issues Test,* may be obtained from the author at the Department of Psychology, University of Minnesota, Minneapolis.

5. The interview forms have changed from year to year as the staff has gained experience with them. The latest version can be obtained from the Moral Education Research Foundation, Cambridge, Mass.

6. See Kohlberg's discussion of the nature of a stage in references cited in note 1.

7. E. Turiel, "Developmental Processes in the Child's Moral Thinking," in P. Mussen, J. Langer, and M. Covington (eds.), *Trends and Issues in Developmental Psychology,* Holt, Rinehart and Winston, Inc., New York, 1969, pp. 92–133.

8. Kohlberg's original cross-sectional research is described in his still-unpublished doctoral thesis: Lawrence Kohlberg, *The Development of Modes of Moral Thinking in the Years Ten to Sixteen,* University of Chicago, 1968.

9. For a summary of this cross-cultural research, see L. Kohlberg and E. Turiel, "Moral Development and Moral Education," in G. Lesser (ed.), *Psychology and Educational Practice,* Scott, Foresman and Company, Chicago, 1971, pp. 436–439.

10. J. Rest, "The Hierarchical Nature of Moral Judgment: A Study of Patterns of Comprehension and Preference of Moral Stages," *Journal of Personality,* vol. 41, pp. 86–109, March 1973. Also see J. Rest, E. Turiel, and L. Kohlberg, "Level of Moral Development as a Determinant of Preference and Comprehension of Moral Judgments Made by Others," *Journal of Personality,* vol. 37, no. 2, pp. 225–252, June 1969.

11. Kohlberg, "Stage and Sequence," op. cit.; Turiel, "Stage Transition in Moral Development," op. cit.

12. Kohlberg, "Moral Stages and Moralization," *Collected Papers,* vol. I, op. cit.

13. Kohlberg, "From Is to Ought: How to Commit the Naturalistic Fallacy and Get Away with It in the Study of Moral Development," in T. Mischel (ed.), *Cognitive Development and Epistemology,* Academic Press, New York, 1971, pp. 151–235; Kohlberg, "Why a Higher Stage Is a Better Stage," *Collected Papers,* vol. II, op. cit.; Kohlberg, "Education for Justice: A Modern Statement of the Platonic View," in Nancy F. and Theodore R. Sizer (eds.), *Moral Education,* Harvard University Press, Cambridge, 1970.

14. Kohlberg, "Stage and Sequence," op. cit., and Turiel, "Stage Transition in Moral Development," op. cit., contain perhaps the best accounts of factors involved in stage transition.

15. J. Rest, "Developmental Psychology as a Guide to Value Education: A Review of 'Kohlbergian Programs,'" *Review of Educational Research,* vol. 44, pp. 241–259, 1974; Kohlberg et al., "Secondary School Moral Discussion Programs Led by Social Studies Teachers," *Collected Papers,* vol. II, op. cit.

16. For a discussion of pedagogical techniques, see Barry Beyer, "Conducting Moral Discussions in the Classroom," *Social Education,* vol. 40, no. 4, pp. 194–202, April 1976.

17. Kohlberg et al., "The Just Community Approach to Corrections," *Collected Papers*, vol. II, op. cit.; Kohlberg, Kelsey Kaufmann, Peter Scharf, and Joseph Hickey, *The Just Community Approach to Corrections: A Manual,* parts I and II, Moral Education Research Foundation, Cambridge, Mass., 1974.

18. Elsa Wasserman, "Implementing Kohlberg's Just Community Concept in an Alternative High School," *Social Education,* vol. 40, no. 4, pp. 203–207, April 1976; Kohlberg et al., "The Just Community School: The Theory and the Cambridge Cluster School," *Collected Papers,* vol. II, op. cit.

19. By far the best account of the relationship of moral judgment and action is in Roger Brown and Richard L. Herrenstein, *Psychology,* Little, Brown and Company, Boston, 1975, pp. 287–340.

20. Kohlberg, "From Is to Ought," op. cit.

21. These sets of goals represent the Kohlberg group's thinking based on a number of publications: Task Force '74, *The Adolescent, Other Citizens, and Their High Schools,* McGraw-Hill Book Company, New York, 1975; *National Assessment of Educational Progress Citizenship Objectives,* Education Commission of the States, Ann Arbor, Mich., 1969; *Social Education,* vol. 38, p. 5, May 1974; J. Gillespie and John J. Patrick, *Comparing Political Experiences,* American Political Science Association, Washington, D.C., 1974; F. Newmann, *Education for Citizen Action,* McCutchan Publishing Corporation, Berkeley, Calif., 1975; Edwin Fenton, *Teaching the New Social Studies in Secondary Schools,* Holt, Rinehart and Winston, New York, 1966; Donald W. Oliver and James P. Shaver, *Teaching Public Issues in the High School,* Houghton Mifflin Company, Boston, 1966.

22. Kohlberg, "Why a Higher Stage Is a Better Stage," *Collected Papers,* vol. II, op. cit.

23. Dan Candee, "The Moral Psychology of Watergate," *Journal of Social Issues,* vol. 3, no. 2, pp. 183–192, 1975; Kohlberg, "Lessons of Watergate," paper presented at the American Psychological Association, New Orleans, 1974.

24. A number of research reports claim that high school, and even elementary school, students exhibit Stage Five or even Stage Six thought. These results can be accounted for in one of two ways. Some of them came from people who used the scoring system developed by Kohlberg for his dissertation. (Revisions in that system adjusted stage responses downward.) Other researchers simply did not understand the scoring system. They took the use of words such as justice or liberty to indicate Stage Five or Stage Six thought without probing sufficiently to determine the real structure underlying the use of these words. For examples of misleading research reports, see several articles in *Social Education,* vol. 39, no. 1, January 1975.

25. Kohlberg and his colleague Robert Selman have produced two series of sound filmstrips for the elementary schoolchild and are preparing two additional series particularly for a middle or junior high school audience. All these materials have been or will be published by Guidance Associates, Harcourt, Brace, Javonovich, New York. They are *First Things: Values,* 1972; *First Things: Social Reasoning,* 1975; and *Relationships and Values,* 1976.

26. Rest, "The Hierarchical Nature of Moral Judgment," op. cit.

27. See transcripts of classroom dialogue in Kohlberg et al., "Secondary School Moral Discussion Programs," op. cit.

28. See proposals listed in note 2. None of these proposals envisions an attempt to develop cognitive, perspective taking, or moral capacities.

29. E. Fenton, *A Rationale for the Second Edition of the Holt Social Studies Curriculum,* Holt, Rinehart and Winston, Inc., New York, 1973.

30. Alan L. Lockwood, "Moral Reasoning and Public Policy Debate," in Likona (ed.), *Moral Development and Behavior,* op. cit., pp. 317–325; Kohlberg, "Moral Development and the New Social Studies," *Social Education,* vol. 37, no. 5, pp. 368–375, May 1973.

31. D. Kuhn, L. Kohlberg, J. Langer, and U. Haan, "The Development of Formal Operations in Logical and Moral Judgment," *Genetic Psychology Monographs.*

32. Stephen K. Bailey, *Education for Civic Responsibility,* Albany, New York, 1974 (mimeographed). Bailey suggests that students should develop minds that can relate things to each other, the ability to negotiate, and what he calls "ratcheting skills"—the capacity to make agreements stick, to strengthen the rule of law, and to live up to contracts.

33. See proposals by Newmann and Gillespie-Lazarus (note 2) for promising techniques.

34. Nancy Biron, *Progress in the Cluster School: An Analysis of the Responses of Ten Students,* Harvard University, Cambridge, Mass., 1975 (mimeographed); *Three Community Meetings Dealing with the Drug Rule,* Harvard University, Cambridge, Mass., 1975 (mimeographed).

35. Beyer, op. cit.

36. Sidney B. Simon and Polly DeSherbinin, "Values Clarification: It Can Start Gently and Grow Deep," *Phi Delta Kappan,* vol. 56, no. 10, p. 680, June 1975.

37. Louis E. Raths, Merrill Harmin, and Sidney B. Simon, *Values and Teaching,* Charles E. Merrill Books, Inc., Columbus, Ohio, 1966, pp. 205–

229; Howard Kirschenbaum, "Recent Research in Education," in John R. Meyer et al. (eds.), *Values Education,* Wilfred Lauriers University Press, Waterloo, Ontario, 1975, pp. 71–78.

38. Philip E. Jackson, *Life in Classrooms,* Holt, Rinehart and Winston, Inc., New York, 1968; Robert Dreeben, *On What Is Learned in School,* Addison-Wesley Publishing Company, Inc., Reading, Mass., 1968; Norman V. Overly (ed.), *The Unstudied Curriculum,* Association for Supervision and Curriculum Development, Washington, D.C., 1970.

39. Fenton, *Moral and Civic Education: In-Service Implications,* Pittsburgh, 1975 (mimeographed).

40. Kohlberg and Fenton have prepared basic materials (*Values in a Democracy* and *Universal Values in American History*) for a six-hour in-service workshop for teachers who wish to learn how to lead moral discussions: *Teacher Training in Values Education: A Workshop,* Guidance Associates, Harcourt, Brace, Jovanovich, New York, 1976. The Civic Education Project staff at Carnegie-Mellon University is developing English and social studies courses for a three-year curriculum in civic education. These materials will be available beginning in 1977 when the first two courses will have been tested in the schools.

41. The Harvard project has additional funds from the Joseph P. Kennedy Foundation, and the schools associated with Carnegie-Mellon University have received a grant under Title IV, Part C of PL93-380.

42. Ralph Mosher, *The Brookline Moral Education Project: A Report for Year I: 1974–75,* Brookline, Mass., 1975 (mimeographed).

43. See accounts cited in note 18.

44. Fenton, *The Development of Civic Education Schools: A Proposal,* Pittsburgh, 1975 (mimeographed).

45. The outline of the seminar will be made available after the core staff members have had an opportunity for evaluation. They expect to be able to reproduce cheaply all required materials for staff-development seminars in other institutions.

46. Fenton, "A Developmental Approach to Civic Education," in J. Meyer, Brian Burnham, and John Cholvat (eds.), *Values Education: Theory/Practice/Problems/Promises,* Wilfred Lauriers University Press, Waterloo, Ontario, 1975, pp. 41–50.

Citizenship Education through Participation

⑧

DAN CONRAD AND DIANE HEDIN

Could you figure out how to count all the trees in your town? Neither could the city council of a medium-sized Midwestern city. The count was necessary in order to obtain federal assistance for control of Dutch elm disease. After being stymied for two years, the council was rescued by a veritable army of tree counters which completed the job in less than four weeks. Who were they? Citizens concerned about the welfare of their community who happened also to be elementary and junior high school youth—trained and organized by students in a high school social studies course.

The story illustrates the major contentions of this chapter: Young people are citizens *now*, not merely preparing for citizenship; as citizens, adolescents can contribute significantly to the welfare of their communities; schools can facilitate youth participation in community affairs. From these contentions emerges our primary recommendation—that youth participation should be a central ingredient in the process of citizenship education.

The case will be made more by example than through philosophy, and the general arguments—and biases—will be summarized only as an introduction to, and in order to establish a framework for, these examples. To avoid repetition, more complete rationales for the general value of youth participation are left to other writings devoted to that purpose.[1]

CITIZENSHIP

Having no desire to engage in a heady platonic discourse on the nature of citizenship does not excuse the authors, however, from giving some indication of the kind of "citizens" which they believe schools should be encouraging—and educating—students to be. For some peculiar and obscure reason, the idea of citizenship, and citizenship education, is nearly always associated with social studies generally, and with the process of government particularly. Yet when most people think of the "good citizen," they do not only think of the person who knows and cares about politics and government, who votes regularly, who can tell you which state has a unicameral legislature, or who can unhesitatingly and unerringly distinguish between separation and division of powers. The image which arises is of the person who acts decently, who knows and cares about the affairs of his community, and who demonstrates this concern through overt actions.[2]

It is the notion of citizenship as "membership," implying a recognition of mutual interest with all other members, a sense of shared concern for the welfare of the total community, and a willingness and ability to contribute to the well-being of that community.

This conception of democratic citizenship is deliberately not limited to a legally prescribed set of rights and duties; to the performance of clearly defined "political" acts such as voting or attending party caucuses; and, most importantly, to the "if the shoe pinches" notion of democracy, which tends to elevate selfishness to a virtue, implying that the interests of all are best promoted when each individual works diligently and skillfully for his or her personal well-being.[3]

YOUTH PARTICIPATION

Since the purpose of this chapter is to make a case for *youth participation* as a central element in this wider conception of citizenship education, another definition is in order. By youth participation is meant the direct involvement of adolescents in the life of the community, ideally in activities concerned with ameliorating or solving social issues and problems.[4] The goal is not just to *talk* about public issues, but to *do* something about them. Because participation can take so many forms, it is difficult—and probably of limited value—to define it more precisely. However, there are some criteria by which we may be able to assess the relevance of participatory programs for citizenship education, the central one being that they should supply the conditions for the growth of democratic values *and* an orientation and commitment to act upon those values. Such conditions include, at a minimum, the opportunities for young people:

• To perform tasks that both the students and the community think are worthwhile

- To have some responsibility to make decisions within their project or placement
- To have others depend on their actions
- To work on tasks that challenge and strengthen their thinking—cognitively and ethically
- To work with peers and adults on group efforts toward common goals
- To reflect systematically on their experience.[5]

Youth participation activities which meet these conditions include volunteer service, internships, social and political action, community studies, and student projects to improve the school or community.[6]

YOUTH PARTICIPATION AS A METHOD OF CITIZENSHIP EDUCATION

This belief that youth participation should be a major component of citizenship education grows out of these four observations:

- The schools' traditional emphasis on preparing youth for citizenship has largely ignored their current status as citizens.
- The very nature of the classroom milieu unavoidably limits what can occur there to a few very similar "treatments" which begin to lose their power upon repeated application.
- Youth participation can serve as an antidote to the current trend toward selfishness and narcissism being advocated in both school and society.
- Youth participation is compatible with and can enhance classroom-based approaches to citizenship education.

Citizenship versus Preparation for Citizenship

Along with the emergence of prolonged adolescence and extended schooling has come the notion that this stage of life is a holding period, an interval during which youth are expected to bide their time, observe but not participate in adult life, and most of all, enjoy themselves and keep out of trouble. There is something wrong with our socialization process when adolescence, the stage of life during which energy and sometimes even idealism are highest, has become a time when waiting is the central task. This is damaging both to the community and to the adolescent. The community is denied the contribution that youth can make. The adolescent is denied the satisfaction that comes from making a contribution. While everyone wants to feel that he or she makes a difference, this wish particularly is strong during adolescence. Youthful apathy, cynicism, hostility, and even delinquency, are some of the consequences of treating youth as incompetent and childish.

If youth participation programs did nothing more than fulfill the young person's need to be, and to be recognized as, a contributing member of society (that is, a participating citizen), that would be justification enough for their place in the schools. But there is hope for even more—that the skill and habit of democratic participation will carry over into the adult years. Since people are inclined to repeat satisfying experiences, and since young people engaged in participatory programs generally report that their participation was significant and productive, there is cause to expect that they will repeat such involvements in later life. Longitudinal data that might support (or refute) the claim that youth participation will lead to continued civic involvement are, unfortunately, nonexistent. In their absence, one can at least hypothesize (and believe) that this approach would have this consequence as much as, or more than, would the promulgation (or even "discovery") of traditional fare through lectures, movies, readings, discussions, and simulation games.

The Classroom Milieu

Unhappily, educators are not more inclined than anyone else to apply what they teach—or preach. As exhibit A, consider the principle all learn in "Economics I," called the law of diminishing returns. A reasonable translation of this principle is that successive applications of similar material by similar methods in similar settings (by similar people?) will have progressively less impact on the students and may even reach the "point of negative returns." Contrasting the wide-eyed enthusiasm of first graders to the glazed-eyed boredom of twelfth graders gives painful and compelling evidence of the decreased power of the classroom experience. By the time students are seniors in high school, they have already sat through more than 12,000 rather similar hours of classroom instruction. They have become immune to the method and weary of its setting. It is little wonder that a new course in or a slight alteration of the citizenship curriculum does not substantially affect student knowledge, attitudes, or actions.

Before taking the preceding observation as the cue of a ritual breast beating, another lesson from undergraduate days should be considered applicable, namely, the distinction drawn by C. Wright Mills between personal troubles and public issues. While his purpose in proposing the distinction was not to assuage guilt, people may perhaps be pardoned for seeking comfort in the notion that they are not personally to blame for all the predicaments in which they find themselves. Some are thrust upon them. In this case, curriculum writers and teachers, regardless of their zeal, talents and imagination, simply cannot produce enough gimmicks to counteract the tedium and sameness of the classroom experience. The problem is not so much that the teaching is uninspired (though it sometimes is) or that the materials are dull (which they often are), but rather that young people are offered a steady diet of classroom lectures and discussions on topics which seldom really touch their lives. Trying to teach an abstract set of concepts (or even facts about the major issues) in a stuffy room to "antsy" adolescents whose insides are churning with fears, frustrations, doubts, and anxieties about who they are, and what for, makes about as much sense (and has as great a chance of success) as the infamous seminars on Western democracy which the military held for groups of starving, frightened, and wounded Vietnamese peasants. Even the latest project materials and snappiest simulation games will not beat those odds!

Despite the daily reminders that they are faced with the impossible task of entertaining a hostile audience for thirteen years of their lives, educators somehow hold on to their faith in classroom instruction.[7] They would do well to consider Arthur Schlesinger's gentle admonition:

> We alone know how limited and marginal our impact generally is on the boys and girls, the young men and young women, delivered by their families to our passing and inevitably superficial care. We do the best we can, but we do not have it within our power to repair all the inadequacies of the family, the church, the marketplace, the media, and other social institutions, although they have it within their power to blame us for not doing so.[8]

A modest suggestion is that a qualitatively different method, such as youth participation, is more likely to engage and motivate the student than will another dose of classroom instruction. Youth participation is no more a panacea than any other single method, but for most young people, community involvement activity in any of its forms—teaching first aid to young children, lobbying at city hall, or painting the home of a poor family—is a completely new experience. Because of the novelty and accompanying challenge, such experiences are generally satisfying and enjoyable and stand a chance of being meaningful to them. A seventeen-year-old told her classmates: "The last three months have been the most important time in my life. I never knew how much people needed help or how much help I could give them."

The Trend toward Narcissism

The usual reaction to such a student statement is to doubt its sincerity. The less cynical might only be embarassed. Some will dismiss such expressions as naïve or "uncool." The more sophisticated may label it as symptomatic of the "good boy, good girl" syndrome, a sure sign of arrested moral development![9] An even more blatant indication of the trend toward selfishness is seen in the popularity of two recent books, preaching the necessity of ignoring altruistic instincts and using manipulation and intimidation in relationships with others.[10] The popular trend in therapy is toward a "deification of the isolated self."[11] One of these new therapies, Erhard Seminars Training (EST), exhorts its participants to realize that each person is all powerful, that truth is identical to belief, and that those who are poor, hungry, or powerless must have consciously chosen that fate. California schoolchildren have even been trained in EST under a federal grant.[12] Soon "assertiveness" will replace "shows a concern for others," as a characteristic of good citizenship.

Selfishness and narcissism masquerading as enlightenment and liberation should alarm those who are concerned with citizenship education. The health of a democracy is dependent on the capacity of its citizens to consider moral complexity, to accept responsibility for the fate of others, and to be willing to confront and alter injustices— whether their own or someone else's. While youth participation will not alone reverse this trend toward the denial of human reciprocity and community, it can, at the very least, serve as a first step toward counteracting this overemphasis on the self. It will show students that *educators* believe that concern for other people, a sense of responsibility for the fate of other human beings, and the "humane application of knowledge" (Herbert Thelen's profound phrase) deserve a place in the curriculum.

Youth Participation and Academic Learning

While it is strongly advocated that community participation be included in the repertoire of methods in citizenship education, there is no suggestion that it supplant other approaches. Rather, it is compatible with and can enhance other emphases in the field such as critical thinking, moral reasoning, the social science disciplines, the legal-political structure of government, and social problems. An experience-based learning model can make these traditional citizenship education approaches more effective in the following ways.

First, the opportunity to do something with and about what is taught in the classroom can increase the student's *motivation,* as he begins to see the connection between what he learns in school and experiences in the world. For example, the authors have had students sit with rapt attention while they read the state regulations on nursing home standards. They listened because they were angry about the treatment given to the elderly in a facility in which they volunteered. Their motivation to learn the state regulations came from their personal relationship to the problem, their felt need for the information, and their serious intent to apply what they learned.

This suggests, secondly, that in youth participation programs, students would have the opportunities to generalize and *transfer* their school learnings to problems confronting them outside school. For example, critical thinking skills, including moral deliberation, become more than an academic exercise to fill class time when a student must decide whether to challenge a policy about the treatment of children in an institution for the retarded. One student was shocked when children who misbehaved were put in a dark closet, euphemistically known as the "quiet room." She had to weigh the consequences of challenging this policy (including the risk of being fired) against keeping quiet and maintaining her volunteer role. She had to look at whether it was more important to speak out against inhumane treatment of people, regardless of their IQ, or to be considered a "troublesome" volunteer.

Furthermore, youth participation programs give students the opportunity to *gather their own data* about a social or political issue and to *reality-test* both their own conclusions and those presented in the classroom or text. For example, a student interning in a city attorney's office was able to observe how race and social class can influence the pattern of sentencing, and then compare this reality against the textbook's version of equal rights for all Americans.

FORMS OF YOUTH/CITIZEN PARTICIPATION

More than most educational "innovations," youth participation has developed at the grass-roots level. Here and there across the country teachers, administrators, students, and parents, alone and in concert, have initiated programs to meet their own interests, objectives, and needs—and those of their community. Thus the programs do not fall into neat categories. Some are for credit, others not. Some are attached to particular disciplines or subject areas, others are not. Some include a significant classroom component, others do not. Similar forms of student action may be a means to quite different objectives. Strikingly different student actions may be a means to quite similar objectives. While this creates problems for people who thrive on neat categories—such as professors of education and writers of articles and position papers—it is probably just fine with everyone else. What matters is that the participants of any particular program are clear about what they are after and have a reasonable plan for getting there.

Examples have been categorized by the general nature of the student action described. The typologies are not meant to be taken with great seriousness, as the categories unavoidably overlap and programs could reasonably be placed in more than one section. The criteria used for selection are that the authors have some firsthand knowledge of them, and that they are reasonable illustrations of how students are *acting* as good citizens to the benefit of the community—and themselves.[13]

Voluntary Service (within social agencies)

It is a measure of the narcissistic cynicism of the day that volunteer service is self-righteously attacked as demeaning labor, recreation for the rich, the "Band-Aid" approach, nice but not very important, and a way to divert energy from the really crucial issues of the day. What the detractors miss is that there are all too few examples of people reaching out to one another, of acting on deep-felt concerns, of admitting that one may owe something to others, of helping another without expecting payment in return. Voluntarism has played a vital role in the history of American social welfare, is still the most common form of direct community participation, and is the most common vehicle of youth participation in the general community.

In Hopkins, Minnesota, an old industrial town now nested among Minneapolis' western suburbs, the twelfth-grade social studies course begins with a community involvement fair. Representatives from some thirty community agencies (from the police department to a hotline for troubled youth) sit at tables in the streamer-bedecked library explaining to students the needs of their agency, how the students can help, and arranging mutually satisfactory volunteer commitments. Each fall, between 80 and 95 percent of the seniors choose to make such a commitment as part of their social studies course, and some 350 sixteen- to eighteen-year-olds are thus added to the pool of people working to improve life in that community. In commitments ranging roughly from two to twenty hours a week, students volunteer in nursing homes, elementary schools, day-care centers, the Red Cross, schools for mentally and physically handicapped children, and many others.

What the students actually do in these placements varies widely. In a nursing home, for example, some primarily provide companionship, others help feed those who need such help, others organize a recreation program, others conduct daily physical exercises, others help decorate rooms, and much more. In the other agencies a similar variety takes place with students matching their energy, skills, and imagination with the needs of the agency and the people served by them.

Such programs are being seen more and more often in Minnesota and elsewhere. In Robbinsdale, Minnesota, a social studies program (which served as a model for the one described above) sends some 600 students into volunteer service each year. Two hundred junior and senior high school students in the Duluth Cathedral community commitment program contribute 600 hours of service each week to 2,000 people in fifty-eight different agencies. Last year their program was named the outstanding volunteer group in the city. At Regina High School in Minneapolis, service to the community has become the unifying theme for the entire school, and each department seeks ways to use what is taught in its classes to help others inside and outside the school. In the Minneapolis Public Schools a major project is underway to make youth participation an integral part of its secondary school program, across all grade levels and all subject-matter areas. Volunteer service is the largest part of this program. Elsewhere, in programs small and large, thousands of young people are being initiated into citizen participation through service as volunteers.

Volunteer service makes sense as citizenship education for the following reasons:

a. It can break down barriers between institutions and groups in the community, getting students involved with people who might otherwise be mere statistics in a social problems course. (One girl said recently to one of the authors: "The kids I work with are severely handicapped, and I was really scared of them the first day. I realized how much I had changed when Kelly and I took some of the kids to see Santa. People stared like we were freaks on parade. A lot of them looked really disgusted, and one couple even said, real loud, 'They have no business here; let's go home.' I was so mad I wanted to slug them, but I was sad too because I realized I might have grown up just like them if I hadn't worked with these kids myself.")

b. It can give students the experience of truly making a difference to someone, an experience that may be necessary in developing a sense of personal efficacy that one must have to believe it is worthwhile to try to change anything in society. (Another student reported: "My job was to try to communicate with a woman who hadn't said a word to anyone in almost two years. You can imagine we had some pretty weird visits as I sat there day after day talking a solo. On about my tenth visit she actually said hello, and later said my name and a couple of other things. It was the biggest thrill of my whole life!")

c. Putting students in positions of responsibility may lead them to develop or discover the competencies they need for all kinds of citizen participation. ("The most important thing I learned was that I could be a leader and take charge of things. Up until now I always figured I was strictly a follower.")

d. It involves students as active citizens, meeting current community needs. (A course evaluation included the open-ended question, "Should this class be offered next year?" All said yes, with a majority volunteering one form of the comment "because this community really needs our help. That's reason enough.")

e. Plus the usual reasons: that it can provide application and illustration of classroom learning about citizenship, give firsthand experience with various means and institutions for dealing with social problems, give a feeling of caring for others, and provide an issue to care about—thus serving as an impetus for working for changes in social policy.

Community Projects

The student projects included in this category fall somewhere between the agency volunteer work above and the social-political action which follows. They are volunteer work, but not with an agency; they include social action, but action directed toward ameliorating a particular need and not primarily toward influencing public or institutional policy. In large part, they are projects which have been initiated, organized, and "manned" by high school students with minimal assistance from adults and with little or no connection with community organizations. One of their strong merits is that they provide the experience of organizing and participating in group efforts toward common goals—a critical skill for citizens in this, or any, society.

Teenage Health Consultant is an organization initiated and run by high school and college-age people in the Twin Cities area. It began with young people who were involved with local teen clinics and who were dissatisfied with the quality of health care and advice available to other youth. Of particular concern was the absence of accessible and accurate information on sexuality. They organized themselves to provide such information and referrals, appearing before school classes, producing video tapes, and so on. To reach more people they have begun, with professional advice and help, to train other students to be health consultants to their peers. Students first participate in an eighteen-week training course and then share their newly learned knowledge about health through staffing a counseling office in the school, making presentations to classes and student groups (with emphasis on junior high), developing educational materials, and working in health clinics and on youth hotlines. Recently they received two small grants to continue and expand the program.

Teen Corps is another youth service organization run entirely by teenagers. It was begun in the late sixties by high school students wanting to mobilize youth power to attack poverty in Minnesota and elsewhere. During the school year they raise money and recruit volunteers, and in the summer they use both for rather spectacular projects such as building an entire camp for retarded and handicapped children. That such youth involvement in citizenship can have carry-over effects is spectacularly illustrated by the fact that the person who started Teen Corps as a high school student later became the youngest mayor in Minnesota. He is currently serving his second term as mayor of Bloomington, Minnesota, the state's fourth largest city.

Not surprisingly, youth projects come in a variety of sizes and styles. In an inner-city neighborhood, which has the highest burglary rate in the city, high school students organized to assist police in educating the public about "Operation Identification." The students, who received credit through their social studies class, went from door to door telling about the program, demonstrating the procedure for labeling valuables, and persuading people to register their items with the police. Elsewhere students manage and operate the only available recycling center in their community; in other communities they plant trees and clean up streams; in others they produce and distribute a community newspaper; in yet others they are building parks and using their talents to add a touch of artistry to their neighborhood. Industrial arts students redecorate and perform minor repairs in the homes of low-income, elderly residents; home economics students provide meals for elderly residents near the school; students in science have advised their city government on a location for a bicycle trail through a marsh with minimal disturbance to local ecology—and on, and on, and on.

Social/Political Action

The most obviously relevant category of participatory citizenship education is this one, which focuses on student efforts to influence public decision making. The most common form of such action is for students to become involved in political campaigns, attend caucuses and political meetings, and to join party and candidate organizations—usually on the urging of their social studies teacher. While educators applaud such participation, and unashamedly urge their own students to engage in such activities, they do not do so with any illusion that these are particularly potent forms of citizenship education. Most political meetings are boring and rather meaningless. Most campaign jobs are tedious and trivial—with young volunteers getting the worst of a poor lot. Many of the incentives which attract adult actives (personal or organizational obligation, habit, desire to be with friends, vested interest in an issue or candidate, and so on) do not operate for youthful participants. And while campaign work gives some students a clearer picture of the tedium of political life and may generate a long-run political interest in others, it seldom brings them close to the real mechanisms of public policy making or gives them either skills or experience in influencing community decisions. For these a different level of involvement is required— and not so easily arranged.

One way for students to perform a more active political role is to join an active citizen organization. Minnesota has a rather effective Public Interest Research Group, which depends on student involvement and regularly assigns high school students tasks of considerable responsibility in investigating pollution, consumer fraud and safety, and the like. Another avenue is for students to work directly with state legislators or city councilmen or to form their own research and lobby groups around a particular issue. The authors worked with one such group of students who lobbied intensively for the eighteen-year-old civil rights bill and who later, when it became clear the bill would pass both houses with or without their further involvement, combined their knowledge of the legislation with their sensitivity to student concerns to produce a pamphlet explaining the new law to other students. The Governor saw the pamphlet and liked it so much that he ordered 80,000 to be printed and distributed statewide.

Most political action must take place closer to home. In one school (the St. Paul Open School) students became tired of breathing the stench that wafted over the school. They traced the source of the pollution to a large paper company. The students contacted executives of the polluting firm, researched pollution laws, wrote complaints, circulated petitions, elicited legal support, and testified before the Pollution Control Agency. Ultimately, the industry was found to be in violation of antipollution regulations and was directed to find a more efficient way to filter its industrial emissions. More recently, students at the same school have formed an "Action Line" which receives student (and community) complaints about assorted "rip-offs" and attempts to find redress for the offended party. In another form of political activity, students at the New City School in St. Paul can participate in a public service video class. They learn to use television as an instrument of social influence through such means as producing documentaries of local problems. Finally, experience in influencing policy can sometimes be gained within the school system itself, and innumerable examples exist of students using their influence to eliminate dress codes, alter suspension policies, create smoking lounges, and the like.

While it is possible to generate a respectable list of examples of young people exerting political influence, the truth is that this is still a relatively rare phenomenon. There are many reasons for this, the most critical of which are: most students are not very "political" in the sense that they feel burning concern for an issue that they believe can be solved through the political system; they (often realistically) have little confidence that their actions could be consequential; and they lack the skill to mobilize what actual power they might be able to exert.

Part of the contention of this chapter is that through the less obviously "political" actions (such as volunteer service and community projects), students may be most likely to develop a concern for serious social problems and to build a sense of confidence that their actions can make a difference. As for skills, there is not much available in schools to prepare students realistically for effective political action should they have the concern and confidence motivating them to try it.[14]

Community Study

A less engaging but clearly worthy approach to participatory citizenship education is through a firsthand study of the community. Again this can take several forms; three are illustrated here.

One form is the survey of community attitudes. In one suburban community, the city council wanted to know how people were reacting to two recently completed public housing projects. In a rural community the council wanted to know how the people felt about six prominent community issues, and in what order of importance they should place them. In both cases rather accurate surveys were taken by social studies students and the results presented to the councils. While the authors are not awed by the value of learning survey research techniques, the students did learn something about this method and about community attitudes on particular issues. In the second example, the students' efforts had some influence on their council's policy making.

Another form has been spurred partly by the success and publicity attending the Foxfire project in Georgia and partly by the Bicentennial year. In large numbers of communities young people are researching the history of their area; interviewing older citizens; and producing newspapers, pamphlets, and the like. In some they are relearning the skills of the past, restoring old structures, rebuilding log cabins and sod houses, and in other ways helping the community reclaim and preserve its heritage—while gaining for themselves a sense of pride and belonging in their own city or town.

A third form is the firsthand study of community institutions. Students learn about criminal justice in jails, courts, and attorneys' offices; about health in hospitals; about economics in banks and welfare offices; about city politics in council chambers and neighborhood action centers. As these are so commonly discussed (though not so often done), the authors will not comment further on them here.

Internships

Finally, something should be said about internships in which students may spend from a few hours a week for a quarter to full time for a year with an individual or in some significant role in a community organization. At their best, internships are a way to get inside an organization, to experience an occupation firsthand, to get an in-depth view of how community decisions are made, and to test one's competence to fill an adult role. At their worst, they are exercises in tedium in which the student's task is to watch a boring bureaucrat attend lifelessly to trivial duties, in which both the student and the bureaucrat are never given an assignment they can care about or in which their own actions make any difference. For such an experience the student might as well stay in school.

In Oregon the state government has opened slots in virtually all its state offices, and in the past few years hundreds of Salem area students have had internships (or extended observations) as part of the Governmental Responsibility and Student Participation (GRASP) program. Students also have extensive classroom study of the state government to give them an overall picture of the decision-making process and to help them to see how "their" department's activities fit into a larger picture. In Minnesota, internships with state legislators are available through a program which provides three days of orientation followed by placement with a particular legislator or lobby organization which has requested student help. This experience can last from a week to a full semester, depending mostly on the student's ability and desire to arrange time away from school.

In these states and elsewhere students act as interns with city officials, judges, lawyers, newspaper editors, artists, businessmen, welfare workers—and even school officials. The quality of these experiences varies so widely that it is difficult to make any valid generalizations about them, except that their value depends on identifying slots that have the potential for significant action by a high school student (associating with a judge may be interesting for a while, but what can you *do* for him or her?) and on finding adults who can recognize and actualize the potential in the job (what would a high school student do with you?).

PROGRAM MODELS

Good ideas in education are superfluous if they cannot be translated into actual school programs. Even when it is possible to convince educators that both the student and community will benefit from the direct participation of youth, and that there are a multitude of significant involvements for young people in the social and political arena, educators may still doubt whether such programs can be incorporated into their school structure. Such skepticism is not unfounded. Those attempting to include experience-based learning into the curriculum will be faced with a myriad of obstacles— traditional beliefs concerning the caretaking role of the high school; the presumed immaturity of the students; rigid curriculum requirements; problems of time, transportation, and liability; inflexible schedules; skeptical parents, staff, and students. Yet hundreds of high schools are offering community service and social action programs, so the problems need not be insurmountable. It should be helpful, then, to look at the ways in which schools have managed to integrate youth participation programs into sometimes inhospitable academic structures.

The strategies can be divided into six basic types, distinguished by the manner and degree in which the work is integrated to the regular academic program of the school. Other criteria would be as useful and valid, but the chief purpose here is to illustrate the ways in which many schools have approached the structural problems.

The continuum below represents a movement from least integration on the left to most on the right. Distinctions between programs are based on their structure, not their merit. The type names are rather clumsy, but their very roughness may at least demonstrate that youth participation is not yet developing an obtuse argot to befuddle an unsuspecting public.

Volunteer Bureau	Community Action Credit	"Lab" for Existing Courses	Community Involvement Course	Action-Learning Center	Sequence of Courses and Experiences
1	2	3	4	5	6

Volunteer Bureau

In this type of program, students volunteer for the intrinsic value of volunteering (and perhaps to break the tedium of the school day) and receive no academic credit for doing so. In some cases, the work is done during the student's unscheduled time, after school, or during a study hall (especially if it can be placed near lunch or at the end of the day).

Another way of carrying out a volunteer program, but one that requires more support from and coordination with the rest of the faculty, is to release students during their classes (usually a day or half-day a week) or rearrange their schedules to allow them to work in the community. At Folwell Junior High School in Minneapolis, eighth- and ninth-grade students may be excused from their classrooms for up to one full day each week to intern in the community on a volunteer basis. Students choose from a wide variety of placements or invent their own where they have the chance to explore careers and to learn and achieve in ways not possible within the school itself. They have worked in a congressman's office, an airport, nature centers, medical labs, elementary schools, and many more places. Students must receive permission from their parents and from all teachers involved before the internship begins and must arrange to make up missed classwork. No formal credit is awarded for participation, but a record of the participation is included in each student's file. In both types of volunteer programs a coordinator, either on a full-time or part-time basis, identifies and places students in involvement opportunities and follows up and reviews the student's work.

Community Action Credit

In this second category community experience is not only facilitated and encouraged by the school, but it is also accredited. Often a community service credit is given for an established number of work hours. For example, 100 hours equals one semester credit. This may or not be used in lieu of some other credit such as social studies or humanities. A common procedure in this kind of program would be for a student to prepare a proposal outlining what he wants to do, for how long, for what purposes, and with what product (if any) to be produced in the end. This proposal would be reviewed by a faculty adviser or program coordinator. If approved, the student acts on the proposal in the time blocked out. For some it may be one full school day a week; for others it may be an after-school activity; in some cases, students may be given from a month to a semester away from school to participate.

The key point, however, as far as this continuum is concerned, is that the community service is not performed within the context of a regular school course. It is essentially an off-campus experience with minimal supervision by school personnel. There may be an occasional seminar or "rap" session with an adviser and/or other participants, but the learning is seen as being in the doing. Formal orientation and training is the responsibility of the receiving agency, and the role of the faculty adviser is to check on the student occasionally and to talk with him about what he is doing and learning. Put somewhat crudely, it is credit for experience and for services rendered. In structure it is very similar to the various independent studies options available on most college and some high school campuses.

Such special learning opportunities as the Executive Internships of America, Close-Up, and the Political Action Project in New Jersey—organized, staffed, and administered outside the student's home school—also fall into this category. The school's responsibility in these cases usually is limited to releasing the student for the necessary time and granting credit for the experience. In the Executive Internships Program the staff locates internships with top executives of business, government, museums, and so forth; runs a weekly seminar for the students; and evaluates the student's final project. While programs such as these offer exceptional opportunities to students, they can rarely have much impact on the teaching style and curriculum of individual secondary schools. They do, however, establish precedents, because they assume that community members who are not certified teachers may be competent to arrange and evaluate accredited learning experiences.

Laboratory for Existing Courses

This kind of program has enabled many schools to introduce a community action component into their academic program with little or no immediate change in curriculum, school structure, or staff deployment. In this model, students in existing courses use either long-term community action or extended observation as a way to reality-test course content, gather data and examples, and make use of what is learned in the class. Students may engage in the community activity during school hours or after school depending on the student's schedule and agency need. This often is done in lieu of a more distasteful requirement such as a research paper. In most cases the course curriculum is left much as it would be without the experiential component. Often, however, this procedure leads to a gradual altering of topics and approaches to coincide with kinds of experiences students are having in the community. A healthy pressure develops to provide useful information, generate techniques for systematic observation, and propose theories to explain the rich but varied data gathered through community experience. Generally, the classroom teacher is responsible for helping students find appropriate off-campus experiences and for general supervision. In some cases one day a week is set aside specifically for talking about the involvement activities.

Options in volunteer service and social action can be worked into almost any curriculum area. Students in a consumer math course researched, developed, and printed a guide to citizen action—detailing what to do and where to call for help with problems ranging from fraudulent sales practices to lost pets. They distributed the pamphlet in the neighborhood around the schools. Students in home economics have established free day-care service in the school building for low-income families. Retirement homes, mental hospitals, and elementary schools provide laboratories for English students to encounter and work on very real communications problems.

Community Involvement Course

This model represents an attempt to combine the strongest features of the previous two into a course which exists as an integral part of the school's academic program. Here the community experience forms the heart and is the central focus of the course. It is combined with an ongoing classroom experience where the emphasis is on providing some information, skills, and generalizing principles. In this way students are assisted directly in interpreting their experiences and in operating more successfully in their placements. There is a strong assumption in this model that whereas experience *can* be educational, it is neither necessarily nor automatically so. Experiences can be miseducative as well as educative, and it is part of the role of the teacher to help make them the latter.

At Central High School, an inner-city school in Minneapolis, a course entitled "Student-Community Involvement Project" is offered as a regular social studies option. The class meets two hours every day and the student receives two class credits. For three days of the week the students report to the class and leave immediately for their placement in a nursing home, senior citizens' residence, elementary school, junior high school, or facility for retarded adults. Here they work until they must return for their next class. On the other two days they are in a class in which the subject matter is related directly to their experiences and to the kinds of people with whom they are working. Students working with the elderly, for example, may receive information about and discuss the problems of senility (and other problems that often may be mistaken for senility) and both receive and share specific ideas on things to do when they return to the nursing home. Alternately the students may be given help in improving their observational and data-gathering skills, time may be given for writing in diaries, or they may reflect on some of the personal implications of involvement. In short the classroom experiences may have a variety of formats and focuses, but all would relate to, and be integrated with, the community experience.

A variation on this model, and a way to create a larger block of time for the student to be in the field, is the interdisciplinary course. Since social problems seldom fall neatly into categories entitled "biology," "sociology," "English," and so on, such an approach also provides a more realistic way to relate community experiences to course offerings. For example, an archeological project could relate to social studies (the historical background and value of the artifacts), to art (the relationship of the items unearthed to other styles of art), and to science (conducting chemical analysis to determine the age of the artifacts).

Action-Learning Center

The fifth approach, a districtwide learning center, allows for more specialized and varied community involvement programs than a single high school can usually offer. In this model, students from several high schools have the option of attending a learning center for a part of the day. Typically a student might spend half of the school day for a semester at the center.

There are several advantages to such an approach. It allows the teachers who have skills and experience with youth participation programs to work with students from all over the district. It provides a mechanism for initiating action learning without the dissension that changing the curriculum and the schedule might cause in some schools. It increases the available pool of students for specialized offerings; an action-learning center can afford to offer courses that a single school could not justify in terms of student demand.

In St. Paul, the New City School offers an enviable array of programs, including working on a magazine of local history, participating in politics, providing community service, and using film and television as a tool for political and social action. Students from all the high schools in the city attend the center on an elective basis. They attend in the morning or afternoon for two and a half hours during one trimester. They remain in their home school for the other half-day and for the rest of the school year.

Sequence of Courses and Experiences

This is the most ambitious model, which may explain its infrequent appearance in secondary schools. Where such models do exist, their goal is often directed toward the development of the skills, motivation, and competencies of effective social activities. This goal, according to proponents of this approach, can be accomplished only over a considerable period of time and through an integrated sequence of classroom and community experiences. Usually, such a curriculum combines formal courses on such topics as social problems, communication, politics, values, and ecology; community-oriented assignments in these courses; and a practicum experience, providing sustained participation in a community project.

At Stone Ridge School in Bethesda, Maryland, students are required to complete a six-year curriculum aimed at progressively building skills related to social action. It begins with a communications lab in which seventh graders are exposed to the dynamics of group participation and cooperation, skills essential to working in community settings. Eighth and ninth graders continue to work on leadership and problem-solving skills in the classroom and begin to identify community projects in which they wish to participate. The students occasionally conduct community studies, but their major involvement in the community takes place in the tenth through twelfth grades. Senior high school students are released from classes for one afternoon per week for field experiences in human service agencies, in governmental or cultural organizations, in school-based activities or in independent projects. Each student keeps a log and shares his experiences with classmates in weekly discussion groups. Students are encouraged to evaluate and reflect upon their personal growth—as well as the impact of their project on the school or community.

A concluding note is suggested by John Dewey, who said most of what is worth saying about education. In *Experience and Education,*[15] he argued that the qualities of a truly educational experience are two: that it is immediately enjoyable, and that it leads to further educational experiences. Youth participation can be justified as educationally sound on these two counts—and perhaps on one more.

There is another important dimension beside "enjoyment" that is characteristic of an educational experience. "Worthwhile" or "important" comes close as a description of it. Now, enjoying oneself in a school activity is not a trivial outcome, but repeatedly students have been observed whose immediate reaction to a social problem or agency was not pleasure but shock, sadness, or anger; but who nevertheless became deeply involved and committed to working on that problem. One student helped clarify this difference when he explained how he felt about working at the nursing home. In response to a question about whether he had enjoyed going there he responded: "No, I didn't like it, but I feel bad about having to stop going there at the end of the semester. I hope we can find some other kid who will take my place because it's important that somebody go there." He is not only on his way to becoming a good citizen, but already is one!

NOTES

1. James S. Coleman, "How Do the Young Become Adults," *Review of Educational Research,* vol. 42, no. 4, pp. 431–439, Fall 1972; Daniel E. Conrad, "Arguments for Educators: A Rationale for High School Service-Learning Programs," *Synergist,* vol. 3, no. 3, pp. 9–13, Winter 1975; John Dewey, *Experience and Education,* Macmillan Publishing Co., Inc., New York, 1963.

2. This is the conception of "good citizen" described by T. V. Smith and Eduard C. Lindeman in their small classic, *The Democratic Way of Life,* reprint ed., The University of Chicago Press, Chicago, 1965.

3. The problem is that the foot that gets relief is usually already encased in an expensive, soft-leather shoe.

4. This is not to say that elementary-age children cannot effectively participate in community affairs. There are many examples of children performing valued service in their communities, but limitations of space and the authors' experience confine focus in this paper to adolescents.

5. In this view of youth participation, action is not separated from thinking. Rather, thinking in the forms of careful observation, perceptive questioning, and synthesizing of the immediate experience with accumulated knowledge is a prerequisite for effective citizen action.

6. These are similar to guidelines suggested by the National Commission on Resources for Youth in *New Roles for Youth in the School and the Community,* Citation Press, New York, 1974, pp. 226–230.

7. Recently, a school administrator suggested that all referees who officiate at school district basketball games should be required to take a human relations course. This, he felt, would be sufficient to eliminate the virulent antiblack attitudes that some of the referees had exhibited!

8. Arthur Schlesinger, Jr., "What Do We Tell Our Students? Thoughts after Watergate," *School Review,* February 1975, p. 179.

9. This is not meant as a criticism of Lawrence Kohlberg, who writes movingly about the importance of empathy as a condition for moral development, culminating with a capacity to live by universal principles of social justice. The authors are reacting to the common misinterpretation of Kohlberg's theory which assigns altruism to Stage Three thinking and confuses a deep-felt concern for the welfare of others with "being nice" and "pleasing others."

10. Robert Ringer, *Winning through Intimidation,* 2d ed., Los Angeles Publishing Company, Los Angeles, 1974, and Michael Korda, *Power! How To Get It, How To Use It,* Random House, Inc., New York, 1975.

11. Peter Marin, "The New Narcissism," *Harpers,* October 1975, p. 45.

12. Mark Brewer, "We're Gonna Tear You Down and Put You Back Together," *Psychology Today,* August 1975, p. 35.

13. For a wider selection of more complete program descriptions, see Daniel Conrad and Diane Hedin, *Action Learning in Minnesota,* Center for Youth Development and Research and Minnesota Association of Secondary School Principals, Minneapolis, 1975; *25 Action Learning Schools,* National Association of Secondary School Principals, Reston, Va., 1975; *New Roles for Youth in the Schools and Community,* National Commission on Resources for Youth, Citation Press, New York, 1974; National Student Volunteer Program, *Synergist* (all issues).

14. One hopeful approach has been outlined by Fred Newmann in *Education for Citizen Action,* McCutchan Publishing Corporation, Berkeley, Calif., 1975; a thoughtful proposal that hopefully may find expression in actual school programs.

15. Dewey, op. cit.

Citizen Participation: Lessons for Citizenship Education

9

LUVERN L. CUNNINGHAM

The roots of citizen involvement extend deeply into the history of this nation. The first citizens committee for education in Chicago was formed in 1834 by private citizens who shared a concern about financing the fledgling Chicago Public Schools.[1] The town meeting tradition is based on an assumption that everyone should have a voice in the resolution of a community's problems. Town meetings have given way in most places to boards and councils, representative forms of local government.

But citizen perspectives may not be reflected adequately through boards and councils; citizen supplements are required. Citizen participation in public affairs has become a national preoccupation in recent years. Government at all levels has involved citizens in many ways, and federal policy requires citizen participation in planning many federal programs (including those in education). The forms of involvement range from presidential commissions to citizen advisory councils at the school building level. State, regional, city, county, and special district governments have recruited citizens to aid and abet decision processes or to buttress political support. School systems have created supplemental citizen structures relating to policy and decision processes. Such groups vary in purpose, composition, leadership, term, staffing, and fiscal support.[2]

A wide range of differences exists within and among school systems on the matter of citizen participation in school affairs. Some are able to integrate broadly held as well as narrowly conceived perspectives into decision and policy processes. School administrators and teachers in those systems are at ease in relating to their publics. Communication channels are open. Parents, students, and citizens express satisfaction about their opportunity to participate as well as about the meaning of their participation.

Other school systems and school officials find that participation is a trial. School personnel are uncomfortable with citizens and often are intimidated by them (especially when the citizen group includes students). Projecting an image of openness, they are in fact closed to effective participation. Many are simply unwilling to share or relinquish power.

Still other school systems and school officials are incredibly open, seeking input from every conceivable source. They are inundated with input, but they don't know what to do with it. Busy seeking, listening, and accumulating points of view, ideas, and suggestions, they have little time to sift and sort and abstract from the sea of suggestions. Inundation leads to frustration and paralysis or to constant ferment. Each idea seems to be as meritorious as every other idea. Each *new* perspective automatically becomes *the* perspective. Board members and administrators find themselves making new policy, new decisions, with almost reckless abandon. Each board meeting, each staff meeting, has little relationship to meetings of last week, of last month. Such school systems give the appearance of being adrift, even when they are not in fact adrift. There is little consistency in policy or practice.

Educators have come a long way toward achieving effectiveness in their relationships with diverse and often emotional constituencies. Some have learned more than others.

One form of citizen involvement is beginning to capture the imaginations of volunteers and officials in large cities: third-party, problem-solving groups. The Detroit Education Task Force, the St. Louis Education Task Force, and the San Francisco Public Schools Commission are examples of such groups. They are supplementary organizations, more than advisory, composed of highly motivated, competent citizens. (For three years this author worked intensively with the citizens' groups in Detroit and San Francisco, and occasionally with the citizens' group in St. Louis. Their participants endured inconvenience, missed meals, awkward meeting times—devoting many hours to organized problem-solving activities for their schools.) They function as mediators between the public and the school systems.

The basic function of a third-party group is to identify and define manageable problems. A second central function is that of a convener. A third is to provide a forum. A fourth is to serve as a proxy for disparate community interests. A fifth is that of a linkage function channeling important sources of power and influence. A sixth is as a legitimizer of goals and directions for an institution. And a seventh function is leadership.

INCORPORATING THE STUDENTS

In 1969, on commission from the National Urban Coalition then headed by John Gardner, Luvern Cunningham directed a study of citizen participation in thirteen major cities.[3] He and his colleagues discovered a wide range of mechanisms for participation. (More recent surveys have located even more.[4]) They sorted out the most prominent objectives these groups hoped to achieve.

The first purpose was to develop community understanding and support for educational objectives. There is clearly a place here for student involvement: students, especially at the secondary level, have views about the quality of their educational experiences. The process of reflecting and giving voice to their judgments is itself educational for young people—an exercise in citizenship with values which should endure.

The second purpose was to supplement school staff in the pursuit of educational objectives. Here again student involvement is certainly desirable. Older students can be a resource to teachers and staff working with younger students. Growth in citizenship and skills results from student participation in program planning, in choosing instructional strategies and preparing instructional materials, in work as tutors, as assistants in playgrounds, and in home visits.

A third purpose was to articulate citizen expectations for schools and to insist upon accountability for educational objectives. Students as citizens have their own expectations for schools but seldom are asked to spell out their views and preferences for change. Active, focused student involvement in identifying citizen preferences about schooling holds promise for citizenship education.

These purposes are not easily achieved. In this 1969 study[5] difficulties were noted in determining group membership, in selecting participatory modes and strategies, in judging effectiveness, in locating leaders, in school system responsiveness, and in formulating third-party roles.

All these problem areas are also areas of opportunity for student participation. The question of representativeness is not new to students and faculty in traditional school life. Debates long have raged about the representativeness of student councils, athletic teams, cheerleaders, and the staffs of student newspapers. Many schools significantly involve at least a few students in their planning process. Some student governments work; they are more than window dressing or the tools of the administration. There are successful student advisory groups to superintendents, principals, and boards of education. But the full potential is seldom realized.

FORMS FOR STUDENT PARTICIPATION

Various ways can be found to produce the benefits of participation for more students.

Students as School Board Members

ELECTION TO A SCHOOL BOARD UNDER EXISTING
STATUTES

There are a few examples of eighteen- and nineteen-year-olds (high school graduates) serving as elected members of boards of education. One example was in Council Bluffs, Iowa, where two young men ran successfully for the board. As board members they were aggressive and strong advocates for conservative educational practices. Their election attracted a national television network to Council Bluffs. The program that ensued captured the attention of several million viewers. The program highlighted conflicting local opinions about the matter, but left no doubt that the two young board members were influencing life in the schools of Council Bluffs.

Students who are eighteen may have this option available to them. New legislation may not be required; permission from school officials may not be necessary. Barring specific statutory prohibition, students can run for office, and if elected, enter political places formerly occupied by older people.

DESIGNATING SCHOOL BOARD MEMBERSHIP FOR
STUDENTS

Voting memberships. Another option is to earmark for students one or two school board seats with voting privileges. State statutes need to be changed for this to occur. Students can be involved in the development of the necessary legislation and in developing policies and procedures for local elections.

Voting membership on a board will be demanding for the success-ful student candidate, who will have to plow through reports and documents of all sorts. The presence of a student member should be a constructive influence on other board members. Certainly many matters directly relevant to students will not coast through boards as they do now.

Nonvoting memberships on school boards. Nonvoting board membership can be achieved at the option of any local district. Student members can engage fully in discussions, raise questions, respond to questions, report on student perspectives, provide data, and seek support for their views. Their participation can be effective even without the vote, and the election process can have citizenship benefits for large numbers of students.

The San Francisco Unified School District Board of Education added a nonvoting student member early in 1976. The membership rotates among participants in the Student Advisory Council to the Superintendent. The entire council retains an active interest, and many students attend board meetings and coach their member from the sidelines. Caucuses sometimes are called on high-stake issues and advice passed on to student board members while meetings are in progress. The San Francisco arrangements are flawed, but have worked well enough to sustain student interest and to generate proposals for change. In fact, San Francisco students are lobbying the legislature for a law to give voting privileges to student members.

The San Francisco board is exceptionally politicized in a period when school affairs generally are very political; student board mem-bers feel themselves in the big leagues in a political sense. They are into "action learning,"[6] although school board participation makes heavy demands on student time. Board meetings are held at night beginning at 5:00 P.M. and sometimes run as late as 4:30 A.M. Committee meetings may conflict with classes. Teachers and admin-istrators do not always give special consideration to these students; board membership competes with traditional uses of student time.

Student Involvement on Education Citizen Committees

Students can and should be part of citizen committees whether they are third-party, problem-solving groups or more conventional study or advisory bodies. In Detroit and San Francisco, where there were

no student members, student views were found to be important—
and hard to get.

Student interests are not the same as adult interests, and priorities are different. Except for questions of teacher evaluation and
teacher tenure (which they oppose), students stress matters that are
more pragmatic and of the moment: fixing broken windows, clean-
ing up the rest rooms, improving security, acquiring better athletic
equipment, and achieving stronger school spirit. Adult problem-
solving groups, on the other hand, focus on problems of finance,
management, intergovernmental relationships, collective bargaining, integration, and so on.

Student and adult interests are not irreconcilable by any means.
Each age group informs and educates the other when there is
adequate time and a proper setting for discussion. And student
involvement in citizen efforts need not be limited to education: there
is every reason to encourage student participation in groups working on other public interest matters (environment, atomic fuels,
public safety, abortion, energy, public finance).[7] In June 1975, students in Detroit played a major role in designing and conducting a
citywide conference on youth employment. Students and adults
alike were sobered by the seriousness of youth employment problems and by the desperately thin solutions that were found. The
conference was an act of responsible citizenship for the community
and had deeply personal benefits for those who took part.

Student Problem-solving Task Groups

Student problem-solving groups can address questions which fall
outside the concerns of adult groups. Their work may include some
of the problems ordinarily on the agenda of student government—
the activity calendar, smoking privileges, behavior in the lunch-
room, and library privileges. Or the agenda can include such issues
as racial, ethnic, or sex-based discrimination; problems of desegregation and integration at the building level; program changes consistent with student needs; and teacher evaluation. Such groups can
collect information; hold hearings and take testimony; prepare analyses and recommendations for change; present and defend their
proposals to school authorities; help with implementation; and provide monitoring services to the student body, teachers, administrators, and community.

The initiative for the formation of student problem-solving groups ought to reside with students, but for such groups to be successful they will need support from teachers and administrators.

Student-sponsored Forums on Public Issues

In San Francisco, the Superintendent's Student Advisory Council together with the San Francisco Public Schools Commission has sponsored several forums, including one on teacher evaluation. Students were in charge; they framed the issues and established the boundaries for discussion. The heads of teacher and administrator organizations, the superintendent and staff, board members, representatives of the media, and an audience, gathered in the assembly room of the board of education for the forum. The session was video taped. Discussions were spirited and provoked substantial interest, especially in the area of teacher tenure. Proposals were advanced which may lead to new state legislation regarding teacher licensing and approaches to protecting teacher rights, short of tenure.

CONCLUDING THOUGHTS

A perennial issue in participation is power:[8] How much of it do citizens have as individuals or as auxiliary groups? If school professionals or board members ignore or turn their backs on citizens, then why expend the effort? However, third-party groups do possess power; they are influential. In Detroit, San Francisco, and St. Louis they earned respect, had access to the media, could gain the ear of board members and superintendents—and were persistent. Problem solving is tough but heady business. For students it can open vistas that otherwise might never appear.

NOTES

1. *Citizen Participation in Public Education,* Committee for Citizen Involvement in Public Education, The Chicago Community Trust, Chicago, 1975, p. 9.

2. Richard W. Saxe, *School Community Interaction,* McCutchan Publishing Corporation, Berkeley, Calif., 1975, chap. 11.

3. Mary Ellen Stanwick, *Patterns of Participation,* Institute for Responsive Education, New Haven, Conn., 1975, p. 5.

4. David A. Straus, *Notebook,* Citizen Involvement Network, Charles F. Kettering Foundation, Dayton, Ohio, 1974. Also Stanwick, op. cit.

5. Raphael O. Nystrand and Luvern L. Cunningham, *The Dynamics of Local School Control,* U.S. Department of Health, Education, and Welfare, National Institute of Education, ERIC Reports, Educational Reports Information Center, Washington, D.C., 1973, pp. 35–36.

6. Richard Graham, "Youth and Experiential Learning," in Robert J. Havighurst and Philip H. Dreyer (eds.), *Youth,* The Seventy-Fourth Yearbook of the National Society for the Study of Education, University of Chicago Press, Chicago, 1975, chap. 9.

7. See Chap. 8.

8. Saxe, op. cit.

The Role and Responsibility of Television in Civic Education

10○

DOUGLASS CATER

One can approach this subject from several perspectives. The first, a visionary one, perceives television's capacity to make this nation into a sort of Greek forum of democracy. Households with television sets number almost double the total circulation of daily newspapers. According to the rating experts the average set burns as much as six hours a day, compared to the twelve to fifteen minutes which the average citizen devotes to his newspaper reading. The citizen can see his leaders in living color in his living room. Roper Research Associates tells us that 65 percent of viewers claim they get most of their news of the world from television; 36 percent rely exclusively on television. Over half are "inclined to believe" television more than other media.

A second perspective, more pessimistic, perceives the evidence of a decline in citizenship over the period of television's greatest growth. During the past four presidential elections, the percentage of voting age population that actually voted has gone down steadily from 62.8 percent to 55.7 percent. From 1960 to 1972, when approximately 30 million citizens came of voting age, the voter ranks grew by less than 9 million (and the drop-off was dominantly among the young). In the 1974 congressional elections, two out of three eligible citizens failed to exercise the franchise.

One cannot prove a causal relationship between the rise of television and the decline of voting, yet it is evident that television has not kindled fresh enthusiasm among citizens to participate in this most important function of democracy. Of course, there is heartening evidence of increased citizen-group activity of a more focused nature (such as Common Cause, League of Women Voters, and Nader's Raiders). Indices for this sort of civic action are not available, but it engages no more than a very small fraction of the total citizenship.

A third perspective perceives a growing disinclination on the part of television broadcasters to deal with citizenship issues. This has been spurred by the rise of the audience expert who specializes in advising stations about how to maximize their revenues. His advice on news and public affairs programs can be summarized: Keep it exciting, keep it human conflict oriented, and keep it brief. He has spawned the "happy news" programs whose anchor persons recite even the most morbid of community happenings amid an atmosphere of wisecracks. A Los Angeles station recently employed a tap dancer to deliver the news in an entertaining fashion.

The results of this trend were revealed by an analysis of the 1974 California gubernatorial campaign ("The Hidden Campaign" by Mary Ellen Leary). Immediately prior to the general election, an eight-week survey of the six dominant television stations in California's four major markets showed only 2.3 percent of news was devoted to the contest between Jerry Brown and Houston Flournoy. Only a few stations carried even one of the five debates between the two candidates. During the primary, candidates had difficulty purchasing time segments longer than the thirty-second spot from the major stations. According to this broadcaster perspective, politics is an audience loser which should be ignored as much as possible.

On the networks, news and public affairs departments have fought hard for prime time schedules. There is evidence that financial restraints have brought reductions in the professional staff devoted to worldwide news coverage. Westinghouse Broadcasting, which has long taken pride in the quality of its news operations, has recently substituted Associated Press coverage for its own correspondents abroad.

A fourth perspective cites disturbing evidence of television's impact on the citizen. At a recent symposium Mervin D. Field, a thoughtful analyst of public opinion in California, spoke of growing evidence of citizen disillusionment. Field claimed that

Research shows that TV viewers, far from being enlightened, seemed to be overwhelmed by the full coverage of conventions and other events. Instead of feeling that they are "in the know," viewers often experience an uneasy feeling that they are being kept out. . . . Full disclosure seems only to confirm the darkest fears of those who habitually take a conspiratorial and sinister view of politics.

Field picked up a theme sounded by Dr. Michael Robinson, a political scientist, who prepared a study for the Aspen Institute Program on Communications and Society. This study analyzed public opinion surveys and concluded that the rise of television has led to a marked decline in citizens' belief in the legitimacy of American political institutions:

> Television journalism, with its constant emphasis on social and political conflict, its high credibility, its powerful audio-visual capabilities, and its epidemicity, has caused the more vulnerable viewers first to doubt their own understanding of their political system. But once these individuals have passed this initial stage, they enter a second phase in which personal denigration continues and in which a new hostility toward politics and government also emerges. Having passed through both stages of political cynicism, these uniquely susceptible individuals pass their cynicism along to those who were, at the start, less attuned to television messages and consequently less directly vulnerable to televisual malaise.

From a series of interviews Robinson has found,

> Even when examining respondents with similar levels of education, the greater the dependency upon television, the greater the personal confusion and estrangement from government.

These four perspectives suggest at the very least that the subject of this chapter—television and citizenship education—is a complex one. It cannot be accommodated neatly to either of the polar positions regularly argued: television is a powerful medium for education and should be cajoled, shamed, or bullied into meeting citizenship responsibilities; television is a medium ingeniously sensitive to the desires of its publics and any effort to impose citizenship obligations is elitist nonsense.

The challenge is to consider fresh approaches which avoid these polar arguments. One might start by examining certain conditions which need to be understood better and investigated more extensively:

1. The age of television has brought a notable shift in the way a citizen learns. He no longer gets the bulk of his information from the printed or the spoken word. Television has been categorized too easily as merely one of the "mass media." In fact, it is significantly

different not just in its reach but in its peculiar coding of sight and sound, reaching the brain with a speed, continuity of flow, and volume, which makes it unlike any other medium of communication. More fanciful analysts have speculated that the brain does not decode television information in the same way that it handles Gutenberg information. Tony Schwartz, a producer of television political commercials, argues that truth is a Gutenberg concept requiring the linear logic and the elaborate comparisons of textual communications. Television, Schwartz maintains, is an instantly evocative form of communication. Its primary function is to call forth impressions already stored in the brain. Schwartz believes that entirely new standards must be developed for measuring and evaluating television's effects on the thinking process.

Somewhat less speculative are the findings in brain research indicating that the differences between Gutenberg man and television man may be one of hemispheres. Gutenberg man is left-brain dominant—relying heavily on the hemisphere which controls sequential, analytic tasks based on the use of propositional thought. Television man relies more on the right hemisphere which appears to be biased toward appositional thought. Youth growing up in the television society may be crossing a cerebral watershed. Very little is known about what this means for citizenship education. The optimist would argue that thought is being unleashed from Gutenberg constraints of sentence and syntax. The pessimist would argue that television thinking makes impossible the disciplines of comparison, of rumination, of review that gave meaning to print communications.

2.   Television has political consequences not yet fully appreciated. It diverts the trickle-down flow, by which political information passes through a succession of informed elites to ever larger publics. It creates the illusion if not the reality of direct democracy. When the citizen can see the far-off leader or the distant event at his hearthside, he no longer needs to rely on community elders to interpret for him. Instead television has created a new breed of elders—the national storytellers. They constitute a surrogate system for providing the nation's continuity. Even though the day's events are charged with calamity, there is Walter or John or Harry to reassure viewers "that's the way it is."

More needs to be known about the role of these television storytellers. What is their educative potential? Cronkite may tell it the way it is, but he assiduously avoids appearing to instruct on what to do about it. Because he and his colleagues must eschew editorial conclusiveness, the cumulative impact of their stories is that the world is filled with insoluble dilemmas.

The television news story must have a beginning, middle, and end, unlike print news which typically puts its punch in the lead and gradually peters out with ever more trivial detail. Print news appeals to publics who make conscious selections among the fare. Television news is more apt to engage the inadvertent viewer, who is exposed to a series of stories whether or not he is interested in or understands them.

3. Television has enormously complicated the job of the politician in performing his educative role. The increased flow of electronic information bits has not been accompanied by increased opportunity to deal with political complexities. By its emphasis on brevity and movement, television has reinforced the politician's age-old temptation to deal in images rather than issues. This has provoked the recent efforts of such citizenship groups as the League of Women Voters and Common Cause to demand that candidates wage their campaigns on more substantive content.

This is easier said than done. The United States has laws and regulations which tighten the flow of television political discourse during precisely the period when it should flow most freely. Most advanced nations have worked out rule-of-reason formulas for allocating political broadcast time among the leading contenders. In the United States, Section 315 of the Communication Act imposes a rigid requirement of "equal opportunity" which means that major candidates must share free time with fringe candidates or else all be denied. In a perverse way, this law operates to benefit incumbents as well as those broadcasters who prefer not to meet any citizenship obligation.

To those who denounce the politician's use of spot commercials, it should be pointed out that rarely does he get more time to explain his positions in the news and public affairs format. Even when he is interviewed at greater length, it is subjected to the encapsulations of television editing. This can provoke the disillusionment of thoughtful men like Walter Mondale, who remarked, at the time when he withdrew his candidacy from the presidential competition, that he felt incapable of blurting out views on weighty issues in accordance with the dictates of television.

One hopeful development is the recent Federal Communications Commission (FCC) reinterpretation of Section 315 to permit more flexibility for television interview shows and for coverage of full-fledged debates sponsored by nonbroadcast organizations. The League of Women Voters initiated its series of candidate forums in response to this ruling.

4.   The television viewer appears to be making an effort to accommodate himself to the limitations of the medium. According to Mervin Field, the viewer is likely to judge a candidate less on how he deals substantively with issues than on such basic character assessments as "honesty" and "sincerity." There is only scant evidence of how well television communicates these basic virtues. Some advocates argue that it is a relentless exposer of the politician's character, citing as evidence the ultimate downfall of Joseph McCarthy. Yet it should be remembered that despite his publicity skills, McCarthy was a demagogue of an earlier generation. What is difficult to assess is how well television can penetrate a more subtle demagogy which is skilled in projecting an image of candor.

5.   Undoubtedly television has increased the number of information bits reaching the citizen's eye in the course of his day. According to the calculations of *Scientific American,* the eye has the capacity to transmit instantly 10 million bits of information to the brain. Yet the brain, the editors report, has the capacity to assimilate only 27 bits of information per second. These are the raw statistics of communication within the human anatomy. This chapter's attempt to analyze television's educative function must differentiate between the sheer volume of communication flow and the human capacity to sort and make use of information. It may be witnessing a societal phenomenon of information overload. Or perhaps the more apt description is assimilation overload.

Sir John Eccles, the Nobel Prize physiologist, commented that the most important frontier of brain research involves the study of inhibition—the capacity to censor stimuli in order to prevent overload. Sir John made a comparison: "It is like sculpture. What you cut away from the block of stone produces the statue." American journalists, both on television and in print, are committed to the proposition that society thrives by the communication of great gobs of unvarnished truth. Yet it is only dimly understood how, in an all-enveloping informational environment, man chisels his little statues of perceived reality.

6. The phenomenon of memory needs further exploration. In 1971 the Graduate School of Journalism at the University of California in Berkeley conducted an experiment: Viewers in the San Francisco Bay Area were interviewed directly after the network evening news programs. Of those who had watched all or part of a program that evening, 51 percent could not recall, unaided, a single story. The average unaided recall was one story per half-hour newscast. Only 6 viewers out of the 232 sampled recalled any commentary. Soft news—that is, feature stories lacking in dramatic conflict—also rated very poorly.

The Berkeley experiment has not been continued, nor is it known that it has been explored elsewhere. Obviously, certain video images persist longer in the memory than certain print images. There are not even beginning theories about how to make the distinctions, much less to program the medium to compensate for the decline of literal memory.

7. Over the centuries, mankind has painfully acquired at least partial awareness of the capacity to manipulate and mask meanings in print. He is still in his infancy when it comes to critical awareness of electronic deception. Tony Schwartz was producer of the infamous "daisy commercial" which portrayed a small child picking flower petals as countdown to a nuclear explosion. The message was never explicitly stated; the name of candidate Senator Barry Goldwater, against whom this commercial was directed, was not even mentioned. Yet its evocation was so Orwellian that the Democratic sponsors withdrew the commercial after a single showing.

8. Stanford University for several years has carried, via ITV channels to industries in the Bay Area, a curriculum leading to the master's degree in engineering. Rigorous testing has produced the conviction that televised instruction can be comparable to that of the actual classroom. More recently Stanford has provided video tape lectures to industry outside the broadcast range. For certain groups, a tutor was also provided who was encouraged to stop the tape every few minutes and promote discussion to clarify understanding. (The tutor was not a trained educator; simply someone already familiar with the course material.) Test results for these groups showed achievement significantly *above* that of participants of the live classroom instruction, even for group participants who had lacked sufficient grade averages to be qualified for campus enrollment. This would appear to demonstrate an ancient educational lesson which has been neglected too often in the universities: learning cannot be a one-way flow but requires collegiate activity permitting the student to test himself against his peers.

The Stanford experiment should have a special meaning for television as an educational medium. Perhaps television's greatest threat is to turn the citizen into a passive spectator in the ferment of democracy; the challenge to the new technologies should be to make communication an interactive process.

9. It is instructive to review the experience of the Surgeon General's committee which inquired into television and social behavior. After three years and a sizable expenditure on research, the social scientists who served on that committee reached limited conclusions: that there was "tentative and preliminary evidence" of a causal relationship between televised violence and aggressive behavior on the part of *some* children. They were unprepared to estimate whether a large or small number of children were affected.

Subsequent research by Dr. George Gerbner, of the Annenberg School in Philadelphia, indicated that heavy television viewers are more apt to have an exaggerated notion of the crime incidence in their community. Other research demonstrated that prosocial programs such as *Mister Roger's Neighborhood* have had measurable effects on children's behavior in group activities. Behavioral science has only begun to provide meaningful insight into television's effects on society. Surely it is a continuing challenge to the social scientists to carry forward this research and, more specifically, to attempt to determine what factors contribute to public cynicism toward citizenship responsibilities.

10. One condition should be made explicit: Broadcast television as now performed in the United States should not be taken as a constant. Technology and entrepreneurship are pushing hard toward a future with more channels of telecommunications. How these will be harnessed remains to be determined. One strong possibility is that on some channels the consumer will be permitted to pay directly for programs of his choice. This could create a vastly different marketplace of television. At last it may open up vast new opportunities for televised education. (In California, the Consortium of State Colleges and Universities is presently developing a curriculum to be carried statewide on cable. For tuition the enrollee will be able to earn a baccalaureate degree without entering the actual classroom.)

The communications future offers the prospect of greater diversity, new program formats, and even a two-way information flow. Viewed pessimistically, it offers the possibility that television programming may be further sensationalized in the effort to appeal to more fractionated audiences. A specific challenge will be felt by the networks, which presently spend approximately $150 million a year on worldwide news coverage. It should be a matter of intense public concern whether in facing the new competition the networks decide to build on this accomplishment.

The above is a beginning survey of conditions which must be taken into account in developing fresh approaches to the role of television in citizenship education. It suggests that this is indeed a frontier area. Much more needs to be known. There is a need for more experiments and more testing of results.

Televised citizenship education is not likely to be accomplished by fiat of the FCC or even by act of Congress. But society cannot remain content to regard television as an immutable force which must be left to shape its own destiny without regard for social values. A decade hence the uses to which this medium will be put may be quite different. In attempting to chart the future one would do well to establish certain values which, hopefully, can be reinforced by television. Three of these values include:

First, to define more clearly what is meant by the civic virtues to be communicated. No one expects a monolithic approach to patriotism, loyalty, or even citizenship obligation. Rather, the objective should be to stimulate searching discussion about the complex and often contradictory nature of what it means to be a citizen.

Second, to reinforce a sense of history in all communications. So far television has tended to consign viewers to the theater of the immediate. It will require acts of will as well as creative genius to stretch the historical perspective.

A third value which grows out of the second is to develop a sense of stewardship for the future. Henry Steele Commager remarked on the occasion of the Bicentennial that this concept of stewardship is the virtue most notably lacking in the present age, compared to the time during which the Republic was founded.

No one can prescribe a program schedule or even precise guidelines by which television can take on this citizenship challenge. Efforts of a purely propagandistic nature are doomed to failure. But one can strive to stimulate that divine discontent which leads to creativity—in formal education institutions as well as in the media. Ways can be searched out by which new communication technologies and new entrepreneural techniques will call forth creativity. And better ways must be found of recognizing and rewarding creativity when it appears.

Alternative Approaches to Citizenship Education: A Search for Authenticity

FRED M. NEWMANN

We live in a period of profound distrust and disillusionment, where platitudes about the noble purposes of public institutions are often cynically dismissed. The tragedy of specific public policies (Vietnam), general patterns of corruption (Watergate), worldwide problems that seem insoluble (the energy crisis), and apparent failures in the United States educational system (where so much confidence has been placed) all leave a legacy of hypocrisy, fraud, phoniness, failure; to summarize, a general lack of authenticity that understandably elicits suspicion toward talk of the goals of education. What must be done to build authenticity in a citizenship education program?

Education has undertaken many missions. The economic mission, for example, concentrates on the student as a producer and consumer of goods and services; the psychological mission tries to facilitate individual cognitive-affective growth; the cultural mission aims at transmission of broad aspects of the human search for truth, beauty, goodness; and the political mission defines the student's relationship to the political-legal structure. A first step in building criteria for citizenship education programs is to take the word citizenship seriously; that is, to recognize the salience of the political mission and focus attention on it.

The political mission of public education in this society should be to teach students to function in a political-legal structure characterized as representative democracy. An authentic approach to citizenship education should manifest a consistency between the general political mission (in this case, building representative democracy) and the process of education itself. (If the educational process violates the political-legal vision, the learner rightfully will come to distrust both.) As a first step in working toward this consistency, central principles of the political-legal ideal ought to be outlined, then educational criteria derived from these principles should be sought.

Equal liberty and consent of the governed are the two most fundamental principles behind representative democracy. These convey the value judgments that all people equally are entitled to the liberty requisite for human dignity and that this requires, as a minimum, the right of people to govern themselves.

Equal liberty refers to each person's inalienable right to personal determination of life-style, religious beliefs, occupational preferences, political philosophies, aesthetic interests, and so on. To the extent that persons seek to fulfill their individual identity through a group, collective or communal heritages also must be guaranteed equal protection. Because centralized, monolithic state power is likely to deny such liberty to some individuals, limits must be placed on what the state can do even with the consent of the governed. A Bill of Rights generally can limit the state's potential infringement on individual freedoms; a system of "due process of law" can help to guarantee special protections when the individual comes into direct conflict with the state; and a system of checks and balances can try to restrain the internal machinery of state.

The consent principle can be derived from the principle of equal liberty. That is, one way to prevent the state from exercising power in ways that deny equal liberty to some citizens is to guarantee to every citizen an equal voice in choosing leaders or in otherwise influencing the course of public policy. Since in this sense government itself derives its authority from consent of the governed, the rights of every citizen to participate in governance must be guaranteed. As conflict among citizens arises, the consent ideal can be maximized through the principle of majority rule, which in turn is limited by constraints indicated above.

FROM POLITICAL–LEGAL PRINCIPLES TO EDUCATIONAL CRITERIA

The search for educational criteria must be guided not simply by the question, "What should all students be taught?" but by, "How can we teach citizenship for representative democracy in an authentic way?" Six criteria seem to be required. To authenticate the principle of equal liberty, citizenship education programs should give students *choices* among the problems of citizenship they study, and maintain an atmosphere of *intellectual openness*. To authenticate the consent principle, citizenship education programs should focus directly on *problems* faced by students in their role as citizens trying to function with influence in the political-legal system, and place students in *active roles* where they can use their knowledge to participate in the consent process itself, taking responsibility for their actions. Two further criteria are central to the authentication of each principle. Citizenship education programs should include study of the *issues arising out of the two principles* of consent and equal liberty; and encourage significant *local input* from students, parents, and teachers into curriculum content.

Equal Liberty

Student choice. As students explore citizenship, diverse interests and diverse styles in approaching problems will emerge. Interest may generate in substantive problem areas such as environmental policy, racial conflict, and administration of the juvenile justice system. There will be varying tastes for reading, discussion, writing, and venturing into the community. To force a standard body of content and a single learning process on all is not only pedagogically ineffective, but it also violates the spirit of equal liberty.

Often it is assumed that all students should learn the same material. Standard content for all is justified usually on the grounds that the integrity of the subject under study requires it (math or history really cannot be learned if important topics are omitted); that it is administratively unfeasible to have students learning different things (how can a classroom be managed); that diversity confounds the evaluation process (how can students be tested and compared if they are all involved in different learning tasks); or that it threatens social unity (students need a common background for them to communicate with each other and work cooperatively toward common goals).

An equal liberty philosophy, however, finds value in diversity. Differing and competing interests act as antidotes to complacent acceptance of a party line. Conflict emerging out of diverse interests may be healthy. Moreover, each individual should have a right to choose which aspects, if any, of civic life are important enough to pursue.

Intellectual openness. The democratic commitment to openness derives largely from the belief that on many questions, especially on those of public policy, the "correct" answer has not been discovered; and that truths often must be seen as tentative, changing, imperfect, rather than conclusive or absolute. With this sense of indeterminacy it is important for the educational system to teach students to evaluate competing claims for themselves, to think critically, to make independent decisions.

This is not to suggest that there is ignorance on all matters or that no question has a "right" answer. It is possible, of course, to produce overwhelming evidence to show that many claims are rationally far more justifiable than others. Rather than simply manipulating the student to accept these "truths," educators must teach them in a way that respects the student's intellectual autonomy. Educators may proclaim allegiance to critical, independent thinking; but if the student's central task in most lessons is to "figure out what the teacher wants" him or her to say, the intellectual fraud is outrageous. Nor can they defend the manipulation which lets students "discover" a conclusion by examining various pieces of evidence stacked so that only one conclusion is likely to emerge (although beyond the classroom the matter may be contested legitimately). If students can make a reasonable case for alternatives, they should not be penalized for failing to reach the precise conclusions of authorities.

Intellectual openness should not be equated with indecision. The citizen role requires action in the face of uncertainty. While one may not be able to justify his or her actions or preferred policies exhaustively and absolutely, one must ground them in reason and evidence to the extent possible—despite a gnawing suspicion that in the future he or she may be proven wrong.

Consent

The problems of the citizen. As citizens, the individuals in a representative democracy ask themselves what they want the government to do (or stop doing), and how they can influence the government to do it (or stop it). To answer these questions intelligently one needs background on how the political-legal system actually functions, information about the social issues to be resolved, historical precedents, and social philosophy that clarifies alternative positions. The selection of specific content cannot be settled once and for all by any one scholar or central commission, but it can be determined only tentatively and through consultation with educators and lay people in each locale.

School programs concentrate on conveying information (often irrelevant to citizens' problems). But facts alone cannot answer

value questions about what *should* be done, or questions of definition crucial to the citizen's relation to government. (What is meant
by an "unreasonable" search, "national security," or "equal opportunity"?) To study adequately the citizen's role, all three types of
issues (factual, definitional, value) must be dealt with.

Responsible participation. The second criterion suggested by the
consent principle is active participation. Students must have an
opportunity to develop skills of participation, in which knowledge of
social issues can be applied to the advocacy of policies. "Responsible"
participation implies the capacity to justify actions publicly through
rational statements, and a prospect that the student may be affected
personally by the outcomes of action.

Participatory roles for students are not unknown in American
education, but the activities are rarely structured with this definition of responsible participation in mind. They rarely attempt the
central task suggested by the consent principle: to help students
exert influence in public affairs.[1] A commitment to meeting graduation requirements, possible liability for personal injury to students
outside of school, and a reluctance of the school to endorse student
involvement in political controversy—all these stand in the way of
the kinds of student participation the consent principle requires.

Criteria for Both Equal Liberty and Consent

Content on equal liberty and consent. Having emphasized
equal liberty and consent so strongly, certainly it must be recommended that students study the principles themselves. Cases of
potential conflict between the principles should be aired: for example, cases when in the name of majority rule a group discriminates
against a minority, or cases when in the name of liberty an individual refuses to abide by duly established rules. There are, of course, a
number of ways in which the principles may be studied—histori-
cally, philosophically, sociologically, and through the lens of constitutional law. The effects of the economic system and technological
development are also crucial.

Local input into curriculum. Public education must reflect the
idiosyncracies of the local communities that support it. This
requires citizen involvement in the *development* of the educational
program, not simply in the choice of products developed elsewhere.

But the consent and equal liberty principles do not compel acceptance of all policies favored by a local community, for the principles themselves are universal and contain limitations on what citizens can do to each other through the consent process. Since every person is entitled to the rights implied by these principles, communities cannot decide, for example, to abolish representative government or to deny individuals due process of law. If a local community decided, for example, to deny students the right to study the meaning and justification of these principles, or to deny them the right to learn skills to participate in the consent process, or to deny them the opportunity to disagree with the teacher about public issues studied in the classroom, it would be using practices which violate the principles of equal liberty and consent as applied to education. The community's right to local input into the curriculum is important, but it is derived from the more general principle that all persons are entitled to these rights. The community, therefore, may not govern itself in a way that takes these rights away from its own members.

CURRENT APPROACHES TO CITIZENSHIP EDUCATION

The educational criteria, having been derived from central principles of the democratic enterprise, can serve as indices of authenticity, or of the extent to which educational practice is consistent with professed political ideals. Programs of citizenship education thus should be judged with reference to the criteria. Currently eight general approaches are found: the academic disciplines of history and the social sciences, law-related education, social problems, critical thinking, values clarification, moral development, community involvement, and institutional school reform. Instructional programs or curriculum projects may manifest more than one of the general approaches; so in practice they are not mutually exclusive. Still, within any given curriculum it is usually possible to identify one or a few of these themes as more salient than others.

Academic disciplines (history and the social sciences). This approach tries to teach facts, concepts, and generalizations about social phenomena (past and present and across cultures) as such knowledge has been generated through scholarship in the academic disciplines, especially history and the social sciences. In the last fifteen years special attempts have been made to teach not only the findings of these disciplines, but also the methods of inquiry employed by the practicing scholar. Rather than focusing on specific problems that the citizen might face, the approach assumes that mastery of developed scholarly systems will help the citizen understand unforeseeable, particular problems in civic matters as they arise.

Often, the teaching of the disciplines is not advocated on grounds of direct relevance to the exercise of active citizenship. Instead, it has been argued that disciplined scholarship reveals the best thinking educators have to offer in the human search for truth. In spite of a plethora of proposals to relax the dominance of history and social science in citizenship education, these disciplines remain the staple, prevailing approach in secondary curricula and in the preparation of teachers.[2]

Law-related education. The earliest forms of law-related education emphasized the Constitution, the Bill of Rights, the structure of federal, state, and local government—often in a ninth-grade civics course or a later course in American government. More recently a major national effort, supported by such groups as the American Bar Association and the Constitutional Rights Foundation, has tried to revitalize and expand the teaching of fundamentals of legal process.[3] The movement offers diverse projects on legal concepts—particular controversies arising out of the Bill of Rights, the system of juvenile justice, techniques of legislative lobbying, judicial reasoning in case law, laws that apply particularly to youth, problems of law enforcement agencies, and other topics. The projects produce curriculum that can be inserted into existing courses as well as materials that stand on their own as separate courses in legal process. Projects vary in depth, detail, self-sufficiency, and the extent to which they encourage students to adopt a critical posture or one of unquestioning obedience and respect. In contrast to the disciplines approach, the goal of law-related education could be characterized not as a search for truth and understanding but as an effort to preserve and make more just the role of law in a democratic society.

Social problems. This approach concentrates on particular social issues of current or predicted importance in the students' lives, such as war, crime, discrimination, poverty, pollution, drugs, and energy. Knowledge from the disciplines and about legal process may be used to clarify such problems, but the problem (not the discipline or the legal material) is the focus of study. The assumption here is that to deliberate adequately on social problems, the citizen needs practice in grappling with the specifics of actual social issues. (How should consumers be protected? What alternatives to welfare are available? What are the effects of racial busing?) This approach has been adopted in "Problems of Democracy" courses, and more recently in separate, discrete courses on problems like those just mentioned.[4]

Critical thinking. Like democracy and motherhood, critical thinking in citizenship education is endorsed by almost everyone. The critical citizen is portrayed as someone who cannot be deceived or manipulated by leaders and the media, but who reaches autonomous conclusions and can rationally justify them to others. He is aware of basic assumptions in his own position, the possibility of bias or selective perception, and incompleteness of information. To arrive at this point, the citizen needs to learn a thinking process that helps distinguish among different types of issues, a process that offers a method for testing and evaluating empirical claims, logical inferences, definitional statements, value judgments, and so on.[5]

Separate courses on critical thinking are rare; the requisite skills, if taught at all, are taught usually in connection with a particular subject such as history, economics, or social problems. The teaching of inquiry skills in the social sciences often is equated with critical thinking, but some scholars have suggested that the specific intellectual operations required for critical thinking about citizenship differ in important ways from those of other kinds of critical thinking.[6] In this sense the critical thinking approach has as much potential for diversity as any of the approaches reviewed thus far.

Values clarification. To the extent that civic problems result from confusion over values, educators might relieve personal and social stress by helping individuals clarify their own ultimate values. The goal of values clarification is to help people to become "purposeful, enthusiastic, and positive," and to direct their lives autonomously through a process of deliberate "choosing, prizing, and acting."[7] Students try to discover what they value by making their own decisions in various dilemmas and trying to determine whether their decisions were actually freely arrived at, with due consideration of alternatives. They try to determine whether they prize their decision, would proclaim it publicly, and would act on it consistently. Values clarification exercises may be added to existing courses or taught in special courses on values. The issues called up for scrutiny in this approach can include, but need not concentrate upon, problems of public policy.

Moral development. Kohlberg and associates see moral development not as preaching but as progress along a naturally occurring psychological path, which leads from the lower "preconventional" to "conventional" to the higher "principled" forms of moral reasoning. It is alleged, for example, that the principles enunciated in the Declaration of Independence, the Constitution, and the Bill of Rights, can be understood only by people who have attained higher stages in cognitive development. Kohlberg argues that the higher, principled types of reasoning are ethically and epistemologically better than the lower stages. The higher stages signify a concern for social contract, equal liberty, and more generally the principles of justice that a democracy presumably aspires to attain.[8]

In this approach students are presented with moral dilemmas (such as a man trying to decide whether to steal an overpriced drug to save his dying wife), and are asked to reason with each other about the morally right solution (see Chapter 7). According to the theory, students will discover inadequacies in their reasoning as they confront persons who reason at higher stages. The desire to resolve conflicts and move toward a consistent position will lead to adoption of more sophisticated reasoning patterns. In contrast to values clarification (suggesting a relativistic, nonjudgmental philosophy in which all student responses are supported by the teacher), moral development recognizes certain types of reasoning as universally better than others and seeks to advance students from the lower to the higher levels.

Community involvement. All six approaches above call for instruction in the school and a style of learning based largely on abstract analysis and verbal communication. Concerned that such curricula tend to isolate students from experience in the "real world," advocates of community involvement try to move students into the nonschool community in order to observe social process as it occurs, to make surveys on community needs and problems, to render volunteer service to social agencies, to create new youth-operated programs, to participate in electoral politics and community organization, and to participate in other forms of direct citizen action. Involvement and participation are emphasized not as substitutes for study and reflection, but as insurance that study and reflection will be directed toward social realities and participation skills.

Community involvement curricula can reflect different ideologies. Volunteer service in social agencies could be promoted, for example, as an attempt to build altruistic behavior, as a way to give students a sense of worth and to enhance self-esteem, as a technique for raising student consciousness about contradictions and injustice in society, or as a method of pacifying and co-opting youth rebellion. All the ideologies have in common a belief in "learning by doing," "experiential learning," or dealing with concrete "here and now" realities.[9]

Institutional school reform. The structure and general quality of life in school may have more impact on citizenship education than does the official curriculum or course content. Critics who agree that the "hidden curriculum" is educationally dysfunctional may differ as to the appropriate direction for institutional reform. Liberal critics claim that one cannot teach democracy in an authoritarian institution and that the school should, therefore, be reformed to give students full rights of citizenship. This would include a meaningful role (not necessarily unilateral power) in the governance of the institution, and the right to all the constitutional protections afforded adult citizens. In exercising responsibility for their own education and resolving inevitable conflicts in governing a public institution, students would learn better how to function responsibly in the society.[10]

Conservative critics, on the other hand, claim that formal education implies an authoritarian structure. Students are required to attend school precisely because they are judged incompetent to perform the role of responsible adult citizens. One should not mislead students into believing they have full rights of citizenship, but should teach them to obey and to respect the authority that legitimately governs them until they gain their citizenship rights (by either earning a diploma or reaching the age at which the society judges them "mature" enough to participate). While some conservatives might endorse expansion of students' rights to due process in disciplinary matters, they would be unlikely to relinquish authority to students for governing the school or for prescribing educational practice.

Six criteria have been suggested and eight current approaches have been reviewed; now each approach (or any given program) should be assessed to determine the extent to which it meets the criteria. In rating each approach against each criterion it was found that no approach met more than three criteria (only community involvement met as many as three), and four of the eight approaches seemed to meet none of the criteria. These are subjective, unreplicated judgments. Nevertheless such criteria may help call attention to a major source of failure of civic education in this country: that regardless of the particular curriculum approaches currently advocated, the central principles behind representative democracy find virtually no support in school-based programs.

That conclusion leads to more fundamental questions. Should it be assumed that youth need citizenship education more than adults do? Perhaps certain groups of adults (such as those in their first full-time job, those who are neither employed nor in school, or those who hold public office) need citizenship education more than youth as a group does. It also should be asked whether citizenship education should be seen primarily as a task for the public schools. One could imagine, for example, a society in which this function is performed by publicly sponsored mass media, by a program of compulsory national service, or by publicly subsidized private organizations such as clubs, businesses, or unions. Studies on the relative ineffectiveness of schooling,[11] on age segregation,[12] and of more general social commentary on the nature of community,[13] should lead us to a much broader conception of citizenship education for representative democracy.

NOTES

1. In this chapter "public affairs" is defined broadly to include virtually any attempt by a citizen to influence what happens in a public institution. Recognizing legitimate reasons for low levels of citizen participation on most publicized issues, the proposed approach aims not at converting all to full-time militant activists, but at helping average citizens to become more effective when they choose to participate. See Fred M. Newmann, *Education for Citizen Action: Challenge for Secondary Curriculum,* McCutchan Publishing Corporation, Berkeley, Calif., 1975, and F. M. Newmann, Thomas A. Bertocci, and Ruthanne M. Landsness, *Skills in Citizen Action: An English-Social Studies Program for Second-*

ary Schools, Citizen Participation Curriculum Project, Madison, Wis., 1977.

Chapter 8 of this book offers a detailed definition of and justification for the ability to exert influence in public affairs as the major goal of citizenship education.

2. The case for discipline-oriented citizenship education is made by Morris Lewenstein, *Teaching Social Studies,* Rand McNally & Company, Chicago, 1963, and Joseph Schwab, "Structure of the Disciplines: Meaning and Significances," in G. W. Ford and Lawrence Pugno (eds.), *The Structure of Knowledge and Curriculum,* Rand McNally & Company, Chicago, 1964.

For a conception of liberal education (the basis of the rationale), see Harvard Committee, *General Education in a Free Society,* Oxford University Press, London, 1946, and Paul H. Hirst, "Liberal Education and the Nature of Knowledge," in R. Archambault (ed.), *Philosophical Analysis and Education,* Humanities Press, New York, 1965.

3. For information, contact Committee on Youth Education for Citizenship, American Bar Association, 1155 East 60th Street, Chicago, Ill. 60637, and the Constitutional Rights Foundation, 6310 San Vicente Boulevard, Los Angeles, Calif. 90048. Both organizations can supply annotated summaries and addresses of major citizenship education projects throughout the country.

4. Often the case for social problems is made in conjunction with a framework for critical thinking, as in Maurice P. Hunt and Lawrence Metcalf, *Teaching High School Social Studies,* Harper & Row Publishers, Incorporated, New York, 1968, and Donald W. Oliver and James P. Shaver, *Teaching Public Issues in the High School,* Utah State University Press, Logan, 1974.

5. For conceptions of critical thinking for citizenship, see Jean Fair and Fannie R. Shaftel (eds.), *Effective Thinking in the Social Studies,* National Council for the Social Studies, Washington, D.C., 1967; Hunt and Metcalf, op. cit.; Oliver and Shaver, op. cit; and Richard C. Phillips, *Teaching for Thinking in High School Social Studies,* Addison-Wesley Publishing Company, Inc., Reading, Mass., 1974.

6. For illustrative typologies of various thinking skills, see Harold Berlak, "The Teaching of Thinking," *School Review,* vol. 73, no. 1, Spring 1965; James S. Coleman, "Policy Research in the Social Sciences," General Learning Corp., Morristown, N.J., 1972; Oliver and Shaver, op. cit.; and Newmann, op. cit.

7. Louis E. Raths, Merrill Harmin, and Sidney B. Simon, *Values and Teaching: Working with Values in the Classroom,* Charles E. Merrill Books, Inc., Columbus, Ohio, 1966, and S. B. Simon, Leland W. Howe,

and Howard Kirschenbaum, *Values Clarification: A Handbook of Practical Strategies for Teachers and Students,* Hart Publishing Company, New York, 1972.

8. Lawrence Kohlberg, *Collected Papers on Moral Development and Moral Education,* vols. 1 and 2, Center for Moral Education, Cambridge, Mass., 1973.

    For summary presentations, see L. Kohlberg, "Moral Education for a Society in Transition," *Educational Leadership,* vol. 33, no. 1, October 1975, and Chap. 7 of this book.

9. The National Commission on Resources for Youth (36 West 44th Street, New York, N.Y. 10036) is a national clearinghouse for youth participation and community involvement projects. Their book, *New Roles for Youth in the School and the Community,* Citation Press, New York, 1974, offers illustrations of different projects.

    In Newmann, op. cit., App. A contains a list of organizations supporting community involvement curriculum. See also F. M. Newmann and D. W. Oliver, "Education and Community," *Harvard Educational Review,* vol. 37, no. 1, 1967.

10. John Dewey, *Democracy and Education,* The MacMillan Company, New York, 1916. For a recent interpretation, see Michael Apple, "Toward Increasing the Potency of Student Rights Claims," in Vernon F. Haubrich and M. Apple (eds.), *Schooling and the Rights of Children,* McCutchan Publishing Corporation, Berkeley, Calif., 1975.

11. J. S. Coleman et al., *Equality of Educational Opportunity,* Superintendent of Documents, U.S. Government Printing Office, Washington, D.C., 1966, and Christopher Jencks et al., *Inequality: A Reassessment of the Effect of Family and Schooling in America,* Basic Books, Inc., Publishers, New York, 1972.

12. Panel on Youth, Report of the President's Science Advisory Committee, *Youth: Transition to Adulthood,* University of Chicago Press, Chicago, 1974.

13. D. W. Oliver, *Education and Community: A Radical Critique of Innovative Schooling,* McCutchan Publishing Corporation, Berkeley, Calif., 1976.

The Crisis of Global Transformation, Interdependence, and the Schools

12

SAUL H. MENDLOVITZ, LAWRENCE METCALF, AND
MICHAEL WASHBURN

All civic education at this juncture in human history should be set
in a global perspective; and this global perspective must be informed
by just world order values.[1] Furthermore, it is essential to understanding, prediction, and control of a global society based on popu-
list and humane values that people be made aware of the great
social transformation which is taking place in this last quarter of
the twentieth century.

I

One of the signs that the world system is being transformed is the
recent and rapid emergence of a new rhetoric for the discussion of
world affairs. Perhaps the most prominent and captivating new
word is "interdependence," which shows signs of becoming for this
quarter of the twentieth century what "containment of communism"
was for the previous quarter.

It is an inadequate and potentially dangerous word with which to
express a new foreign policy consensus or to inform the study of
world affairs in the schools. It masks a number of fundamental
value issues, blurs important strategic distinctions, and narrows the
range of acceptable policy alternatives.

"Interdependence" does describe contemporary reality better and
more pointedly than other concepts. It does focus attention on a set
of critical world issues, primarily economic ones. Furthermore, the
immediate connotations of the word "interdependence," evoking the
notions of community and mutual assistance, are positive. It taps
the deep yearnings for global community that have been stifled by
the cold war while suggesting an approach to the world that would

189

restore America's self-image and sense of humanitarian mission. In short, interdependence seems to lead to a policy which would positively and creatively resolve much of the strain, fear, and discord associated with the breakdown of the cold war consensus and the rise of the limits to the growth/scarcity spectre.

Massachusetts Institute of Technology Professor Lincoln Bloomfield summarized the reasons for the generally favorable United States view of interdependence in a special study for the State Department:

> Interdependence as a deliberate strategy rests on conceptual foundations with deep roots in Western liberal political-economic philosophy—notably the assumption that world peace would result from an international division of labor based on comparative advantage and a free exchange of goods and services, all presumably reflecting a harmony of pooled, shared interests. . . .
>
> More than a few liberal internationalist-minded Westerners regard interdependence as a desirable halfway house between the narrow and eventually unsuccessful unilateral route and the never-never land of supranational integration. They view it as both an inevitable consequence of technology-driven economics and as a good move toward greater international unity through accelerated functional cooperation.[2]

An Unsentimental Look at Interdependence

Interdependence means that in the last few decades the nations of the world have extended and increased their interrelationships to such an extent that the web of mutual dependencies is for the first time global in scope and of paramount importance for most societies.

While this perception of world reality by Americans in particular may account largely for the growing popularity of the interdependence concept, the fact is that interdependence is really not a new fact of international life. Some scholars, like Berkeley's Kenneth Waltz, have even argued that the economy of Europe and its colonies in the late nineteenth century was even more interdependent than the world economy of today.

The sudden popularity of the rhetoric of interdependence can be explained best by a change in the circumstances of one nation, the United States. The new fact is not the interdependence of nations but the growing *dependence of the United States economy*—on the importing of key natural resources and labor-intensive manufactured goods, and on the production of goods for export to pay for

U.S. NONFUEL RESOURCE DEPENDENCE			
Percentage Currently Imported (estimates vary)	Potentially Self-sufficient	Potentially Partially Dependent	Potentially Completely Dependent
95–100	Manganese	Chromium Cobalt	Asbestos Industrial diamonds Quartz Platinum
84–96	Bauxite		
75–85		Mercury Nickel	Tin
50–55		Tungsten Zinc	
25–30	Iron ore		
20–25			Lead
10–20	Copper		

SOURCE: Department of State Special Report, no. 17, July 1975.

them. The United States is highly dependent on foreign sources for twenty-two of the seventy-four nonenergy minerals necessary for the operation of advanced industry (see the accompanying table). The United States is the major supplier of internationally traded food, and nearly 30 percent of its cropland is devoted to production for export markets (in 1971–1974, 67 percent of the wheat crop was exported and 59.5 percent of the rice crop). And since 1950, while domestic corporate earnings have risen about 50 percent, foreign earnings through direct investment abroad grew more than 450 percent.

The potential costs of global economic instability for the economy of the United States are mounting steadily. At the same time the world economy, and particularly the economy of the advanced industrial nations, has become increasingly complex and sensitive to foreign and domestic policies of individual governments. This in turn has increased the need for consultation and coordination on economic policy among nations. The reality of interdependence is thus spreading rapidly from commercial innovation and expansion to the realm of governmental concern and institutional development.

For the purposes of this brief discussion of what is obviously a complicated matter, there are four basic problems with interdependence as a guiding imagery for understanding the contemporary global, social, and political system.

First, interdependence advocates do not fully comprehend the nature and extent of the global transformation now taking place. Furthermore, they discount the possibility of global catastrophe of both the nuclear and the ecological kind and underestimate the need for planned, fundamental changes in the present world order. Put differently, they overestimate the efficacy of making marginal adjustments to tensions emerging in international political and economic relations.

Second, the positive internationalist view of interdependence tends to assume that most interdependent relations involve mutual or symmetrical dependencies, when in fact many involve relationships in which one side is far more vulnerable than the other (this is particularly true of Third World nations vis-à-vis the developed countries).

Third, interdependence enthusiasts tend to underestimate the difficulty of creating the machinery and institutions needed to manage the complexities and fragilities of interdependence in a world of states among which power, resources, and dependence are so unequally distributed.

Fourth, the liberal view tends to underestimate the extent to which the rhetoric of interdependence could be used by more conservative political forms to mask or justify a strategy of enhancing the power and wealth of the United States and other advanced economies while constructing an increasingly oligarchic and repressive world system.

Interdependence is not the equivalent of peace and justice. In fact, it may lead to peace and justice no more than nuclear deterrence has led to disarmament. The limitations and dangers of employing interdependence as the organizing concept for thinking about the global human system are seen best in the light of a broader look at the changes taking place in the present world order system. To do this, an approach called World Order Studies[3] will be employed. (For a technical definition of world order and a schema for a relatively rigorous statement on transition to a preferred world, see the appendix to this chapter.)

The Challenge of System Transformation

World order thinking starts from a recognition that the present global challenge is fundamental and systemic, that the obstacles to implementing an adequate response are nearly overwhelming, and that time is the scarcest and most precious resource. This alternative to the liberal interdependence approach is summarized in the following paragraphs.

These are the essential features and dynamics of the present world system:

1. In the present global political system the nation-state is, far and away, the dominant actor, controlling nearly all the military power.

2. There is a wide range of domestic governance systems among the state actors and there are patterns of cooperation and conflict among them on matters of ideology, economics, and political power.

3. There is a great inequality among state actors and these inequalities have become formalized over time into a relatively rigid pattern of relationships among them, which places a few in positions of dominance and many in positions of dependence.

4. The domestic and global economic systems are directed toward growth and driven primarily through competition. The economic sphere is dominated by very large private and state-controlled enterprises, the largest and most essential of which operate transnationally.

5. The dominant form of productive system is one which employs sophisticated technology and requires high energy and resource inputs.

The changes that have been taking place in the world system since 1945 have not been simple evolutions in each of these dimensions. Rather, they have been of such magnitude and speed that they add up to a qualitative or basic structural change in the system itself. The central logic of each component of the world system and the nature of the interrelationships are such that within-the-system responses to problems are very likely to make them worse. Each of these key system components—the political, economic, and cultural institutions and assumptions—is being pushed to its limits.

It is very difficult at this juncture to predict the exact nature and extent of the system mutation that is taking place. Among world order thinkers there are at least three views. First is that the world is passing through a period of time in which imperialism and colonialism are being dismantled. A new phase in the life of the nation-state is emerging and the result will be a less hierarchical and more equitable distribution of wealth and power among the 150-200 nation-states which will make up the global system by the end of the century. According to this view, the changes are taking place essentially in the distribution of economic and political power. This view is held by many Third World participants in world order thinking.[4]

A second group argues that the transformation which is taking place is in fact a disintegration of the nation-state system. This group suggests that the changes are as profound as those which occurred when the contemporary state system first emerged out of the feudal society of Western Europe in the sixteenth and seventeenth centuries. To the transformation of economic and political structures seen by the first group, this group adds basic changes in the resource base, the productive system, and the dominant system of values. This is the view held by scholars in the United States, Western Europe, and Japan (all areas where ecological thinking has gained a foothold).

Finally, there is a relatively small third group which believes that human society is moving away from a system of separate agroindustrial units. The trend is toward a more coherent, if not cohesive, global society. The trend that dominates and shapes the whole change process, according to this view, is the changing cultural/value system. Thus the long-term trend is toward a planetary civilization.

All these groups agree that transformation from the old system to the envisioned new one is not inevitable, easy, or without conflict. In fact, they are pessimistic about the chances for a violence- and catastrophe-free transition process. To understand why requires a sharp look at the imperatives of the state system, each of which leads away from the kinds of solutions most likely to effect a peaceful and more just system. These imperatives of the state system include:

1. *Competition.* It is generally assumed that the fulfillment of national destiny is ultimately dependent upon the frustration of the goals of rival governments, and it is assumed that rival governments are never completely trustworthy.

2. *Domestic Interests.* Major internal interests dominate state goals and the policy-making process. The values of external empathy are weak and generally inoperative.

3. *Growth.* Maximum attainable rates of economic growth are a nearly universal first-order priority. Assessment of government performance by key elites and the public is closely related to the provision of material goods for its citizenry.

4. *Short-term Goals.* Governments seek to satisfy immediate desires with little or no regard to the longer-range consequences.

5. *Self-help.* There is little deference to world community values and little reliance on, or faith in, world community procedures and institutions.

Some small, but hopeful, cracks have appeared in recent years in these iron imperatives of the state system. They are the basis for developing a positive model of a desirable world order.

A "Strategy of Hope" must recognize first and foremost the necessity of fundamental change away from the nation-state system. A world order perspective implies the futility of working only with events, moving from public issue to public issue. It also implies the futility of putting all one's efforts into electing new leadership. The real tasks are much harder. They involve transforming the liberal vision and perceptual apparatus on a broad basis among leadership people, young people, and the general public, converting the new consciousness and the new visions into an effective transnational movement for system change.

II

Social integration is a useful conceptual tool for those who would understand a social crisis. Social integration is primarily a matter of cultural unity. The various components of the culture mesh as a meaningful whole. Actually no society is completely integrated, but integration can be said to exist in a significant sense when there is substantial agreement upon basic social postulates. These postulates are of two kinds, the intellectual and the moral. Intellectual postulates tell individuals how to structure and interpret social reality. Gunnar Myrdal has called these the *beliefs* of people. They are propositional as to logical form and are subject to empirical testing. When one asserts what reality is, or has been, one is engaged in the expression of *belief.* Moral postulates are evaluational in nature. They assert what one prefers as social reality, past or present. They tell what kind of social change, in what direction, would be desirable. These are expressions of *value.*

In an integrated culture there is considerable agreement as to the basic ends and means of living. Community consists of the shared *beliefs* and *values* of people. There is a great consensus—even if unspoken—as to what reality is like, and what the good life is. Schools, acting as a dependent variable, take their purposes and programs from the surrounding culture. Schools have no choices to make when moral postulates are clear. Indoctrination, as instruction in morals, is not at issue. The good man and the good society are tacitly or explicitly acknowledged in everything that the school does. Only when a culture begins to fall apart do educators come together (as they do frequently today) in order to discuss the great questions of education, social change, and cultural decay.

In a situation of cultural disintegration, adults no longer have a clear perception of either truth or morality. The outlines of the existing social order are no longer clear to many of the people. Even greater doubt surrounds all value questions—including the question of the kind of social order which would be preferable, given the many alternative social forms evidently available. When this kind of social confusion exists, not only the school is adrift. The very language of the people begins to fall apart. Loss of communication and failures in communication occur regularly, and semantics becomes a serious intellectual discipline. Not only are basic beliefs and values placed in question, but also under scrutiny is the methodology by which questions of truth and morality are solved.

There will be a general retreat from the use of reason as a tool of social analysis and persuasion. There will be frequent references to intuition and mystic experience as sources of personal and social insight. Movements in religious revivalism will not be confined merely to those who want to restore and preserve the contours of a bygone social order. Those who define truth as that which corresponds with experiment and testing will be placed in conflict with those who view truth as that which corresponds with inner feelings. Feeling and thought will be at war within people, as well as between them, and rationality will be blamed for most social difficulties. Personal disorganization and the disaffection of intellectuals will be visible plainly to all, and many will feel they live in a community of the insane.[5]

Social disintegration has been defined by William O. Stanley as an imbalance or maladjustment among life conditions, institutions, and basic moral and intellectual norms.[6] The forces released by the industrial-scientific revolution have destroyed the balance that once existed among conditions, institutions, and norms. It is this lack of adjustment that William Fielding Ogburn once labeled "cultural lag." The international realm demonstrates one of the more striking instances of maladjustment. The nation-state exists as an inherited institution; political independence and territorial security continue as cherished norms. But life conditions today include highly destructive weaponry with delivery systems that flash easily across national boundaries, and against which no defense is adequate. The capacity of the nation-state to provide for national defense and security has been cast in doubt. Widespread public confusion can develop as people begin to sense that the nation-state is less powerful and less sovereign than the needs of national survival demand. Yet, the same public may doubt the wisdom and attainability of a world government capable of controlling threats to human safety and welfare.[7]

There will be strong temptation to attempt to restore the old order. The impotency of the nation-state will be attributed to subversive or internationalizing tendencies and influences. In place of efforts to build a new order characterized by a better balance and adjustment among life conditions, institutions, and norms, one is likely to witness an attempt to apply old solutions to new problems. It may be granted that the bombings at Hiroshima and Nagasaki marked a fundamental change in the nature of international relations, but this will not deter people from trying (with the assistance of politically repressive measures) to solve their problems through application of *prenuclear* beliefs and values. And the more recent pollution crisis has not forced many people to relinquish their *preecological* assumptions.[8]

Clearly, domestic solutions have international consequences. It is equally clear that a generalized intellectual and moral order would color the solutions to problems of economic, social, and international order. What is not so obvious is the central importance to be given to construction of a new international order. Stanley himself did not place international order at the center of things when he first analyzed the crisis almost twenty years ago. More recently, he has acknowledged the absolute importance of addressing the thoughts of leading educators to the problem of world government. An intellectual and moral order that has little or no application to this problem would leave humanity poised at the brink of disaster. In commenting upon this aspect of the crisis, he said

Peace between nations, as between men, depends upon law and order, and law and order, on a world scale, means an effective world government. The basic issue then is how can we establish a world government with the authority and the power to settle international disputes even when such disputes involve the vital interests of the great powers? The capacity to achieve such a world government by mutual consent is an essential condition of the preservation of civilized society, if not human life itself, on this earth. Yet, all I can hear on this most fundamental of issues is a monumental silence.[9]

III

Schools as an Instrument of Social Transformation

What kind of education is to be preferred, as part of the means of moving toward a better system of international relations evolving into a humane global society?

It is proposed that the school become an institution devoted in its social studies to the creation of a climate favorable to drastic change in the international system, and that it create this climate by opening up the classroom to the study of "radical" proposals for changing the character of the existing international system.[10]

The traditionally objective study of war that is limited largely to a careful conceptualization of war as a social institution, followed by a scholarly treatment of the causes and effects of war, is not proposed. It is proposed that war be studied in these objective terms, but that teachers also apply their canons of objectivity to the problem of war prevention. The task of teachers of world order is to help students assess the capacity of existing and alternative international systems to reduce drastically the occurrence of war. With equal objectivity, assessment should be made of alternative systems and institutions for their capacity to solve the other world order crises of global poverty, loss of human rights, and environmental deterioration. This emphasis on drastic change or system transformation is one primary feature of world order studies.

A second feature would be exploration of the interrelatedness of all the world order problems and values. To what extent is war prevention necessary to achievement of ecological balance in the world? Can worldwide economic development take place without a side effect of overwhelming pollution? How many people can the earth support at what standard of living? These are only three of the questions that can be raised in regard to the large matter of interrelatedness.

A third feature of world order studies would be the use of models. Models help teachers and their students to make sense of their data. They will be wise not to accept any model unquestioningly as a picture of international reality. Instead they should try to locate the main features of the model, its basic concepts and principles. Assumptions about humanity and society should be made explicit and examined. One can turn then to other questions of fact and value. Which model comes closest to a description of some existing or emerging system? To a student's preferred system?

For each proposed system change, three questions have to be raised. Is the change necessary? Is it fair to everyone involved or affected by the change? And, finally, is the change possible? The feasibility question is fundamental; it forces one to distinguish between practical and impractical utopias (to borrow a concept from Paul Goodman).

A fourth feature of world order studies is a focus upon long-term planning and policy. What kind of world order would one like to see come into being by the year 2000? Those who teach or study world order must examine present-day short-range policies in order to determine if they point in the right direction. A policy that seems right from a short-run perspective may be the worst possible policy in the longer view of things. If present policies look unpromising for achievement of some preferred form of world order, inquiry would then turn toward a search for alternative policies and strategies of fundamental change.

The Liberal School

It is not unusual for a liberal teacher or school to study the international system from a reformist or gradualist point of view. This kind of study does not usually nurture a climate favorable to the study of proposals for far-reaching system transformation. In fact, it may do the very opposite by supporting the idea that the existing system is fundamentally sound, and that all that is necessary is to reform, slightly modify, or patch up that system. In addition, many liberals perceive system change as a notion too utopian to qualify as a hypothesis deserving serious study.

A possible example of this kind of thinking from the history of domestic politics in the United States is Franklin D. Roosevelt's New Deal. Many historians are saying now that these policies did not transform the United States economic system. Rather, they "saved" capitalism from the "threat" of alternative systems and provided patchwork ameliorations of the problems of unemployment and poverty, while ignoring almost entirely the deep-rooted racist features of the then existing system.[11] Yet, Roosevelt was viewed by many of his conservative critics as a "communist" bent upon destruction of the capitalistic system.

Many a liberal teacher defended Roosevelt against his conservative critics by identifying their inconsistencies and ignorance. This is good education to the extent that facts and logic are straightened out. (And it is important to nurture the fullest possible participation of conservatives who will spotlight inconsistencies in liberal teachers.) But this is bad education to the extent that it shuts out from consideration the many significant social alternatives which involved drastic system change. Did the problems of Roosevelt's day require drastic system change as a solution? How well did New Deal modifications of the American economy solve the problems of unemployment, poverty, economic instability, and racist discrimination? Were more drastic solutions possible at the time?

These are among the questions to be raised by social studies teachers within a school committed to creation of a climate favorable to the study of radical ideas. Thus, it is argued that a school which aims for a climate favorable to the study of radical or utopian solutions is more liberal than most liberal schools, provided that this more radical approach retains the liberal faith in reason and persuasion as ways of social change.

The School as Source of Social Action

Some people would have the school act as a *source* of radical change, training cadres for political action. Students would move into the community as protestors and demonstrators, and would do so under school sponsorship. In recent years, the protest activities of college students have been treated by most authorities as being disruptive of the educational process. But this third view of the school and its social role would include these activities as a piece of the curriculum. Not only would students engage in political activity, but they would learn through research how to assess the political effectiveness of various forms of protest.

Radicals who press for this kind of social role often argue that the socially neutral educational institution is a myth, that schools have to take sides, and that because of this they should take the correct rather than a wrong side. Spokespersons for this movement say that no university can be neutral. It is said that most universities are sexist and racist in their policies, support antiunion sentiments and organizations, and train young people to serve corporate and military interests. Such spokespersons regard training young people to take effective political action in the name of social justice as no more inconsistent with the "principle" of political neutrality than most of what already is being done.

It would be hard to deny that educational institutions have played a political role, and that their political stance has favored the status quo. The radical who claims that schools and colleges have never been politically neutral on important issues is more right than wrong. There appears to be something hypocritical about a university which votes its stock holdings on the side of corporate management rather than for ecological balance, and then uses political or social neutrality as an excuse for "not taking sides" whenever radicals ask it to be socially bold and daring.

Perhaps a few universities could achieve enough independence to choose to disseminate and act upon radical but unpopular ideas. But it is doubtful that public schools have this independence or will ever have it. Even more doubtful is the ethical right of any public school to achieve and exercise such independence. While this ethical question is not likely to arise in an integrated culture, it can hardly be avoided in a society in crisis. Those who advocate a social role for the school which makes it a source of radical change are overlooking an important feature of the social crisis. The crisis means many publics rather than one. Ethically speaking, the school is placed in a dilemma. As a public school, it is meant to be controlled by the public it serves; but it is clear that there is no single public. The so-called public consists of a large number of organized interest groups, each of which has its conception of the "public" good.

The School as a Dependent Variable or as a Brake on Social Change

In addition to liberal and radical activist alternatives to the kind of school proposed, there are those who would have the school play a more conservative role. Conservatives are of two kinds—those who see the school in the role of a dependent variable in society, and those who prefer that the school act as a drag on social change.

The first version (the school as a dependent variable) assumes that schools necessarily reflect established institutions. This descriptive assumption also may function prescriptively. Schools not only reflect established ways; but also, it is desirable that they do so. The school is said to exist *in order to* pass on the cultural heritage, to prepare students for defined and expected roles. Education does not lead or oppose social change. If society changes, schools will change. Teachers have no choice but to do what society expects of them.

This position seems to be saying that if there is consensus in society as to major beliefs and values, the school should indoctrinate, inculcate, or teach that consensus. The school might be critical enough to help students understand and apply acceptable beliefs and values, but its criticism could not include a consideration of beliefs and values alternative to accepted ones—except to demonstrate the inferiority of every alternative. Communism, for example, might be studied in order to give students a greater appreciation for a free enterprise system.

It seems to follow from this view of the relationship between school and society that a culture lacking consensus could not include a school which instructs in crucial areas of belief and value, at least until the crisis had been resolved by the larger society. In other words, a school acting as a dependent variable could not depart from the role of spectator in this culture except by teaching conflicting beliefs and values. It would be logically impossible for the school as a dependent variable to teach societally approved versions of good character and the good life, because the larger society is in turmoil and doubt on all important questions.

There is a valid and deep sense in which the coming of crisis frees the school from the restrictions and dependency of easier times. A crisis usually is viewed as a threat. It can also be an opportunity, a challenge, and a test. A crisis may force school leadership to choose between a school situation that is socially inactive and irrelevant, and one that is a laboratory where social inquiry becomes the heart of the curriculum.

Not much remains to be said about the second form of conservatism, the school as a drag on social change. The school could be opposed to any attempt to examine a social system as a system. It could be just as opposed to the practice of raising questions about the validity and adequacy of given systems. War and unemployment could be studied as isolated and catastrophic events with no attempt to trace their causation to a systemic environment. The social studies could become mere propaganda for an idealized version of the way things used to be. Given a current social analysis at both domestic and international levels, it ought to be obvious why this conception of education is inappropriate. However, it is likely that, as the general social crisis deepens, this head-in-the-sand approach to schooling will be powerfully advocated. It will gain support from many who are disoriented and frightened by the crumbling of value consensus and the inefficiency of social institutions.

IV

There are substantial numbers of people in every part of the world who are fully aware of the global social crisis and the nature of the task of system transformation. They are already working on alternative visions, the creation of a movement, and the cementing of transnational political coalitions.[12] As Soviet dissident (now exiled) historian Andrei Amalrik wrote in the fall of 1975, it may be that the United States will lead the way to a humanitarian world order:

> The U.S. must strive for a transformation of the world if it wants to be more stable. A system that does not set expansionist goals for itself contracts and dies away. The world has experienced many forms of expansion—military, economic, cultural. If the U.S. can become the center of a new expansionism, a humanitarian expansion based on human rights throughout the world, its future would be assured for a long time.
>
> It is interesting that this idealistic element has already, to a lesser or greater degree, been felt in American politics during the entire history of the U.S. The old-fashioned European political mentality—without an understanding of historical perspective and without interest in higher goals—is not likely to long dominate the foreign policy of the U.S. No matter how much more Mr. Kissinger wants to cast aside humanitarian problems, they come to the surface by one means or another.[13]

There can be no denying that the rhetoric and reality of interdependence are a significant and positive step in the direction of a humanitarian global transformation strategy. This chapter has tried to bring out the shortcomings and ambivalences of liberal interdependence thinking, and of the liberal educational philosophy which is likely to guide its introduction into the schools. It has focused on the part of the glass that is half empty, perhaps even two-thirds empty. This critical attitude is not meant to dampen hopes, but to temper them and make them resilient for a long road ahead. Yes, it is a fact that the glass is at least a third full. But that will not be enough to get through the next thirty years.

The basic question is, what must be done to enhance and broaden the basis for a humanitarian system transformation? How can the rhetoric and reality of interdependence be prevented from creating a short-term illusion of progress and security and a long-run incapacity to shape the future? As Mr. Amalrik said, "Americans are a people easily carried away. . . . Haste reflects . . . not only the mentality of Mr. Kissinger himself, but also the features of American mentality in general—the mentality of businessmen who want to see at once the tangible results of their efforts." People must learn first that true progress requires restraint, determination, and adequate preparation. Long-run goals must not be sacrificed for short-term gains. Patience is not a symptom of powerlessness, but rather of strength and wisdom. Schools have long had patience, even reverence, with the past. The task now for social studies education is to foster both a passion for and a patience with the future, a deep commitment to world order values, and adequate preparation for the decades-long task of creating a humanitarian transformation of the world system.

APPENDIX: DEFINITION AND MATRIX
FOR THE STUDY OF WORLD ORDER

Definition of World Order

World order is used here to designate that study of international relations and world affairs which focuses primarily on the questions: How can the likelihood of international violence be reduced significantly? and How can tolerable conditions of worldwide economic welfare, social justice, and ecological stability be created? (In more connotative but less precise terminology the questions would read: How can a warless and more just world be achieved and maintained? and How can the quality of human life be improved?)

So understood, world order encompasses a range of entities— world institutions, international organizations, regional arrangements, transnational movements, nation-states, infranational groups, and individuals—as they relate to the following world political and community processes: peacekeeping, third-party resolution of disputes, and other modes of pacific settlement of disputes; disarmament and arms control; economic development and welfare; the technological and scientific revolutions; the attainment of ecological stability; and the protection of human and social rights.

Methodologically, this inquiry will evaluate *relevant utopias* and culminate in statements of investigators' *preferred worlds*.

A "relevant utopia" is a projection of a reasonably concrete behavioral model or image of a system of world political and social processes, capable of dealing with the set of global problems at some tolerable level of human satisfaction. In addition, relevant utopias must describe, in as rigorous a manner as possible, the trends and prognoses related to these problems over a one- to three-decade period. (Within this context "relevance" means that both the model and the transition must be sufficiently described in behavioral terms, so the intelligent reader as well as the formulator will have a reasonable basis for making a statement about the probabilities of the emergence of such a model. It does not mean the model has been proven to be politically feasible.)

"Transition" is the rubric covering projections of ways the present system is likely to be and/or will be transformed into the relevant utopia. In dealing with transition, special emphasis is given to the possibility of system change without recourse to large-scale violence.

A "preferred world" is the culmination of the preceding investiga-

MATRIX FOR THE STUDY OF WORLD ORDER

| Actor | Year | Impact on Key Processes and Their Elements (can be ranked on a 10-point scale) | | | | |
| | | Minimization of Violence | | | Maximization of Well-being | |
		Arms Policy	Peace Keeping	Conflict Resolution	Per Capita Income	Life Expectancy
World (e.g., the U.N.)	1970 1980 1990 2000					
International	1970 1980 1990 2000					
Regional	1970 1980 1990 2000					
Transnational	1970 1980 1990 2000					
National	1970 1980 1990 2000					
Infranational	1970 1980 1990 2000					
Individual	1970 1980 1990 2000					

Achievement Scale for World Order Values with Minimal-Acceptable-Maximal Range
(−5 to 0 to +5)

PEACE
   total war—to—minimization of violence—to—prevention of violence
ECONOMIC WELL-BEING
   starvation—to—creation of tolerable conditions—to—maintenance of universal prosperity
SOCIAL JUSTICE
   oppression—to—creation of tolerable conditions—to—maintenance of human dignity

Education and Health Guarantees	Maximization of Justice			Maximization of Ecological Balance		
	Participation*	Race Equality	Human Rights	Population Equilibrium	Pollution Control	Resource Balance and Growth

ECOLOGICAL BALANCE
collapse of ecosystems—to—restoration of balance—to—preservation of balance

*PARTICIPATION
totalitarianism—to—self-identity—to—active involvement in achievement of preferences

WORLD ORDER METHODOLOGY				
WORLD ORDER VALUE / **TASKS**	**Minimization of Violence**	**Maximization of Economic Well-being**	**Maximization of Justice**	**Maximization of Ecological Balance**
	PROBLEMS: (a) Population (b) Science and technology			
Value clarification and operationalization				
Diagnosis or present global situation				
Prognosis of existing trends: Positive Negative				
Design and testing of alternative world order systems				
Transition strategies				

tions; it comprises a blueprint of a recommended structure and a list of recommended guidelines and steps for achieving that structure, described in reasonably concrete behavioral terms. It is from testing alternative world order models and transition processes, structures, and strategies (that is, from a set of relevant utopias), that the investigator is able to select or invent his preferred world.

In world order inquiry, formalized authoritative structures and processes of world legal order are given special emphasis, especially as they relate to all the various political, economic, and social processes and structures that either favor or militate against the achievement and maintenance of a warless, more just, and ecologically stable world.

Finally, a continuous effort must be made to define "world interest" operationally, in terms of the central world order problems under discussion.

Richard Falk, in his World Order Models Project book, has formulated a clear synthesis of the transition process. Here his schematic summary, which captures his approach to the elements of time, strategy, and arena, is presented.

- The 1970s: Political   Consciousness   and   the   Domestic
    Imperative

Transition Path $S_0 \longrightarrow S_2$

Problem Focus Change Orientation Institutional Focus Transition Stages Temporal Subscripts / Analytic Stages	War Consciousness Domestic Arena	Poverty Mobilization Transnational and Regional Arenas	Pollution Transformation Global Arena	Human Rights Transformation Global Arena
t_{1970s}	*****	**	*	
t_{1980s}	**	****	***	*
t_{1990s}	*	***	****	***

N.B.: The number of stars in each box is roughly proportional to the degree of incremental emphasis in each t interval.

- The 1980s: Political Mobilization and the Transnational Imperative
- The 1990s: Political Transformation and the Global Imperative

The framework that Falk offers is sensitive to political realities. In the first stage, the emphasis is on value change within domestic societies, particularly the principal ones. The second stage rests upon mobilizing transnational coalitions that have already debated issues of global reform, ironed out the differences, and arrived at a fairly accurate reading of the areas of convergence and disagreement in different parts of the world order system. The third stage is one of social transformation and work within an expanded and strengthened global arena.

NOTES

1. For thoughtful views on the necessity and usefulness of a global perspective in connection with education, see Ward Morehouse, "A New Civic Literacy: American Education and Global Interdependence," Interdependence Series No. 3, Program in International Affairs, Aspen Institute for Humanistic Studies, New York, and Robert Hanvey, "An Attainable Global Perspective," Center for War/Peace Studies, New York.

   For an additional perspective on how research and education concerning these matters might be carried on through a transnational process using just world order values, see Saul H. Mendlovitz (ed.), *On the Creation of a Just World Order,* The Free Press, New York, 1975, introduction.

2. Lincoln Bloomfield, in *Toward a Strategy of Interdependence,* U.S. Department of State, Washington, D.C., July 1975.

3. The world order approach to the study of international affairs derives from an intellectual tradition dating back at least to the Middle Ages and includes such outstanding thinkers as Dante, Rousseau, Kant, Marx, and (in this century) Woodrow Wilson, David Mitrany, Grenville Clark, and Louis Sohn. See W. Warren Wagar, *Building the City of Man,* W. H. Freeman and Company, San Francisco, 1971, and F. H. Hinsley, *Power and the Pursuit of Peace,* Cambridge University Press, New York, 1968.

   The world order methodology combines empirical studies, rational analysis, and explicit attention to values. It is futuristic, looking at alternative preferred and likely world futures, as well as at past and present world order systems. World order is interdisciplinary and has over the last fifteen years produced several score books and materials for teaching at the school and university levels. It has an extensive following in the United States and a growing presence in other regions, particularly Japan, Africa, India, and Europe. The best introductions to world order thinking are Richard A. Falk, "Future Worlds," Foreign Policy Association Headline Series, S. H. Mendlovitz (ed.), no. 229, February 1976, op. cit., and Rajni Kothari, *Footsteps into the Future,* The Free Press, New York, 1974.

Additional information may be obtained from the Institute for World Order, 1140 Avenue of the Americas, New York, N.Y. 10036.

4. It should be noted that Eastern European scholars and political analysts hold a similar but noncongruent view of these matters. One should recall that spokespersons for the People's Republic of China frequently speak of "The great disorder under heaven" which is bringing about beneficial social change.

5. Cf. William O. Stanley, *Education and Social Integration,* Teachers College Press, Columbia University, New York, 1953, chap. 3.

6. Ibid., p. 89. By life conditions, Stanley means the physical, biological, economic, and technical conditions under which social life must be lived. Institutions affect the social relationships of people, define various statuses and roles, and enter into the channeling of many societal activities. Intellectual and moral norms provide the basis for individual and collective judgments.

7. The state's weakened role concerning national security can be accompanied by a strongly repressive role concerning individual liberty.

8. The cultural crisis contains an implicit and generally unrecognized conflict between ecology and economics. See Barry Commoner, *Closing the Ring,* Alfred A. Knopf, Inc., New York, 1971, pp. 250–292.

A similar conflict exists between ecology and the existing international system, according to Harold and Margaret Sprout, *Toward a Politics of the Planet Earth,* Van Nostrand Reinhold Company, Inc., New York, 1971, pp. 13–31.

9. W. O. Stanley, "Education and Social Integration—Fifteen Years Later." (Unpublished paper.)

10. With some people "radical" is an unpopular expression connoting communism. This definition is inadequate. In this society there are many radicalisms besides communism, and in a communistic society communism would not be considered radical. The definition in *Webster's New*

World Dictionary is preferable: "Of or from the roots or root; going to the foundation or source of something; fundamental; basic (a radical principle)."

11. Howard Zinn, *The Politics of History,* Beacon Press, Boston, 1970, chaps. 7, 10, and 11.

12. The Institute for World Order alone has produced a long list of books and periodicals on this subject, among which are Ali A. Mazrui and Hasu H. Patel (eds.), *Africa in World Affairs: The Next Thirty Years,* The Third Press, New York, 1973; W. W. Wagar, op. cit.; Jagdish N. Bhagwat (ed.), *Economics and World Order,* The Macmillan Company, New York, 1972; R. A. Falk in collaboration with Johan Galtun, R. Kothari, and S. H. Mendlovitz, *First State of the Globe Report,* North Holland Publishing Company, Amsterdam, 1975; R. Kothari, op. cit.; S. H. Mendlovitz (compiler and ed.), *Legal and Political Problems of World Order,* Institute for World Order, New York, 1962; S. H. Mendlovitz, *On The Creation of a Just World Order,* op. cit.; R. A. Falk and S. H. Mendlovitz (eds.), *Regional Politics and World Order,* W. H. Freeman and Company, San Francisco, 1973; George Lakey, *Strategy for a Living Revolution,* Grossman Publishers, New York, 1973; R. A. Falk and S. H. Mendlovitz (eds.), *The Strategy of World Order,* Institute for World Order, New York; R. A. Falk, *A Study of Future Worlds,* The Free Press, New York, 1975; R. A. Falk, *This Endangered Planet,* Random House, Inc., New York, 1971; Grenville Clark and Louis B. Sohn, *World Peace through World Law,* 3d ed., enlarged, Harvard University Press, Cambridge, Mass., 1966; *Alternatives, A Journal for World Policy,* quarterly publication by North Holland, Amsterdam; Louis René Beres and Harry R. Targ, *Planning Alternative World Futures,* Praeger Publishers, New York, 1975; and *Bulletin of Peace Proposals,* edited at the International Peace Research Institute, Oslo, under the auspices of the International Peace Research Association.

13. Andrei Amalrik, in *The New York Times,* Oct. 22, 1975, p. 45.

Appendix

Citizenship Test for Secondary Schools

GEORGE GALLUP

GALLUP CITIZENSHIP TEST

To better prepare young people for the responsibilities of citizenship, a coordinated effort to correct the situation requires more than just a blind plunging headlong into new programs of civic nature. There first need to be some evaluation studies on a district-by-district, or better yet, school-by-school basis to determine the "political literacy" of the students.

The Task Force staff cooperated with Dr. George Gallup, chairman of the Gallup Poll, in the development of a test vehicle designed to enable teachers, principals, and local school boards to see for themselves areas of undeveloped learning. This test is reprinted here as a convenience for teachers interested in assessing the knowledge of high school youngsters about civic affairs.

GOVERNMENT

1. Who is the governor of your state? ————————————

2. How many U.S. Senators come from this state? ——————

3. What are their names? ——————————————————

4. Please name the representative in Congress from your Congressional district. ——————————————

5. Do young persons under the age of 18 have the right to write articles attacking the local educational system, or would they have to wait until they reach voting age? ——————————————

6. If the President and the Vice President were both removed from office, who would succeed them in the presidency? _____

7. "We, the people of the United States, in order to form a more perfect union, etc." These are the opening words of what governing document? _____

8. Can the Supreme Court nullify a law passed by a majority of both Houses of Congress and signed by the President? _____

9. What are the three main branches (divisions) of the federal government? _____

10. Who is now Chief Justice of the Supreme Court? _____

11. Who is now U.S. Secretary of State? _____

12. Who were the 3 men who served as President of the United States immediately before President Ford? _____

HISTORY

1. In what year did Columbus discover America? _____

2. In what year did the United States declare its independence? _____

3. From what nation did the United States declare its independence?

4. In what city was the Declaration of Independence signed? _____

5. In what war was the issue of States' Rights a major issue? _____

6. How many states now comprise the United States? _____

7. Name 3 nations that fought on our side in World War I. _____

8. Did Russia fight on our side or against us in World War II? ———

9. What document guarantees the right of a free press in this country?

10. With what does the Equal Rights Amendment deal?   ————

11. Can an employer, in an advertisement, specify that he is looking for a male or a female to fill the position? ————

12. What is the percentage of black people in the total population of the U.S.? ————

GEOGRAPHY

1. What is the capital of your state? ————

2. What county do you live in? ————

3. What is the distance in air miles between New York and San Francisco? ————

4. Oregon is on the coast of the ———— Ocean.

5. New Jersey is on the coast of the ———— Ocean.

6. What is the population of the U.S.? ————

7. What state in the U.S. has the largest population? ————

8. Which were the last 2 states to be admitted to the U.S.? ————

9. Where is Angola? ————

10. What nation in the world has the largest population? ————

11. Name 2 nations that produce a large surplus of grain to sell to other nations. _____

12. If oil tankers cannot use the Suez Canal, by what route do they get from Saudi Arabia to the U.S.? _____

13. If the Panama Canal were closed, by what route would ships go from New York to San Francisco? _____

14. What language is most widely spoken in Brazil? _____

15. What language is most widely spoken in other Latin American countries? _____

16. Which has more people—Mexico or Canada? _____

17. What is the capital of Canada? _____

THE ELECTORAL PROCESS

1. At what age do American citizens become eligible to vote? _____

2. The final selection of the Presidential candidate of each major party is made by _____

3. Do persons who wish to become their party's candidate for the Presidency have to win the most votes in state primaries? _____

4. If you vote for the Presidential candidate of one party in the general election, do you have to vote for candidates of the same party for other offices? _____

5. Do the majority of members in the U.S. Senate at this time belong to the Democratic or the Republican party? _____

6. What about the majority in the House of Representatives—is it Democratic or Republican? _____

7. Who was the Democratic candidate for President in 1972? _____

8. How many Senators are there in the U.S. Senate? _____

9. What determines how many representatives in the House of Representatives come from a given state? _____

10. How can you vote in an election if you don't happen to be in your home district on election day? _____

11. Does the Presidential candidate who gets the most popular votes in a national election always win the presidency? _____

ECONOMIC ISSUES

1. Is the federal government spending more money than it takes in? That is, is it operating at a deficit? _____

2. The economy of Russia is described by economists as communistic; that of Sweden as socialistic. How is ours described?

3. Just your best guess, what is the federal income tax on corporations with net earnings of $1,000,000? _____

4. About how much federal income tax does a married couple with no children (and no personal deductions) have to pay on an income of $20,000? _____

5. About how much does this same couple pay on an income of $100,-000? _____

6. If you buy a new car and take out a loan through the auto dealership, about what annual interest rate do you have to pay? _____

7. Just your best guess, how much profit, in percent, does the average corporation typically make today on its total sales? _____

8. In early years of the nation about 3 percent of the nation's total income went to pay for the costs of government. What percent of the nation's total income now goes to pay the costs of government? _____

POLITICAL ISSUES

1. Which political party—the Republican or Democratic—is more in favor of States' Rights today? _____

2. In general, which party—the Republican or Democratic—follows the wishes of organized labor more closely? _____

3. In general, which party—the Republican or Democratic—follows the wishes of the business world more closely? _____

4. In general, which party—the Republican or Democratic—wants the federal government to reduce spending on social programs? _____

5. Does the U.S. Constitution permit a woman to be President? _____

6. Does the U.S. Constitution permit a black person to be President?

7. Can you belong to the Republican party or to the Democratic party without paying membership dues? _____

8. Does a person who cannot read nor write have the right to vote? ___

9. Suppose someone wished to start a new party in the United States

called the "Center" party. Does the Constitution permit an individual to start a new political party? _____

10. Can people on welfare vote in national elections? _____

FOREIGN POLICY

1. Name 3 nations in Eastern Europe that were taken over by the Russians after World War II. _____

2. What is meant by the word "detente" as applied to our present foreign policy? _____

3. What is NATO? _____

4. The typical family in the United States has an annual household income of $11,000. What is your guess as to the annual household income of a family living in India? _____

5. Name 2 basic commodities that the U.S. buys in large quantities from other nations. _____

6. How many nations belong to the United Nations? _____

7. Name the 5 nations that have permanent seats on the Security Council of the United Nations. _____

8. Name 2 agencies through which the United Nations Organization carries on its work throughout the world. _____

9. What 2 nations are in conflict over Cyprus? _____

10. What large nation entered the Korean War on the side of the North Koreans? _____

11. Where is the Sinai desert? _____

WORLD FIGURES

Please identify the nation with which each of these individuals is associated:

1. Harold Wilson   _____

2. Anwar Sadat   _____

3. Indira Ghandi   _____

4. George Wallace   _____

5. Leonid Brezhnev   _____

6. Adolph Hitler   _____

7. Golda Meir   _____

8. Marshal Tito   _____

9. Jefferson Davis   _____

10. Winston Churchill   _____

11. Joseph Stalin   _____

12. Julius Caesar   _____

13. James Monroe   _____

14. Napoleon Bonaparte   _____

15. Thomas Paine   _____

ENVIRONMENT

1. The productivity of the soil has been damaged in many countries by cutting down the trees. What kind of damage does this do to the soil?

2. Will you name one common form of air pollution? _____

---

3. Can you name any animal or bird that is threatened with extinction?

---

4. It is claimed that the gas from aerosol cans destroys something in the atmosphere. What is it? _____

As can be seen by the content of the test, the students are quizzed on their basic knowledge of American history, government, geography, the electoral process, economic issues, political issues, foreign policy, recognition of world figures, and environment. The reason the test is so broad in scope is because the American citizen of today must keep informed on technological advances (as a result of the current knowledge explosion), and must understand the complexities of how decisions made at the local, state, or national level can have a domino effect on people around the world.

It is easy to see, in retrospect, how such incidents as the Arab oil embargo or the cancellation of the American SST had catastrophic results—but day-to-day decisions are not always as clear. It is for this reason that a broad-based test vehicle was developed. Citizens must have at least the ability to analyze decisions with sufficient background knowledge to form a good data base. Note that the test has no value-laden questions—only straight facts. While most decisions in an adult's life require some value or moral judgment, this is not the purpose of the test vehicle.

As had been expected, the preliminary field testing revealed a shocking lack of knowledge; specifically, in geography, foreign policy, and economics. The potential value of the test, however, lies not in its ability to embarrass one or a group of students. Rather, it serves as a pathfinder for teachers in reorganizing course structures, in order to help students gain knowledge needed to cope with the problems of citizenship.

Index

Absolute monarchy, 39
Abuse of power, 92
Academic disciplines, 56–57, 139, 180–181
  political leadership and, 41
Accommodation of interest groups, 35
Accountability, 159–160
Action-learning centers, 152–153
"Action-rich" curriculum, 39
Administration of comprehensive educational system, 23–25
Adversary system, 87
Advisory groups, 122–124
Agribusiness, 90
American Association of School Administrators, 62, 63
American Bar Association, 181
  Special Committee on Youth Education for Citizenship of, 77
American Historical Association:
  Commission on Social Studies of, 61
  Committee of Seven of, 57
American Legion, 61
American Political Science Association (APSA), 57
  Committee on Pre-Collegiate Education of, 77, 80
Analysis of society, 79
Aristotelian philosophy, 30–32, 39
Arithmetic, 15
Arrests of adolescents, 72
Attendance, compulsory, 56
Attitudes:
  about government, changes in, 73
  nonschool influences on, 17
  survey of, 146
Authenticity, 175
Authoritarian educational structure, 184

Beliefs, 195
  mainline, 71

Bible reading, 84, 85
Bill of Rights, 84, 86, 87, 181
  ratification of, 93
Blacks:
  discrimination against, 89
  during post-Civil War era, 55
  special courses for, 71
Brain research, 168, 170
Brookline High School project (Massachusetts), 120–121
Busing, 89

Cambridge High and Latin School (Massachusetts), 106–107, 121–124
Campaign work, 144
Candidates, assessment of, 170
Capitalism, 199–200
Censorship of student newspapers, 87
Central High School (Minneapolis), 151
Checks and balances, 91–92
Child labor, 56
Civil War, 54–55, 70
Classroom milieu, 136–138
Clientele-service-oriented public administration, 44
Cognitive moral development, 97–98
Cold war, 63, 75
Common schools, 54, 55
Communication skills, 115, 153
Communism, 63
Community action credit, 149–150
Community boards, 23–24
Community involvement, 134, 183–184
  course on, 151–152
Community meetings, 106–107, 115–116, 122–124
Community projects, 143–144
Community School Association, 22
Community schools, 22
Community study, 146–147
Competition, international, 194

Complexity of moral issues, 109
Comprehensive educational
   environment, 23–25
Compulsory attendance laws, 56
Computational skills, 15
Conference on Political Education in the
   Federal Republic of Germany and
   the United States, 78
Congress, U.S., power base of, 92
Consent:
   informed, 111
   principle of, 178–179
Conservation, 62
   (See also Environmental concerns)
Conservatives, 184
   on social role of schools, 201–203
Constitution, 53, 57, 83, 181
   drafting of, 93
   equality provisions of, 88–89
   mixed and balanced government
      concept in, 32, 91
   moral basis of, 102–103
      comprehension of, 110–113
   Preamble to, 29
   rights and liberties guaranteed by, 9
   understanding of principles
      underlying, 97
   (See also Bill of Rights)
Constitutional Rights Foundation, 181
Consumer law, 90
Contracts, 89, 90
Conventional level:
   of moral development, 98
   of perspective taking, 104
Cooperative education, 21–22
Correctional institutions, 97
   participatory democracy units in, 106
Corruption, political, 31, 35–36, 83
Creative work, 45
Crime, 4–5, 73, 83
   inequality as cause of, 31
Criminal justice, 87
Critical judgment, 62
Critical thinking, 182
Cultural lag, 197
Curriculum:
   "action rich," 39
   engineering model and, 80–81
   "ethnic studies" in, 71

Curriculum (Cont.):
   experience-based learning in, 148,
      150, 151, 153
   local input in, 179–180
   materials for, 78
      classroom milieu and, 137
   moral education, 120–121
   negotiation exercises in, 39
   during 1950s, 64
   during Progressive era, 57
   projects for development of, 66
   public administration and policy, 42–
      44
   social studies and English, 122–124,
      126–127
   syndetic exercises in, 38
   for work-study programs, 21–22
Cyclical theme of history, 30
Cynicism toward public officials, 73

Data-gathering, 115, 139
De jure segregation, 88
Deception, electronic, 171
Decision-making, interest-group
   participation in, 35–36
Declaration of Independence:
   equality doctrine in, 32
   on justice, 87
   on liberty, 84
   moral principles of, 99, 102–103
Defense strategy, 75
Deification of isolated self, 138
Dependent variable, school as, 201–
   203
Desegregation, 88–89
Detroit Education Task Force, 158
Devotion to democracy, 63
Diffused responsibility, 109
Direct political participation, 33
Disciplinary specialists, 41
Discipline committee, 123, 124
Divine right, 39, 71
Domestic governance systems, 193
   interests of, 193
Due process of law, 87–88
Duluth Cathedral community
   commitment program (Minnesota),
   141

Ecological balance, 206
Economic literacy, 63
Economic system:
  domestic and global, 193
  New Deal modifications of, 200
  property relationships and, 90–91
  reorganization of, 89
  test questions on, 217–218
Economic well-being, 206
Education citizen committees, 161–162
Educational environment, 15–25
  comprehensive, administration of, 23–25
  nonschool components of, 16–19
  public mood and, 15–16
  reconstruction of, 21
  social class differences in, 19–21
Educational Policies Commission, 62
Electoral process, test questions on, 216–217
Electronic deception, 171
Elementary schools, 10
Employment, educational role of, 16–18
Energy crisis, 45, 175
Engineering model, 80–81
English, 10
  curriculum for, 122–124, 126–127
Environmental concerns, 9, 45
  impact on beliefs and values of, 197
  propertied interests in conflict with, 91
  test questions on, 220–221
Equal liberty philosophy, 177–180
Equal Rights Amendment (ERA), 74
Equality, 83–84, 88–89
Erhard Seminars Training (EST), 138
Ethical values, 9
"Ethnic studies," 71
Executive Internships Program, 150
Experience-based learning, 139, 148, 150, 151, 153
Expression, freedom of, 86
Expulsion from school, due process applied to, 88

Federal Communications Commission (FCC), 170
Federal educational legislation, 24

Federal role in civic education, 11
Federalist doctrines, 48–49, 52–53
Financial resources, 78
Folwell Junior High School (Minneapolis), 149
Food exports, 76
Foreign investments, 76
Foreign policy, test questions on, 219
Formal operational thought, 115
  moral development and, 103–104
Forums, student-sponsored, 163
Foxfire project (Georgia), 146
Free enterprise system, 90–91
Freedom, historical views of, 30–32

Gallup Citizenship Test, 213–221
Geography, test questions on, 215–216
Global interdependence, 75–76, 78, 189–191
  economic aspects of, 190–191
Government, test questions on, 213–214
Governmental institutions, 71–72
Governmental Responsibility and Student Participation (GRASP), 147
Grain exports, 76
Great Depression, 61, 92
Greek philosophy, 30–32
Growth, economic, 195

Hemispheres of brain, 168
Heterogeneous student groups, 9
Hidden curriculum, 10, 123, 184
History, 180–181
  of community, researching, 146
  cyclical theme of, 30
  mode of inquiry for, 114
  sense of, television and, 173
  study of: during Progressive era, 55–60
    during Revolutionary era, 48
  test questions on, 214–215
Home, education in, 16–18
Human rights, 9, 99
Humane application of knowledge, 138

Ideologies:
    of community involvement, 184
    extreme, 28
Immigrants, 53, 55, 70
    Americanization of, 56
    assimilation of, 60, 71
"Impartial manager" as public service
    ideal, 42
"Independent" voters, 73–74
Industrial-scientific revolution, 196
Industrialization, 53, 70
Inequality:
    as cause of civil unrest, 31–32
    among nation-states, 193
Information overload, 170
Informed consent, 111
Inner city, 19–20
    youth projects in, 144
Inquiry, modes of, 114
In-service training, 81
    of school-within-school staff, 123
Institutional school reform, 184–185
Institutions:
    crisis of confidence in, 83
    firsthand study of, 146–147
Instrumental relativism, 98
Integration, 88–89
Intellectual openness, 177–178
Intellectual skills, 113–115
Interdependence:
    global, 75–76, 78, 189–191, 203–204
    of nations, 10
    of peoples, 9
Interdisciplinary courses, 152
Interest groups, 35
Internships, 147
Interpersonal sharing, 98
Isolated self, deification of, 138

Jacksonian outlook, 50, 51
Jeffersonian outlook, 48–49
Judgment, critical, 62
Judicial review, 92
Just Community Schools, 109
Justice, 83–84, 87–88
    criminal, 87
    social, 62, 206
Juvenile justice, 87–88

Knowledge, 110–113
Kohlberg scale, 124

Labor organizations, 90
Laboratory for existing classes, 150–151
Landlord-tenant disputes, 90
Latent power of citizens, 33
Law:
    observance of, 63
    practical, 73
    rule of, 30–31
"Law and order" candidates, 73
Law-related education, 66, 181
    materials for, 77
Leadership, 40–44, 153
League of Women Voters, 170
Left-wing ideology, 28
Legislation, political process
    surrounding, 72
Liberals, 184
    views on world order of, 199–200
Liberty, 83–87
    equal, 177–179
    nineteenth-century attitudes toward,
        52
Literacy, faith in, 48
Literature, social issues in, 23
Lobbying, 145

Mainline values and beliefs, 71
Majority rule, 37
Management-oriented public
    administration, 42
McCarthyism, 63, 64, 170
Meaningful work, 44
Media:
    political role of, 35
    role of school in evaluation of, 23
    (See also Television)
"Melting pot" notion, 5, 71
Membership, citizenship as, 134
Memory, 171
Metropolitan task forces, 24
Middle class, 19
    domestic tranquility and, 32
Militarism, 55
Military alliances, 75

Minneapolis Public Schools, 141
Modes of inquiry, 114
Moral development, 183
  cognitive, 97–98
  goals of civic education based on, 110–120
    development of self-esteem, 116–120
    intellectual skills, 113–115
    knowledge, 110–113
    participatory skills, 115–116
  levels and stages of, 98–104
    interview to determine, 99–100
    invariant sequence of, 103–104
    natural, 101–102
    as organized systems of thought, 100–101
    preference for highest stage comprehended, 102–103
  perspective taking and, 104–109
    cognitive conflict, 105
    deliberate attempts to facilitate change in, 106–107
    moral judgment and action, 107–109
  trend toward narcissism and, 138
Moral education, 10, 15
  curriculum for, 120–121
Moral reasoning, 80
Motivation in youth participation programs, 139
Multinational corporations, 76, 90
Municipal League, 57
My Lai incident, 109

Narcissism, trend toward, 138
Nation-states, 193
  disintegration of system of, 194
  impotency of, 197
National Association of Secondary School Principals, 21
National Commission on Resources for Youth, 21
National Council for the Social Studies, 64, 77
National Education Association (NEA), 62
  Commission on the Reorganization of Secondary Education of, 57
  Committee of Ten of, 57

Nationalism, 55, 75–76
"Natural political world of children," 80
Natural resources, 75
Negotiation skills, 13, 39
New City School (St. Paul, Minnesota), 145, 152
"New culture movement," 70
New Deal, 61, 199–200
New Social Studies projects, 65, 113, 115
News, television, 165–169
Newspapers, student, 87
Nonpartisan public interest organizations, 74
Nonschool education, 16–19
Nonvoting school board membership, 161
Nuclear weapons, 75
  impact of, on beliefs and values, 197
Nursing homes, voluntary service in, 141

Obedience, 98
Objectives:
  accountability for, 159–160
  clarification and reassessment of, 9–10
Oligarchy, 32
"Operation Identification," 144
Out-of-school educational programs, 21–22

Paddling, 88
Parochial schools, 84, 85
  desegregation circumvented by, 89
Participation, 32–37, 133–154, 206
  academic learning and, 139
  classroom milieu and, 136–138
  forms of, 140–147
    community projects, 143–144
    community study, 146–147
    internships, 147
    social and political action, 144–146
    voluntary service, 140–142
  program models for, 148–154
    action-learning centers, 152–153
    community action credit, 149–150

Participation, program models for (Cont.):
  community involvement course,
    151–152
  laboratory for existing courses,
    150–151
  sequence of courses and
    experiences, 153–154
  volunteer bureau, 148–149
  responsibility and, 179
  skills of, 9, 115–116
  Progressive era emphasis on, 59–60
  by students in school affairs, 157–163
    education citizen committees, 161–
      162
    problem-solving task groups, 162–
      163
    school board membership, 160–161
    sponsorship of public issue forums,
      163
  trend toward narcissism and, 138
Participatory democratic units, 106–107
Party identification, 73–74
Patriotism, 48, 61
Peace, 206
Penal system, 45
Personal efficacy, 142
Perspective taking, 104–109
Philosophical inquiry, 79
Philosophy, ancient Greek, 30–32
Piagetian scale of cognitive
  development, 103
Pittsburgh area project, 124–127
Platonic philosophy, 30–32, 39, 43
Plea bargaining, 87
Pledge of Allegiance, 84, 87
Pluralistic society, 5
Police:
  experience of adolescents with, 72
  power of, 91
Policy analysis emphasis in public
  administration, 43
Policy recommendations, 24
Political action, 144–146
Political issues, test questions on, 218–
  219
Political corruption, 31, 35–36, 83
Political-legal principles, 175–180
  of consent, 176, 178–179
  of equal liberty, 176–179

Political participation, direct, 33
Political-process-oriented public
  administration, 43
Political skills:
  development of, 37–40
  informal organization of schools and,
    80
Political system, knowledge of, 9, 112
Pollution, 145
Poverty, 83, 90, 143
  inner-city, 19–20
  rural, 21
Power, 84, 91–93
  greed for, 31–32
Practical law, 73
Prayers in schools, 84, 85
Preconventional level:
  of moral development, 98
  of perspective taking, 104
Preferred worlds, 205
Presidential elections, 93
  voter turnout in, 165
Press, freedom of, 85–87
Principal, role of, in civic education, 12
Principled level of moral development, 99
Private schools, desegregation
  circumvented by, 89
Problem-solving skills, 153
Problem-solving task groups, 162–163
Productive system, dominant form of,
  193
Productivity, 17
Professional specialists, 41
Progressive era, 55–60
Project orientation, 78, 79
Prolonged adolescence, 135–136
Property rights, 83–84, 89–91
Protestant outlook, 48
Public assistance, 83
Public Interest Research Group, 145
Public policy:
  complexity of, 41
  mode of inquiry for, 114
Public schools:
  establishment of, 48–50
  nineteenth-century, 54, 55
Public service video class, 145
Punishment, 98
Puritan outlook, 48

Quality of life, 91

Radicalism:
  school as source of social action and,
    200–201
  study of, 200
Raw materials, 75
Reading, 15
Reality testing, 139
Reconstruction, 55
Reformers, 33, 35–36
  clientele-oriented public policy of, 44
Regina High School (Minneapolis), 141
Regional task forces, 24
Regulation of interest groups, 35
Relevant utopias, 205
Religious institutions:
  educational role of, 16, 18
  separation of state and, 84–85
Representation, 35
Republican doctrines, 49
Responsibility, 17
  competencies discovered through,
    142
  of leaders, 40
  participation and, 179
  rights and, 2, 9, 12
Revolutionary era, 47–50
Right-wing ideology, 28
Rights:
  of accused, 72
  responsibilities and, 2, 9, 12
Role taking, 104
Rural children, 20–21

St. Louis Education Task Force, 158
St. Paul Open School, 145
San Francisco Public Schools
    Commission, 158
San Francisco Unified School District
    Board of Education, 161
School boards:
  role in civic education of, 11
  student members of, 160–161
Schools-within-schools, 97, 106–107,
    121–124
Science, social application of, 63

Secondary schools, 2, 10
  citizenship test for, 213–221
  Progressive influence on, 57–60
Segregation, 88–89
Self-esteem, development of, 9, 116–
    120
Self-help, 195
Self-made man, image of, 56
Selfishness, 138
Seminars, staff development, 125–126
Separation of church and state, 84–85
Separation of power, 91–92
Sex education, 78
Short-term goals of governments, 195
Situational stress, 109
Slavery, 54
Small towns, 20
Social action, 144–146
  school as source of, 200–201
Social activity, 62
Social agencies, voluntary service in,
    140–142
Social applications of science, 63
Social change, 70–71
  school as brake on, 201–203
Social class, 19–21
Social contract, 83, 99
Social integration, 195–198
Social justice, 62, 206
Social perspective, 104
Social problems approach, 181–182
Social sciences, 180–181
Social skills, development of, 18, 38
Social studies, 10
  curriculum for, 122–124, 126–127
Social transformation, schools as
    instrument of, 198–199
Social understanding, 62
Socialization, link of schooling to other
    agencies of, 78, 79
Societal maintenance, 99
Societal perspective, 112–113
Socioeconomic status, 89
Spanish-American War, 55
Speech, freedom of, 85–86
State governments:
  internships with, 147
  role in civic education of, 11, 24
Stewardship, 173

Stone Ridge School (Bethesda, Maryland), 153
Student choice, 177
Suburban children, 19
"Sunshine laws," 36
Superintendent, role in civic education of, 11
Supreme Court:
　desegregation decisions of, 88–89
　due process decisions of, 2, 88
　freedom of speech in school decision of, 85
　moral-ethical pronouncements of, 92
　religion in school decisions of, 85, 93
Survey of community attitudes, 146
Suspension from school, due process applied to, 88
Syndetic skills, 38
System Development Corporation, 22

Task forces, regional, 24
Teachers, role of, in civic education, 12
Teachers College Citizenship Education Project (CEP), 64, 65
Teen Corps, 143
Teenage Health Consultant, 143
Television, 12–13, 165–174
　candidate assessment and, 170
　critical awareness of electronic deception in, 171
　educative role of politicians and, 169–170
　freedom of press and, 86
　influence of, on thought process, 168
　information overload from, 170
　innovations in, 172–173
　instructional, 171–172
　memory and, 171
　news coverage on, 165–169
　public service video class, 145
　social behavior and, 172
　values influenced by, 17, 19
Textbooks:
　in Civil War era, 54–55
　nineteenth-century, 50–54
　during Progressive era, 57
　during Revolutionary era, 48
Therapy, popular trends in, 138

Third-party problem-solving groups, 158
Tolerance, 62
Totalitarianism, 61
Town meetings, 157

Underground newspapers, 86, 87
Universal ethical principle, 99
Urbanization, 70
Utopian solutions, study of, 200
Utopias, relevant, 205

Values, 10, 196–197
　changing, 70
　clarification of, 182–183
　cultural, changing system of, 194
　mainline, 71
　negotiation skills and, 40
　nineteenth-century, 52
　nonschool influences on, 16–17
　reconstruction of educational environment to influence, 22
　working-class, 20
Vietnam war, 61, 83, 175
Violence, 83
　juvenile, 88
Vocational education, 21
　employer support for, 77
Voluntary organizations, 24
Voluntary service, 10–11, 140–142
Volunteer bureau, 144–149
Voting, 93, 160–161
　party identification and, 74
　in presidential elections, 165

Wars:
　eradication of, 45
　just and unjust, 83
　(See also specific war)
Watergate scandal, 3, 61, 83, 175
Welfare, 90
Women:
　discrimination against, 89
　enfranchisement of, 70
Work-study programs, 21
Working-class families, 20
World citizenship, 63

World figures, test questions on, 220
World order:
    challenge of system transformation in,
      192–195
    definition of, 205, 208–210
    liberal point of view on, 199–
      200
    matrix for study of, 206–207

World order (*Cont.*):
    school as instrument of social
      transformation and, 198–199
    social integration and, 195–198
World War I, 55, 61
World War II, 63

Youth participation (*see* Participation)